ANGELS OF DECEIT

The Masterminds Behind Religious Deceptions

Richard Lee
AND Ed Hindson

Illustrations by James Stoltzfus

ANGELS OF DECEIT

Copyright © 1993 by Richard Lee and Ed Hindson
Published by Harvest House Publishers
Eugene, Oregon 97402

Library of Congress Cataloging-in-Publication Data

Lee, Richard, 1946-
    Angels of deceit / Richard Lee, Ed Hindson.
        p.   cm.
    ISBN 1-56507-163-8 : $8.99
    1. Cults—United States—Controversial literature.
    2. Baptists—Doctrines. I. Hindson, Edward E. II. Title.
BL2525.L437   1993
239'.9—dc20   93-3972
                                                          CIP

Printed in the United States of America.

*To all who are sincerely seeking the light of the TRUTH
that they not be deceived.*

*The Spirit clearly says that in later times
some will abandon the faith and follow deceiving spirits
and things taught by demons. Such teachings
come through hypocritical liars, whose consciences
have been seared as with a hot iron.*

—1 Timothy 4:1,2

*For such men are false apostles, deceitful workmen,
masquerading as apostles of Christ. And no wonder,
for Satan himself masquerades as an angel of light.*

—2 Corinthians 11:13,14

Preface

This is a book about the dangers of false religion. It is also about the spiritual conflict that goes on behind the scenes of the human struggle with false prophets, extremist cults, and fanatical leaders.

It is our hope this study will remind the reader that "our struggle is not against flesh and blood, but against the rulers, against the authorities, against the powers of this dark world and against the spiritual forces of evil in the heavenly realms" (Ephesians 6:12).

People do not join religious cults because they want to believe a lie. They are deceived into believing lies to be truth. In fact, most cultists are sincerely seeking the truth. But they are looking in all the wrong places. Their search for meaning and significance has led them into the snare of the devil and his angels.

It is our prayer that this study will help you understand the cultic mind-set and how to avoid it. Once an individual starts down the wrong road, he or she is going to end up in the wrong place. Even well-meaning Christians at times border on cultic tendencies. That's why you need to recognize the marks of the cults and know how to escape back into the truth.

Ten million Americans are reportedly members of religious cults. By sheer numerical probability, it is highly likely that you will have a personal encounter with the cults. It is very possible that a member of your family will be deceived and taken in by a religious cult. Therefore, you need to know as much as you can about the cults and what they believe.

By definition, a cult is a religious group that claims special revelation from God. *Theologically*, a cult is a group that perverts and distorts the biblical doctrines of historic Christianity. *Sociologically*, a cult is a religious group that tends to isolate itself from other religious bodies. Such cults often become extreme in their beliefs and practices.

The Bible predicts that false prophets will multiply in the last days before the return of Christ. The Scripture says,

> For the time will come when men will not put up with sound doctrine. Instead, to suit their own desires, they will gather around them a great number of teachers to say what their itching ears want to hear. They will turn their ears away from the truth and turn aside to myths (2 Timothy 4:3,4).

We believe that day is upon us now! For the past 150 years, one false prophet after another has arisen. Cult after cult has been formed. And there is no end in sight. Modern Americans, like the ancient Athenians, seem content to listen to one babbler after another in their search for truth. But a century and a half of cultic explosion has left American religion splintered into hundreds of factions of error and untruth.

It is time to call America back to God by calling her people back to the Bible. Only in the time-honored truths of Scripture will we ever find the spiritual light we seek. It is in the pages of God's revealed Word that we will find the answers to life's greatest questions.

We want to express our appreciation to *There's Hope!* and its staff for their commitment to this project. A special word of thanks goes to Mrs. Emily Boothe, the administrative assistant at *There's Hope!* who typed and proofed the original manuscript. We also want to thank Bob Hawkins, Sr., Bob Hawkins, Jr., and Eileen Mason at Harvest House for their intense interest in this project and their help in making it a reality. A word of thanks also goes to our wives, Judy and Donna, for their patience and encouragement.

Richard Lee
Ed Hindson
There's Hope!
Atlanta, Georgia

Contents

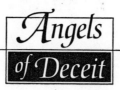

Angels of Deceit

PART ONE

The Process of Spiritual Deception

*Their thinking became futile
and their foolish hearts were darkened.
Although they claimed to be wise,
they became fools.*

—Romans 1:21,22

Falling into the Darkness

*The Consequences of
False Religion*

I just knew he was God's messenger," Kelly kept saying. "His preaching was so powerful and convincing. It was like he was an angel of God," she insisted.

"I joined their Bible-study group searching for the truth," Dave added. "I was really burned out on the secularism in my college classes. I thought this would help me spiritually."

"I always felt uncomfortable with the whole thing," Chris injected. "It was like you could sense something was wrong, but you couldn't explain it to anyone else."

Kelly, Dave, and Chris were discussing their experiences in a religious cult they had joined while they were students at the University of Illinois. Each one had come from a different background. And each got hooked in a different way.

Dave had attended church as a youngster, but had drifted away during his high-school years. He knew something was missing in his life but he didn't know where to turn to find it. Kelly was a professing and active Christian. She thought she was just getting into another youth group. Chris was a skeptic—but an honest one. He appreciated the group's willingness to discuss religious issues and respond to his questions.

But in time, each of the three students realized there were extremist tendencies among the leaders. Strict discipline, rigid schedules, and long sermons were a constant routine. They had little time for their studies, their personal lives, or their parents.

Kelly began to feel uncomfortable when the group constantly discouraged her from going home on the weekends. "All that talk of us being a family made me miss my real family," she said. "But whenever I wanted to go home, even for a few days, they tried to keep me so busy I wouldn't have time to go."

"I got real concerned," Dave admitted, "when they kept talking about defending themselves from government intrusions. When one of the leaders told me he had bought a gun, I knew it was time to leave! But when they realized I might go, they really put the pressure on me to stay."

"I finally realized they weren't really answering my questions," Chris observed. "We had lengthy discussions, but they always turned into indoctrination sessions. I soon found myself accepting their beliefs because I was tired of arguing with them. I guess I caved in to peer pressure and didn't even notice it."

Kelly, Dave, and Chris were fortunate. They got out before it was too late. They had fallen into one of the hundreds of smaller cult groups that exist in America today. The group sounded Christian, studied the Bible, and talked about God, so each of the three assumed it was legitimate.

"We sang and prayed a lot," Kelly added. "It seemed like one big spiritual family. But it almost turned into one big nightmare."

All three students had been drawn into the Christian Vanguard, a neo-Nazi cult, masquerading as a campus Bible study at the University of Illinois. They were all from the St. Louis, Missouri, area and later attended Missouri Baptist College, where I (Ed) was teaching at the time.

Their stories are not unlike those of multiplied thousands of others. They were sincere people seeking the truth, but caught in one of Satan's greatest deceptions: false religion.

Masters of Deceit

The Bible describes Satan as the "father of lies" (John 8:44). He is pictured in Scripture as the ultimate deceiver. His name means "accuser," and he is depicted as the accuser of God and His people (Revelation 12:10). He is opposed to God and seeks to alienate men from the truth. He misled the fallen angels (Matthew 25:41; Revelation 12:4). He tempts men and women to sin against God's laws (Genesis 3:1-13; 1 Timothy 6:9). He denies and rejects the truth of God and deceives those who perish without God (2 Thessalonians 2:10). Ultimately, he "inspires" the false prophets and the very spirit of antichrist (1 John 2:18-23).

The Bible clearly warns us that in the last days people will "abandon the faith and follow deceiving [KJV—'seducing'] spirits and things [KJV—'doctrines'] taught by demons" (1 Timothy 4:1). These false teachings will come through "hypocritical liars" whose minds have been captured by Satan's lies (1 Timothy 4:2). Thus, the process of spiritual deception is clearly outlined in Scripture:

The term *angel* (Greek, *angelos*) means "messenger." God's angels are His divine messengers (Hebrews 1:14; Revelation 1:1) and His true prophets and preachers are called the angels of the churches (Revelation 2:1,8,12,18; 3:1,7,14). By contrast, Satan is pictured as a fallen angel, the leader of other fallen angels, who deceives the whole world (Revelation 12:9). He is revealed as the ultimate power behind the antichrist and the false prophet who deceives mankind with false religion (Revelation 13:14). Thus, the messengers (angels) of deceit are Satan-inspired false prophets and teachers whose messages are the very spirit of antichrist (1 John 2:18).

A century ago, A.T. Pierson, the Bible teacher who often spoke for Charles Spurgeon at the Metropolitan Tabernacle in London, wrote, "Evil spirits acquire their greatest power from their subtilty. They are *masters of the art of deception*, and aim to counterfeit that which is good rather than suggest what is obviously and wholly evil."[1]

The Process of Deception

The lure of false doctrine is that it presents itself as the truth. It appears as a corrective measure to established doctrine. It is propagated by those who are certain they have discovered some new revelation of truth or a better interpretation of old, established truth. Either way, they are convinced they are right and that everyone else is wrong.

That is Satan's oldest trick. He appeals to our *self-conceit* and leads us into *self-deceit*. When he first approached Eve, Satan questioned the integrity of God's command and appealed to her selfish desire to be like God. It was that same desire that had led to his fall in the first place. And there is something selfish enough in all of us to want to believe that we can know what no one else knows.

C.S. Lewis said,

> What Satan put into the heads of our remote
> ancestors was the idea that they could 'be like

> gods' ... and out of that hopeless attempt has
> come nearly all that we can call human his-
> tory ... the long terrible story of man trying to
> find something other than God which will make
> him happy.[2]

The irony of self-deception is that it arises from our own self-conceit. One does not have to look hard to find expressions of self-centeredness in most cult leaders: Father Divine said he was God. David Koresh claimed to be Jesus Christ. Sun Myung Moon says he is "Lord of the Universe." Joseph Smith claimed to receive angelic revelations. Mary Baker Eddy believed her book *Key to the Scriptures* was inspired of God. Herbert W. Armstrong claimed his church was the only one on earth proclaiming "the very same gospel that Jesus taught and proclaimed."

The process of deception works like this:

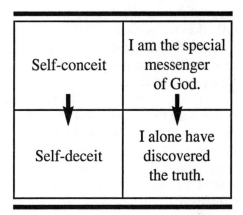

Once the false teacher falls into the illusion that he or she alone is God's messenger and has a corner on His truth, spiritual deception is inevitable. Mary Baker Eddy, the founder of Christian Science, was so convinced she was right that

she said, "Today the healing power of Truth is widely demonstrated as an imminent, eternal science . . . [its] coming as was
promised by the Master, is for its establishment as a permanent
dispensation among men."[3] She actually believed that her
"discovery" of Christian Science fulfilled the promise of
Jesus' second coming!

In the preface to her *Key to the Scriptures*, Mrs. Eddy said
of herself, "Since the author's discovery of the might of Truth
in the treatment of disease as well as of sin, her system has
been fully tested and has not been found wanting."[4] It is
difficult to imagine the sincerity of such self-conceit and spiritual arrogance. The only logical explanation is that she really
thought she was right.

Once *spiritual deception* sets in, it leads to *spiritual darkness*. It is not long before the deceived cult leader begins to
espouse heretical doctrine. Since he or she acknowledges no
one else as God's spokesperson, traditional and orthodox concepts may be challenged or even disregarded. Charles Russell,
the forefather of the Jehovah's Witnesses, was so convinced
that he was correct about the date of the second coming of
Christ (1914), that he became equally convinced of other
unorthodox beliefs as well: He denied the Trinity, the deity of
Christ, the personality of the Holy Spirit, the existence of hell,
and the visible return of Christ.

Pride and arrogance are the sins that lead a person to become spiritually deceived. These sins take us to the second
stage of spiritual deception (as shown in the chart on the next
page). Satan tempts us with our own self-centeredness and
lures us into spiritual darkness with the bait of our own pride.
We really want to believe we are right and everybody else is
wrong. The Bible calls it the "pride of life" (1 John 2:16 NASB).

Having been hooked by our *arrogance*, we are reeled in by
our *ignorance*. Most people who fall into the trap of false
doctrine are ignorant of the implications of their views. Hank
Hanegraaff illustrates this in his epic work *Christianity in
Crisis*.[5] In exposing the doctrinal flaws in the "Faith theology" of Kenneth Copeland, Benny Hinn, Robert Tilton, and

others, Hanegraaff states that many sincere preachers get off the theological track, but don't know enough theology to realize their error at first.

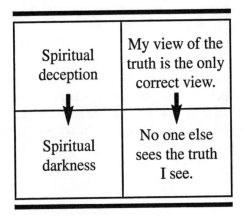

The problems arise when false teachers love their erroneous teaching to the point they will not repent of it even when their error is exposed. This is what leads to *spiritual darkness*. The willful rejection of the truth results in the mind being blinded by Satan. The Bible says, "They are darkened in their understanding and separated from the life of God because of the ignorance that is in them due to the hardening of their hearts" (Ephesians 4:18).

Scripture further explains that Satan himself is the source of spiritual darkness: "The god of this age has blinded the minds of unbelievers, so that they cannot see the light of the gospel of the glory of Christ, who is the image of God" (2 Corinthians 4:4). Thus, Joseph Smith belligerently defied all appeals to rethink his theology of men becoming gods, of marital polygamy being acceptable, or his supposed angelic revelations of *The Book of Mormon*.

Once theological error falls into "ecclesiastical cement" it is virtually impossible to eliminate it. When *false doctrine* is accepted by an organized religious body it will be perpetrated by a *false defense* (apologetic) based upon a false premise. If I honestly believe my dog is a reincarnation of my Uncle Joe, I will look for every possible proof of Uncle Joe's personality in my dog's behavior. When a whole group of followers accept false doctrine as truth, they will organize it, categorize it, and systematize it. But that doesn't make it true!

For example, if I start driving north from Atlanta on I-75, but I really believe I'm heading south, I am not going to end up in Florida, no matter what I think. The spiritually deceived person can believe Jesus returned in 1914, or moved into the heavenly temple in 1844, or that He is coming back this year. But just believing it doesn't make it so. My faith has to be anchored in the truth if it is going to do me any good.

The final stage works like this:

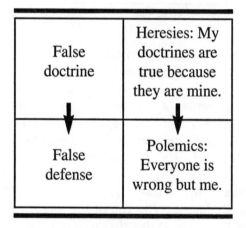

The acceptance of *false doctrine* always leads to a *false defense* or faulty apologetic to defend that doctrine. For example, because Jehovah's Witnesses deny the deity of Christ, they have to reinterpret every passage of Scripture (e.g., John 1:1) that contradicts their false doctrine. Mormons believe that Jews came to America long before Columbus and that millions of Nephites and Lamanites once lived and were killed on the

American continent hundreds of years ago. Therefore, Mormon archaeologists keep looking desperately for any material evidence of these ancient peoples to verify the historicity of *The Book of Mormon.*

Have We Not Prophesied in Your Name?

Jesus spoke often of false prophets and spiritual deception. He told His disciples that spiritual truth could be recognized by its fruits. Then He added, "Not everyone who says to me, 'Lord, Lord,' will enter the kingdom of heaven. . . . Many will say to me on that day, 'Lord, Lord, did we not prophesy in your name, and in your name drive out demons and perform many miracles?' Then I will tell them plainly, 'I never knew you. Away from me, you evildoers!'" (Matthew 7:21-23).

False religion can arise from any source. Hindu-based cults have produced an endless stream of gurus who claim to be *avatars* (incarnations of deity). Sai Baba claims to be the living incarnation of both Jesus and Krishna! Extremist Muslims exist, like Sheik Omar Abdel-Rahman, the deported cleric, whose followers allegedly car-bombed the World Trade Center in New York City. Theirs is a "gospel" of hatred, violence, and murder in the name of God. Jewish Lubavitchers believe Menachem Schneerson is the Messiah, and they are awaiting his declaration of saviorhood.

One might expect false prophets and extremist cults to arise from non-Christian religions that reject Jesus Christ. But when false cults arise from within Christianity, it is especially disturbing. The New Testament, however, is filled with warnings about heretics, false prophets, and false prophecies. Even in apostolic times, the apostle John wrote, "Dear children, this is the last hour; and as you have heard that the antichrist is coming, even now many antichrists have come. . . . they went out from us, but they did not really belong to us" (1 John 2:18,19).

One only has to consider the fiery finale of the Branch Davidian cult led by David Koresh, the grandiose fanatic, to see the powerful influence of false doctrine. Koresh convinced his followers that he alone could properly interpret the seven seals of the Book of Revelation. By "opening" the seals, he further convinced them that he was the Lamb of God—Jesus Christ in the flesh. Therefore, his conflicts with law enforcement agencies were setting the stage for the final battle—Armageddon. He was so self-centered, *Newsweek* noted, "he was consumed by Armageddon and his role in it."[6]

The Infernal Journey

The long-haired, guitar-strumming, one-time rock 'n roller, David Koresh, was the 33-year-old leader of the Branch Davidians, whom he called "God's Marines." Claiming that he was the Lamb of God (Christ), he believed that he personally was to open the seven-sealed scroll of Revelation chapters 6–7, and bring God's fiery judgment upon the world. Described by *USA Today* as "a zealot with a loose grip on reality," Koresh led his followers to one of the most disastrous confrontations in the history of religious cults.[7]

Born and named Vernon Howell in Houston, Texas, in 1959, the self-styled prophet took over the leadership of the Seventh-day Adventist offshoot called the Branch Davidians in 1987. The sect was housed ten miles outside Waco, Texas, in a cluster of buildings on a 77-acre farm called "Mount Carmel," ironically named for the place where Elijah confronted the false prophets of Baal (1 Kings 18). Vernon Howell changed his name to David (for King David) Koresh (Hebrew for Cyrus) in 1990. He rebuilt the cult's rickety headquarters into an interconnecting series of buildings that formed a virtual fortress. He installed generators, a water-supply system, and bunkers to withstand the possibility of an armed conflict. "This compound was built with a siege in mind," said the McLennan County sheriff.[8]

Constant rumors of child abuse, polygamy, and a massive stockpile of weapons circulated around Waco. Ex-cult members claimed that Koresh thought he was the incarnation of

King David and that he was called of God to "build the House of David" by having sex with all the women in the cult. They were considered to be his "wives," while other male cult members were ordered to be celibate.

On Sunday, February 28, 1993, at 8:30 A.M. over 100 federal agents of the Alcohol, Tobacco, and Firearms (ATF) Bureau stormed the Mount Carmel compound. They attempted to serve search warrants and an arrest warrant for David Koresh, who had already stood trial for attempted murder six years earlier in a shoot-out with George Roden, a former Branch Davidian cult leader.

Bullets from Heaven

What was planned as a two-minute operation quickly turned into a bloody 45-minute gunfight in which four ATF agents were killed and 16 wounded. The battle now stands as the single bloodiest day in FBI history since the days of Prohibition! Several cult members were also reported killed inside the compound, including a two-year-old child.

Federal agents said they came under fire immediately upon arriving at the compound Sunday morning. Koresh, on the other hand, later claimed in a CNN interview, "They fired on us first." The assault came one day after the *Waco Tribune-Herald* began publishing a series of articles on the Branch Davidian cult. Witnesses said the federal officers stormed the building, throwing concussion grenades and shouting, "Come out!" In the meantime, National Guard helicopters circled overhead. "It sounded like a war zone," commented John McLemore of KWTX-TV, who witnessed the shoot-out: "People were being hit. You could hear people screaming with agony."[9]

Federal agents withdrew after failing to breach the complex. They retreated with twenty agents having been hit. Two of the helicopters were also hit, as was a news van. "I cannot tell you what went wrong. It appeared as though they were waiting for us," lamented Ted Royster, head of the ATF office in Dallas.[10]

Koresh told radio stations that he had been shot "in the gut" during the firefight and that his two-year-old daughter had been killed. He called his mother in Chandler, Texas, and left a message on her answering machine: "Hello, Mama. It's your boy. . . . They shot me and I'm dying. . . . But I'll be back real soon, OK? I'll see y'all in the skies."[11] Koresh recovered from his wounds, however, and granted several telephone interviews over the next few days until federal agents cut the phone lines.

Claiming they had undercover information that the Branch Davidians were planning a mass suicide for either Passover or Easter Sunday, the ATF attempted to justify their assault. But some officials openly questioned the use of such force with women and children present. "They view this as a 'holy war' provoked by an oppressive government," one local official said.[12]

Ranch Apocalypse

For more than a year, David Koresh had predicted an armed confrontation with federal agents. He even nicknamed the compound "Ranch Apocalypse." In a paranoid frenzy, the Branch Davidians had bought or bartered $200,000 worth of weapons, thousands of rounds of ammunition, and a grenade launcher. The initial raid had been met with such a flurry of bullets that the federal agents decided to send heavily armed tanks against the compound to break through the walls and insert massive injections of tear gas into the buildings starting at 6:04 A.M. on the morning of April 19.

The tank incursions were met with volleys of gunfire. Inside, the Branch Davidians donned gas masks and prepared for an apocalyptic confrontation with the "enemies of God." FBI spokesman Bob Ricks explained, "We were hoping by the infusion of gas into that compound that the women would grab their children and flee."[13] Instead, they all bunkered down, put on gas masks, and tried to withstand the siege.

The tanks rammed the building five times between 6:04 A.M. and noon. At 12:05 P.M., flames erupted from the opposite ends of the compound, whipped by 20 to 30-mile-an-hour winds. Within minutes the entire compound was ablaze with flames. By 12:18 P.M., the watchtower collapsed. Shortly thereafter, the ammunitions room exploded in a ball of fire. And by 12:28 P.M., the second floor was engulfed in flames and the roof collapsed. The blazing flames and dark smoke billowed across the Texas sky. Only nine people escaped or survived the fire. All the others perished in the conflagration.

Arguments may persist for some time as to whether the inferno was the result of a mass suicide, an accident, or an act of desperate self-destruction. But the whole terrible mess was the end result of a false prophet whose deceived followers perished for a lie.

It is never the will of God to defend the faith with guns and bullets. Peter attempted to defend Jesus from arrest by the Roman soldiers in the Garden of Gethsemane. Our Lord told Peter to put away his sword because "all who draw the sword will die by the sword" (Matthew 26:52). Later, when Pilate nervously questioned Jesus about being a king, the Lord replied, "My kingdom is not of this world. If it were, my servants would fight to prevent my arrest" (John 18:36).

A false prophet is one who contradicts the true message of Christ, as well as one whose predictions fail to come true. David Koresh was guilty on both counts. A typically self-deceived extremist cult leader, David Koresh perished with nearly 90 of his followers in the flames of Ranch Apocalypse. And in Matthew 23:33, Jesus Christ warned there is a worse fate for false prophets: They will not escape the fires of hell!

The Cultic Mentality

The Development
of a Cultic Mind-set

Religious cults are on the rise worldwide. The violent shoot-out in Waco, Texas, between federal agents and David Koresh's Branch Davidian followers has again underscored the dangers of such cults. They prey on the immature and uninformed, offering group acceptance, a better way of life, special discoveries of truth, and even direct access to God.

Extremist cults are usually schismatic deviations of established religious bodies. They are generally led by a powerful figure who is convinced he has the only true message from God for these days. The result is often a bizarre system of deviant doctrine built upon the claim of extrabiblical revelation. The words of a self-styled prophet, divine leader, or special book are said to replace the authority of Scripture.

Religious cults differ from denominations in that they are heretical schisms from orthodox belief and practice. While cults exist in virtually every religious society and take many varied forms, they all have one thing in common: the belief that they alone are the people of God.

Believers within traditional denominations may have different doctrinal views and polity practices, but they do not exclude all others from the fold of heaven in the way cults do. For example, a Baptist and a Methodist may disagree on their mode of baptism, but they do not consign each other to hell on that basis. A Presbyterian and a Lutheran may differ on the matter of church government, but they do not reject each other as heretical or cultic.

Cult members, however, believe they are the only true people of God. Therefore, they are convinced they have the only true message of God and the only true way to heaven. The cult, instead of the Bible, becomes the ultimate norm of all truth. While the cult may tolerate ignorance of their views by the uninformed, they ultimately believe that all who disagree with them are lost. Thus, the cult group reasons, salvation belongs to them alone. This gives rise to the persecution complex that feeds the paranoia of most cults. They develop the mentality that "people hate us because we're different." Cults expect persecution and often invite it.

This mentality that believes "we alone are right" eventually gives way to uncritical allegiance to leadership. Soon, all disagreement is looked upon as disloyalty and a threat to the purity of the movement. Social pressure and sometimes even violence and physical restraint have been used by cult leaders to hold the allegiance of their followers. Jim Jones of the People's Temple cult is one such example.

Religious cults thrive on biblical illiterates and religious neophytes who become enamored with special revelations, deeper truths, and better methods. They profess to have a special corner on God's revelation and, as a rule, claim to have a book or letter that is the "key" to understanding the Bible. Some say only their translation of the Bible is inspired. Others believe their leader alone has God's final message for the world in these last days.

The idea then develops that God can accomplish His ultimate purposes only through "our" group, since we alone are His people and understand His message. If our movement fails, they rationalize, then God has failed. If we let Him down, they think, His work will never be accomplished. With this mentality, a cult becomes a manufactured religion of human effort. Salvation by allegiance to the cult soon replaces the doctrine of justification by faith, and a "messianic complex" (we alone can save the world) sets the movement in religious cement.

Jim Jones's followers did not commit suicide merely because he told them to do it. Nor did David Koresh's Branch Davidians respond with violence just because he ordered it. They had long before fallen victim to the cultic mentality. The rest was inevitable!

Too Good to Be True

Truth in advertising is a hot issue in our marketing-driven culture. But nowhere is it more of a problem than among the extremist cults. They promise incredible blessings, but often deliver inconceivable bondage. Paul Martin observes, "If it sound too good to be true, then it probably is too good to be true!"[1] He quotes Jeanie Mills, a defector from the People's Temple cult:

> When you meet the friendliest people you have ever known, who introduce you to the most loving group of people you have ever encountered, and you find their leader to be the most inspired, caring, compassionate, and understanding person you have ever met, and then you learn that the cause of the group is something you never dared hope could be accomplished, and all of this sounds too good to be true—it probably is too good to be true!

Jeanie was later murdered for defecting from the cult. Such extremist groups view loyalty as the highest virtue and disloyalty as betrayal. Once you're in, you can't get out. Ample testimonies exist from ex-Moonies to ex-Mormons of intimidation and threats from cult leaders once they decided to leave the cult. The Children of God (COG) sect often has gone so far as to hide potential defectors from their parents in an underground network called "the catacombs."[2]

Heaven Can Wait

Most cults offer no final cures. Religious charlatans keep people in perpetual bondage in order to enforce allegiance to the cult. One can never be sure of eternal salvation until the unrealized future. Cult members are motivated by fear to keep striving, serving, witnessing, praying, and so on, and can never be fully sure of eternal life while alive in this world. Dave Breese notes, "The follower lives in constant fear that he has not done enough, given enough, prayed enough, worshipped enough to be sure of salvation."[3]

The unattainable goals of cult perfection exact every kind of sacrifice from followers. They are expected to work harder, pray more often, give more money, and make more sacrifices than their leaders would ever do. In the process, they prove their loyalty and devotion and fill the coffers of the cult.

Denying themselves every kind of personal freedom and convenience, cult followers blindly throw themselves into the propagation of the cult system. Selling books and flowers may seem harmless enough, but this time-consuming passion brings millions of dollars into the hands of the leadership. Leaders, in turn, often live in opulence compared to the average cult member.

Christopher Edwards, a former Moonie, tells of the incredible lifestyle of their American leaders, Omma and Oppa (Dr. and Mrs. Dust), who were crowned by Reverend Moon as the "True Parents of America." He recalls them being chauffeured in Lincolns, dressed in furs, and bedecked in jewels. "I was dazzled by the image of majesty they conveyed," Edwards says. "They stepped up the stairs like aristocrats from some forgotten age."[4]

Submission or Oppression?

Extremist cults demand loyalty and obedience as proof of one's commitment to God. There is little opportunity for honest questions, critical thinking, or personal freedom. Cult leaders often mask oppressive controls under the guise of biblical submission. But their brand of submission is not biblical at all. They do not call their followers to submit to the lordship of Christ or the principles of Scripture, but to submit to the authority of their own leadership.

The apostle Paul urged the believers at Corinth to "follow my example, as I follow the example of Christ" (1 Corinthians 11:1). Paul recognized that his authority and leadership as an apostle depended upon his faithfulness to the lordship of Christ. Every believer has the right to ask, "Is my spiritual mentor really following Christ?"

All too often, cult leaders deny their members the right to make their own decisions about matters of faith and practice, claiming that they are not yet equipped to make such decisions without help. Attempting to dictate their followers' use of time, as well as their beliefs and personal thoughts, cultists obliterate any true personal freedom. Martin observes, "The lack of freedom lies at the core of cultism. In fact, it is the breeding ground for cultism."[5]

Religious cults usually motivate their followers through fear and guilt. Rejection of the cult's authority, they imply, will send you to hell, ruin your life, condemn your children, or hinder the plan of God on earth. Believe it or not, the latter is often the greatest guilt-motivator. Sincere devotees are led to think they will somehow disappoint God and fail to help His cause if they fail to obey the cult in all its dictates.

Cult detractors are often threatened with eternal damnation, demon possession, the mark of the Beast, incurable diseases, natural disasters, and public ridicule. Many disillusioned cult members remain in the group simply to avoid what they fear may be a worse fate. Some have even been known to commit suicide rather than make the break.[6]

No Questions, Please

Cult leaders themselves are often self-deceived. Believing they have discovered ultimate truth, they love to pontificate on the implications of that truth. But they don't like questions—especially negative questions. They don't mind being asked to further amplify or clarify their ideas, but rarely will cultists allow open and public scrutiny of their views.

Questions that imply rejection of their ideas or authority will almost always be looked upon as arising from spiritual rebellion. Such questions will not be encouraged or appreciated. If the questioner persists, he or she eventually will be denied, rejected, ridiculed, or expelled.

Another favorite cult gimmick is to raise straw arguments against other belief systems and uphold them to open ridicule. This always causes the unsuspecting follower to assume the teacher/leader is correct and that the "other guy" could not possibly answer these objections. Of course, the other guy is never invited to present his own position or to respond in person to the objections that have been raised.

Cult leaders have found that the best way to maintain loyalty is to isolate followers from any outside opinion—secular or religious. Other religious groups are to be avoided at all costs because they are spiritually contaminated. Since they are presumed to be in spiritual darkness, they have nothing to offer and are to be rejected altogether.

Whenever religious leaders try to get you to stay away from other churches, campus groups, fellowships, Bible studies, prayer meetings, or even Christian bookstores, they probably have something to hide. While legitimate Christians may attempt to shield you from the cults, the cults will do all they can to shield you from legitimate Christianity.

There is a fine line between spiritual guidance and cultic manipulation. Even genuine Christians must be careful not to cross that line. All too often we are quick to make statements like these:

"You don't have to understand it; just believe it."

"If it doesn't make sense, just take it on faith."

"Don't read that book; it will confuse you."

"People who ask too many questions usually have a spiritual problem."

"Those people can't be right because they're not one of us."

Closing of the Cultic Mind

A few years ago, University of Chicago professor Alan Bloom shocked the general public with his bestselling book *The Closing of the American Mind.*[7] In it, Bloom argued that modern students have now abandoned rational inquiry for relativism, replacing reason with emotion. Today's students, he observed, don't care what is right or wrong so long as it works. They are more interested in pursuing the good life than in making right decisions.

Bloom laments the self-centeredness of today's student generation, observing, "Students these days are, in general, nice... but they are not particularly moral or noble."[8] He further bemoans, "Today's students are no longer interested in noble causes."[9] He goes on to explain that students who are a product of modern education are not committed to noble ideas and therefore are incapable of developing noble goals. Since relativity prevails, Bloom argues, students are robbed of their spiritual values and are left with an overload of information that cannot change their lives.

It is into this moral and intellectual vacuum that the cults make their greatest appeal to today's generation. They appear to offer answers to life's questions. They provide a structure for moral choices and they demand allegiance to a great cause.

But unlike genuine Christianity, the cults recruit through deception and hold their converts by manipulation. Just try to get the guy selling flowers at the airport to tell you to which group he belongs. He won't do it! Ask those inviting you to a

Bible study or campus group to tell you up front with whom or what they are associated. If they hesitate or are vague, they probably have something to hide.

In his powerful and insightful book *Unholy Devotion: Why Cults Lure Christians,* Harold Bussell makes these crucial observations:[10]

1. *Cults gain control of their followers by demanding that they surrender control of their lives.* This surrender is to be done to the cult itself in order to meet one's needs and accomplish one's goals. This is generally done under the guise of surrendering all to God, Christ, Krishna or some higher being. In Eastern mysticism or New Age cults that surrender is made to a "spiritual master," or a "spirit guide" channelled through some earthly medium. In occult circles, the ultimate surrender is to Satan himself!

2. *Cultic manipulation bases its appeal more on emotion than logic.* Bussell notes that people today are more persuaded by the dynamics of a speaker's personality or delivery than they are by the content of his message. Even in evangelical colleges, he observes, students want to hear the speakers who are the most exciting and entertaining. In cultic circles, this means that even well-educated people can be easily manipulated by powerful appearances, dynamic messages, exciting experiences and emotional expressions.

3. *Cults offer strict guidelines for acceptable behavior.* To a morally bankrupt and confused society, most cults offer very rigid guidelines for moral behavior. Often taking biblical commands to excessive extremes, the cults demand allegiance to a code of conduct that locks the follower into the group. Since no one else makes such demands, it is assumed, we must be right. The more rigid we are the more spiritual our

commitment. Following that logic, the cult can demand almost anything from its followers, who will give up everything from coffee to television to satisfy the convictions of the cult.

4. *Cults often excuse the behavior of their leaders.* The demands of cult submission and the rigid behaviors it requires are so difficult to maintain that even its leaders often fall short. But instead of honest admissions, true confession or genuine repentance, the cults often try to excuse or cover up their leaders' failures. Mormons don't want to talk about Joseph Smith's polygamy. Jehovah's Witnesses never mention Charles Russell's divorce or his "miracle wheat" scam. David Koresh's Branch Davidians weren't concerned about his excessive interest in guns. And nobody at the People's Temple talked about those Kool-Aid communion services—until it was too late!

Mother of Perpetual Obligation

The ultimate hook of the cultic mentality is that of perpetual obligation. The cultist is never free from the cult. The assurance of salvation is never fully realized. The devotee must pray better, witness more, meditate longer, try harder, and work endlessly. Promoters of false religion leave their followers in total dependence upon themselves. They are devoid of any theological structure or biblical truth that offers a sure and lasting salvation.

David Breese makes the insightful observation in his book *Know the Marks of the Cults* that cultists are kept in hopeless bondage to the cult.[11] He observes that Jehovah's Witnesses are never quite sure if they are one of the 144,000. New Agers who believe in reincarnation are never sure whether they are coming back or going on ahead to something better. Krishna devotees live in constant fear of losing their Krishna-consciousness and failing to merge with deity.

Breese comments, "A thoughtful person who examines the preaching and writing of the cults carefully is almost certain to sense a frustrating indefiniteness. He is being strung along, beguiled up a primrose path to nowhere."[12] In contrast to the uncertainty of the cultic appeal, consider the striking words of the apostle Paul, who said, "I know whom I have believed, and am persuaded that he is able to keep that which I have committed unto him against that day" (2 Timothy 1:12 KJV).

The enslaving organizational structure of most cults leaves their followers feeling trapped for life. Jim Morud tells the story of Ashley, who wanted to leave the Mormon Church but felt that if she did she would become an apostate, deny her temple marriage, and lose her children for all eternity. "I felt I had lost my whole identity," she confessed.[13]

The Big Lie

Most cults bind their converts by the lie that they alone have the truth and, therefore, they are the only true people of God. Tragically, this idea often begins with sincere self-deception. Many cult leaders actually believed they had discovered the truth that others had failed to see. Therefore, they quickly concluded that they were the only ones who knew the truth.

Seventh-day Adventists are certain that Sunday worship is a lie of Satan perpetuated by the medieval Roman Catholic Church. Therefore, all who reject the Saturday Sabbath have the mark of the Beast.[14] Mormons believe they are the only true "latter-day saints"; therefore, all other Christians are apostate.[15] Christian Scientists believe the mind can heal the body, so they reject medical assistance to prove the reality of their faith. Those who accept medical help are said to have no faith.[16] Jehovah's Witnesses believe Christ already returned in 1914. Since they are the only ones who teach this, they conclude that they alone are His faithful witnesses. All others are deceived and will be lost.[17] Moonies believe that Jesus failed as the Messiah and that the world is being given another chance to accept God's kingdom through Sun Myung Moon, the new messiah.[18]

Once the cultist buys the lie that "we" alone are right and all others are wrong, spiritual pride and arrogance set in quickly. Since the cult alone has the truth, it can judge all other beliefs as erroneous. All they have to do is evaluate the claims of others in comparison with their own beliefs. Any discrepancy is viewed as a departure from the truth (as understood by the cult). Detractors are quickly denounced as heretics, liars, and deceivers. A former member of the Glory Barn sect remarked:

> Our leader was critical of all established denominational churches and all people who didn't believe as he taught. I became mentally isolated because it was felt that nobody outside of (our) teaching was walking in as much truth as we were and therefore their opinion was not valid. I became cloistered in a world of Bible meetings and spiritual pride.[19]

Such beliefs quickly seduce cult followers into accepting extravagant claims for the group's leaders. Excessive titles soon embellish the leader's power and position. Here are a few examples:

Prophet: Joseph Smith (Mormon)

Apostle: John R. Stevens (The Walk)

Perfect Master: Guru Maharaj Ji (Divine Light Mission)

Father David: Mo Berg (Children of God)

Messenger of God: Elijah Muhammad (Black Muslims)

Master and True Parent: Sun Myung Moon (Unification Church)

Master of the Universe: Elizabeth Clare Prophet
(Church Universal and Triumphant)

Master of the Masters: Bhagwan Shree Rajneesh
(Rajneesh Foundation)

Female Christ: Mother Anne Lee (Shakers)

Jesus Christ: David Koresh (Branch Davidians)

Father Divine: George Baker (Peace Mission)

Manifestation of God: Baha'u'llah (Bahai)

It is difficult to imagine how such extravagant claims can be taken seriously. But the sad truth is that the cultic mind readily accepts such claims as truth. Once believed, this further extension of the lie locks the devotee into a position of unquestioned allegiance. After all, who wants to resist the will of Father Divine or the Master of the Universe?

The New Vocabulary

The acceptance of the lies that "we alone are God's people" and "we alone know the truth" leads to the abandonment of one's self to the exaggerated claims of the cult leader ("I am God" or "I alone can lead you to God"). This, in turn, emerges the devotee into the mind-set of the cult, which becomes the new "world" of the cultist.

Each cult has a vocabulary unique to itself. The longer the convert is isolated by the group, the more he or she will begin to think and talk in the terminology of the cult. In time, new concepts fill one's conversations: "holy discourses," "heavenly handshake," "dreamless sleep," "the force," "spirit guides," "heavenly deception," "according to principle," "spoiling the system," "harmonic convergence," "karma," "mantras," "millennial dawn," "Nephites," "telestial Kingdom," "devas," "mahatmas," "flirty fishing," and "animal magnetism" become common designations, code words, and shibboleths used by cult insiders.

Unfortunately, most cult evangelists don't begin by emphasizing the unique and even bizarre elements of their cult's doctrine. Rather, they tend to start with commonly used religious terminology. Many talk of finding inner peace, spiritual help, and personal salvation. Mormons are big on morality and marital fidelity. They often appeal to one's need for ministry to his or her family. Seventh-day Adventists and Jehovah's Witnesses are concerned about Bible prophecy and appeal to one's need to understand the future. Christian Scientists emphasize the power of the mind and tend to appeal to intellectuals. New Agers want to help you find yourself by finding God.

The Cultic Trap

All this may sound rather harmless at first, but it becomes the hook that lures the potential convert into the cultic world. The more extremist cults then take total control of the convert's life. Some insist that all one's possessions be donated to the cause. Some determine who you can marry, where you can live, and what time you should get up in the morning. The more general cults allow members to possess their own property, live in their own homes, and make their own daily decisions. But they also tend to exert strong control through guilt manipulation, personal intimidation, and even social rejection and shunning.

"The longer I was in the cult," Diane admitted, "the more I was afraid to leave it. Not because they were holding me against my will, but because I no longer had a will of my own. It was just easier to go along with it, rather than make the break." When Ashley tried to leave the Mormon Church to marry an evangelical Christian, she was warned by her bishop that she was marrying an apostate, betraying her parents, and losing her opportunity to inherit "eternal exaltation."[20]

The cult member ends up being intimidated by such threats only because he or she has already believed it! The acceptance of the basic cult lie ("we alone are God's true people") leads to uncritical allegiance to leadership ("I am God's only true spokesman"), and the rest is automatic! Hence, Moonies believe demons sit on their eyelids to make them sleep during lectures because that is what their leaders teach.[21] Many New Agers believe they are reincarnations of famous people because their leaders believe it about themselves.[22] Jehovah's Witnesses won't salute the flag or serve in the military because their leaders believe that Christ has already returned and set up His kingdom, which supersedes all human governments. Believing the church age to have ended in 1914, they meet in Kingdom Halls and denounce all churches as apostate.

Once you accept the false premise of cultic teaching, all the rest falls consistently in line. Believing the basic lie, one closes his mind to the truth and throws away the key of logic. From that point on, anything and everything can and will make sense to the cultic mentality:

> Grab your guns!
> Drink this Kool-Aid!
> Keep flicking those demons off your eyelids!

3

A Crash Course in Spiritual Deception
Traits of the Cultic Paradigm

The morning of Father's arrival dawned bright and beautiful. San Francisco sparkled in the distance. We awakened to prepare for the arrival of the Master . . . the atmosphere was electric. I had never seen Father before, but he seemed much smaller and much harder-looking than I had ever imagined.

I marvelled at my great fortune. Here I was living at the most crucial moment in history, in the center of the richest, most progressive nation on earth, face to face with the most important man in the history of the universe. As the family stood at attention, the Messiah sipped silently from his glass, surveying the crowd with indifference.

The room was circled by guards, huge Asians and Europeans in black suits, well drilled in the martial arts. The doors were locked, the windows tightly shut. Christine shouted, "Bow!" and we complied, all 400 of us simultaneously inclining from the waist for Father. Christine shouted, "Down!" and we immediately sank to our knees, dropping our heads three times for the Master. . . .

Reverend Moon pushed back his chair and stepped up to the microphone beside his translator. The crowd, sitting in rows, applauded wildly, and everybody rose on their knees to get a better look at their Messiah. The chunky Korean began to scream at the top of his lungs, pausing intermittently for his translator to interpret. I looked on in wonder as Father danced across the room, ranting and yelling . . . chopping the air . . . slashing at spirits, wrestling with invisible demons.[1]

So begins Christopher Edwards' account of meeting Sun Myung Moon while a member of the Unification Church on January 1 ("God's Day"), 1976. Like many young cult converts, Edwards believed he had found the truth, only later to realize it was a lie.

The Cultic Paradigm

All cult logic is built on the same faulty premise: We alone know the truth. Believing themselves to have discovered truth that is unknown to others, cultists assume they have a corner on that truth. The cultic paradigm works like this:

We alone know the truth of God;
therefore,
we alone are the people of God.

Other variations of the cultic paradigm derive from this original premise. For example, if we alone know the truth, then all others are in error. If we alone are the people of God, then all others are heretics. If people reject our message, they are rejecting God's message. If people persecute us, they are persecuting the cause of God because our cause is God's cause. Since we are right, and others are wrong, our church is the only true church.

Cult logic, beginning with a fallacious premise, weaves a web of deceit so thick that it entangles the minds and souls of its victims. Canadian anthropologists Irving Hexham and Karla Poewe note that this process often leads to a psychological break which they call *schismogenesis*.[2] They define this concept as a psychological split in one's relation with the world and oneself. This leaves the weakened individual vulnerable to the logic of the cult.

Truth no longer must make sense by the normal criteria of logical investigation. Evidence and proof are unnecessary, since truth must be taken on faith. Indoctrination then replaces research as the method of seeking the truth. The need for evaluation and confirmation of one's beliefs is eliminated. Questioning authority is viewed as gross disloyalty and spiritual rebellion. Thus, conformity to the cult's belief system is the only way to gain acceptance and approval by the other cult members.

Basic Traits

While schismatic cults exist in every religion from Lubavitcher Jews to Muslim extremists, they all have certain characteristics in common.

Extrabiblical Revelation:
"We have a special message from God."

Every religious cult has a sacred book, translation, set of writings, key to interpretation, and perhaps visions, dreams, or voices to validate its beliefs. Muslims believe the Koran is God's final revelation to man through the Prophet Muhammad. Mormons look to *The Book of Mormon* as equally inspired as the Bible. Jehovah's Witnesses recognize only their *New World Translation* of the Bible. Seventh-day Adventists recognize Ellen G. White as an inspired prophet of God. Christian Science reveres Mary Baker Eddy's *Science and Health with Key to the Scriptures* as divinely inspired. The same is true of

Theosophy's devotion to Helena Blavatsky's *The Secret Doctrine*.[3]

While some cultic religions have gone so far as to produce and sanction their own sacred books, others have not. Instead, they claim allegiance to the Bible. But they insist that their interpretation of the Bible is the only spiritually valid understanding of Scripture. The Way International founder Victor Paul Wierwille claims, "God spoke to me audibly, just like I'm talking to you now. He said he would teach me the word as it had not been known since the first century."[4] By contrast, *The Way* magazine condemns the so-called Christian church as being built essentially upon man-made doctrine and tradition.[5] Thus, Josh McDowell and Don Stewart conclude, "The Way International believes Victor Paul Wierwille has the only true interpretation of the Scriptures, and is the only one who can lead fellow Bible students out of the confusion in which traditional Christianity has engulfed them."[6]

The Children of God (COG), also known as the Family of Love, recognize David Berg as "prophet and King" and his "Mo letters" as God's truth. Berg himself has said, "My letters mean exactly what they say, literally, and they don't need explaining away, spiritualizing or reinterpreting by any one."[7] One of Berg's early prophecies concerned an impending earthquake in California in the early seventies that never came to pass, yet he was revered by COG members as "God's prophet and King." Later revelations of sexual relations with his own daughters and other cult members only caused Berg to use his letters to defend his practices.[8]

The Church of Bible Understanding, originally known as the Forever Family, is an example of a Bible-based cult. Founded in 1971 in Allentown, Pennsylvania, and headed by Stewart Traill, this religious group uses orthodox Christian terminology loaded with very unorthodox meanings. Cult observers Una McManus and John Cooper state that Traill's "understanding" of the Bible and its concealed meanings ("figures") are accepted as authoritative for cult members. They note that the group has "declared war on the powers of this world, including government, police, schools, parents, and churches."9

The Church of Armageddon, also known as the Love Family, looks to the visions of its members, including founder Paul Erdmann (also known as "Love Israel"), as its divine authority. Members renounce all worldly traditions of matrimony and are considered to be married to one another.10

In each of those examples, the words, visions, or writings of a human leader are made equal to the Bible. In some cases they are looked upon as being of even greater authority than Scripture itself. Even in some evangelical charismatic circles there is a danger of placing human "prophecies" on a level with divinely inspired Scripture.11 Whenever someone claims to have a new revelation from God, he is making the same claim Muhammad made for the Koran and Joseph Smith made for *The Book of Mormon.*

Presumptuous Leadership:
"I know what is best for you."

Not every cult leader is dangerous, but every one is presumptuous. He thinks that he alone has God's ultimate message for mankind. Therefore, in his mind, it becomes an absolute necessity that he deliver God's message at all costs and eliminate whatever opposition he faces in doing so. Branch Davidian cult leader David Koresh's demand that his 58-minute "message to the world" be aired on radio in Waco, Texas, is typical of such a mind-set.

Early descriptions of David Koresh's and Jim Jones's backgrounds show striking similarities: broken homes, parental neglect, desire for power and control, excessive sexual appetites, and the constant demand for loyalty and allegiance from their followers.

"He'll kill us all," shouted the would-be defectors from the People's Temple cult.12 It was Saturday afternoon, November 18, 1978. From the far end of the field the Temple dump truck, along with a red tractor and trailer, emerged from the jungle.

> Three or four men jumped off. And then the shooting started.
>
> Don Harris was hit.
>
> Bob Brown, the NBC cameraman, tried to stay on his feet, and kept filming even as the gunmen advanced. He was incredibly tenacious.
>
> One or two gunmen stepped in with big guns. Then I saw one of the attackers stick a shotgun right into Brown's face—inches away, if that.
>
> Bob's brain was splattered all over his blue NBC minicam.
>
> I saw Don Harris shot at close range.
>
> Congressman Ryan was lying in the mud in front of the right wheel of the aircraft.
>
> His face had been shot off.
>
> Don Harris lay alongside the middle of the plane.
>
> Bob Brown's body was at the tail.
>
> Greg Robinson, the brilliant young *San Francisco Examiner* photographer of our party was at the left wheel, his body almost jackknifed.

So goes the eyewitness account of the wounded Ron Javers of the *San Francisco Chronicle*.[13]

Before that day ended, over 900 men, women, and children perished in the Jonestown settlement in the jungles of Guyana. The babies were the first to die. The cyanide was squirted into their little mouths with syringes. Then came the older children and adults. They lined up in the central pavilion to accept the cups of Kool-Aid laced with poison. They were all following the orders of "the Father," Jim Jones, who also perished on that fateful day.[14]

Jim Jones and David Koresh may be extreme examples of dictatorial cult leaders. But they are not that far removed from the excessive behaviors of Sun Myung Moon, who dictates the marriages of thousands of his followers to total strangers, or David Berg, who authorized incest within the Children of God. In fact, such excess is not that far removed from Christian Science founder Mary Baker Eddy, who claimed her deceased husband was "mentally murdered."

Like this statement from the egotistical Reverend Ike, who said, "You can't lose with the stuff I use," the blasphemous and extravagant claims of deluded cult leaders are incredible. Here are just a few:

Judge Rutherford (Jehovah's Witnesses): "Jesus Christ has returned to earth A.D. 1914 to establish the Theocratic Millennial Kingdom" (*The Kingdom*, 1933). The world is still awaiting this revelation.

Mary Baker Eddy (Christian Science): "Death is an illusion" (*Science and Health*), 584:9. She succumbed to that illusion on December 3, 1910.

Father Divine (Peace Mission): "I am God Almighty... the Holy Spirit personified... the Prince of Peace" (*New Day*, July 16, 1949). God (George Baker, alias Father Divine) died 1965.

Elijah Muhammad (Black Muslims): "Wallace Farad [Muslim version of Father Divine] is God himself! He is the one we have been looking for the last 2,000 years" (*New York Herald Tribune*, April 3, 1963). Wallace Farad (alias Allah) disappeared in 1934 and was never seen again.

Elizabeth Clare Prophet (Church Universal and Triumphant): "I am that I am" (*Teachings on the Path of Enlightenment*). She claims to be the channel of the "Great White Brotherhood" of "Ascended Masters." She and her followers are awaiting the end of the world in Montana.

Meher Baba (Sufism Reoriented): "I am Jesus Christ personified" (*Parvardigar*).[15] Baba died on January 31, 1969.

Sun Myung Moon (Unification Church): "Jesus Christ will return by being born in the flesh in Korea as Lord of the Second Advent and True Parent of the world family" (*Divine Principle*, p. 501ff.). Moon considers himself to be the Messiah incarnate.

David Berg (Children of God): "Forget not thy King. . . . Forsake not His ways, for he hath the key, even the Key of David! Therefore, thou shalt kiss the mouth of David. For thou art enamored of my words and thou art in love with me, thy Savior!" (*The Kingdom: A Prophecy*, August 20, 1971, LO. NO. 94). Berg is revered as King, Father, and David by his followers.

John Robert Stevens (The Walk): "We are going to turn and become the savior of the Church" (*Living Word*, July 6, 1975). Stevens's followers denounce all churches but their own as the "harlot of Babylon."

Herbert W. Armstrong (Worldwide Church of God): "We grow spiritually more and more like God, until at the time of the resurrection—we shall then be born of God—we shall then be God" (*The U.S. and British Commonwealth*, p. 9).

David Koresh (Branch Davidians): "I am the Lamb of God" (*People*, March 15, 1993, p. 41).

Exclusive Salvation:

"We alone are the people of God;
all others are lost."

This one criteria separates cults from denominations. Various Christian denominations may differ on their methods of ordination, their mode of baptism, or their form of church government. But they generally don't consign each other to hell because of those differences. Cults, on the other hand, are always convinced they are the only ones going to heaven. All others are lost, damned, heretical, or have the mark of the Beast!

Jehovah's Witnesses believe that the church age ended in 1914 with the return of Christ to earth. Therefore, they do not meet in churches, but in Kingdom Halls. They say that only Jehovah's faithful witnesses (the 144,000) know and believe the truth—all others are lost. They clearly teach that only faithful Jehovah's Witnesses (both the "remnant" and the "other sheep") will survive the Battle of Armageddon and see the salvation of Jehovah.[16]

Mormons believe that they alone are the "latter-day saints" of God. Brigham Young said, "Every spirit that does not confess that God has sent Joseph Smith, and revealed the everlasting gospel to and through him, is of Antichrist."[17] Speaking of non-Mormon Christian churches, Mormon apostle Orson Pratt said, "They have nothing to do with Christ, neither has Christ anything to do with them, only to pour out upon them the plagues."[18] That means if you are a Mormon and grandma was a Methodist, she is under the wrath of God!

Seventh-day Adventists believe that the third angel's message in Revelation 14 requires the observance of Saturday Sabbath-keeping in order to guarantee eternal life. They allow that some Christians may live and die in ignorance of the third angel's message, and thus be given another chance to receive it at a special resurrection. But all who refuse will suffer annihilation![19]

Christian Science founder Mary Baker Eddy said, "A Christian Scientist requires my work *Science and Health* for his textbook . . . because it is the voice of truth to this age . . . uncontaminated by human hypotheses."[20] In the glossary of *Science and Health*, the true church is defined as "that institution which affords proof of the apprehension of spiritual ideas and the demonstration of divine science."[21] Since Christian Science views itself as unerring and divine, it presumes that all other churches are erroneous.

Spiritualism declares it is the "highest message of truth which we have as yet grown to grasp."[22] Sir Arthur Canon Doyle said, "Spiritualism is the greatest revelation the world has ever known."[23] But Spiritualism (or spiritism), with its emphasis on communicating with departed spirits, has always opposed every major doctrine of Christianity (inspiration of the Bible, deity of Christ, the virgin birth, the atonement, and the resurrection) as anathema in spiritist theology. Lord Dowling, a strong spiritualist advocate, said, "The doctrine of the

Trinity seems to have no adherents in advanced circles of the spirit world."[24]

Swedenborgians believe that Christ returned in the eighteenth century when their founder received what they claim to be the key to the interpretation of Scripture. They also believe he designated them alone to be the "new Jerusalem."[25] Following the highly speculative ideas of Emanuel Swedenborg, this small but influential cult claims to be the church signified by the New Jerusalem of the apocalypse. The rest of professing Christianity is viewed as "perverted from the truth."[26]

The Worldwide Church of God, under Herbert W. Armstrong and Garner Ted Armstrong, denounces all trinitarians as false prophets. They denounce all other churches as preaching a false gospel and a false Christ. They accuse others of "stupendous errors," "false conceptions," and "spiritual blindness."[27]

The Unification Church (Moonies) teaches that Sun Myung Moon is the second messiah ("Lord of the Second Advent") sent to complete the work of salvation begun by Jesus Christ. Moon says of himself and his church, "No heroes in the past, no saints or holy men in the past, like Jesus or Confucius, have excelled us."[28] Emphasizing his church exclusively, Moon claims, "We are the only people who truly understand the heart of Jesus, and the hope of Jesus."[29]

Once the process of spiritual deception reaches the point where the cult believes they alone are God's people, then it follows logically that whatever they believe must be God's truth. By contrast, then, all who disagree with them are viewed as lost or deceived. Their belief that they have an exclusive corner on truth leads them to think they also have an exclusive corner on salvation.

It was this "we are right/all others are wrong" mentality that enabled the followers of David Koresh to surrender their wives and daughters to him for sexual purposes. It also opened the door for them to contradict the clear teaching of Jesus against self-retaliation and take up arms to kill people in the name of God. It was this same mentality that provoked Muslim extremists from the Al-Salam Mosque in Jersey City, New Jersey, to bomb the World Trade Center in the name of God.

Limited Eschatology:

"Jesus is coming only for us; we alone will be spared."

Christian-based cults have often begun as a result of some prophetic date-setting scheme. In most cases these eschatological prognosticators were sincere in their belief that Christ would soon return. However, when things did not work out the way they expected, they soon devised other explanations for their foiled mistakes. The most notable of these were the Seventh-day Adventists and the Jehovah's Witnesses.

Around 1818, William Miller became convinced that the world would end "in about twenty-five years" (1843).[30] By 1834, Miller was a full-time Baptist preacher teaching that the 2,300 days in Daniel 8:14 referred to 2,300 years beginning in 457 B.C. and ending in A.D. 1843 with the return of Christ to "cleanse the temple." Over the years Miller gained a great following of Adventists who were looking for the return (advent) of Christ in 1843. When 1843 passed, however, Miller was influenced by Samuel Snow to recalculate the date as October 22, 1844 (the Day of Atonement). Our Lord's failure to return on that date led to what is now called the "Great Disappointment" and many, including Miller, gave up the whole enterprise.

In the meantime, one Adventist, Hiram Edson of Port Gibson, New York, claimed to have a vision that Christ came into the Holy of Holies on October 22, 1844, to perform a special work before returning to earth. This vision explained why Jesus did not return on October 22, 1844. Edson himself wrote,

> Heaven seemed open to my view, and I saw distinctly and clearly that instead of our High

Priest coming out of the Most Holy of the heavenly sanctuary to come to this earth on the tenth
day of the seventh month, at the end of the 2300
days, He for the first time entered on that day the
second apartment of that sanctuary; and that He
had a work to perform in the most holy before
coming to this earth.[31]

The vision conveniently explained why Miller and Snow
missed their guess on the date for the second coming. Instead
of coming to earth in 1844, Christ moved into the heavenly
Holy of Holies for the first time. In order to accommodate this
change in emphasis, Adventist theology had to be developed
and rearranged to turn the "Great Disappointment" into the
"Great Day of Atonement." Ironically, William Miller, who
started the whole thing, never accepted this explanation and
never became a Seventh-day Adventist![32]

Given its origin, one should not be surprised that eschatol-
ogy plays a large role in Adventist teaching. Seventh-day
Adventists believe they are the true remnant seed of the church
(Revelation 12) and that God has raised them in the last days
(since 1846) to proclaim the keeping of the Sabbath (the third
angel's message [Revelation 14]) as binding on the whole
church. They also teach that they will be granted a special
resurrection before the glorious return of Christ.[33]

In 1870, Charles T. Russell became influenced by Adventist teacher Jonas Wendell in Pittsburgh, Pennsylvania. Sparked
with a renewed interest in the second coming of Christ,
Russell organized a Bible class, began teaching, and started
publishing a magazine called *Zion's Watchtower and Herald of
Christ's Presence*. By 1881, Russell incorporated Zion's Watchtower Tract Society. By 1886 he began publishing a seven-
volume series entitled *Millennial Dawn*, later called *Studies in
the Scriptures*.

Initially, Russell taught that Christ would return spiritually, not physically, in 1874 and finish the end-time harvest
by 1914. Following the ideas of N.H. Barbour, Russell

believed Christ had returned spiritually in 1874 and that the dawn of the millennial age could be expected in 1914. By correlating historical events with the length of the corridors in the Great Pyramid of Egypt, Russell confirmed his 1874 date for the beginning of the Tribulation. Modern Jehovah's Witnesses reject Russell's calculation in favor of 1914. Cult expert Ronald Enroth observes, "To accommodate the change, a new edition of Russell's *Studies* (1923) simply added forty-one inches to the corridor's length in order to locate the starting point for the final years of earth's existence in 1914."[34]

Since there was no visible appearance of Christ in 1914, Jehovah's Witnesses believe that He revealed Himself only to His faithful witnesses (the 144,000). Initially, Jehovah's Witnesses emphasized that when that number was complete (presumably around 1918), Christ would reveal to the world that He was already here. And today, they teach there are two classes of followers: 1) The "congregation of God" or the true church of Jehovah, and 2) the "great crowd" or "other sheep." The first group is limited to the 144,000 and will live in heaven, while the latter group is larger and will live on earth after Armageddon.[35]

Jehovah's Witnesses teach that they are the 144,000 "associate kings" who will rule with Christ in the millennium. They believe that they are the only ones who know the truth that Christ returned on October 1, 1914, and ended the church age and the rule of nations. Hence, they recognize no church but their own and will not salute the flag of any nation. They also believe that they alone will survive the Battle of Armageddon and enter the millennium as God's true people.

Mormons also believe they hold a special place at the time of Christ's return. Calling themselves the Latter-day Saints, Mormons believe the time of the end is at hand and will culminate in the regathering of Israel in Jerusalem, the regathering of Ephraim (Mormons) at Zion (Independence, Missouri), and the regathering of the ten lost tribes to Zion. Mormons believe they will build the Temple of God in North America and recapture Zion from the Reorganized Church of

Latter-day Saints, who actually hold title to the temple property in Independence after a split from the group that went on to Salt Lake City.

Mormons also believe they will be regathered first since Joseph Smith was a "pure Ephraimite," and that Ephraimites (Mormons) now hold the priesthood, having received the "fullness of the everlasting gospel" in these last days. They also believe that only faithful Mormons will enter the Celestial Kingdom (God's highest eternal order) and live eternally with their wives and children and continue to procreate more children in that celestial state. In other words, Mormons believe they hold center stage in God's eschatological program.

Moonies believe that all humanity will literally be saved by Sun Myung Moon, Lord of the Second Advent. Even departed Christians will return to earth and serve the new Messiah in the "True Family" of eternity. "Everybody who ever lived," notes Jack Sparks in *The Mind Benders*, "good, bad, and indifferent—will participate in that great unified family formed around Moon, his wife and his children." Sparks then adds, "What malarkey! This is one of the most amazing schemes a human being has ever devised to deceive people and to bring them under oppressive domination."[36]

Notice again how one lie leads to another: We alone have the truth; we know what is best for you; we alone are the people of God; we alone will be in heaven. It is this kind of logic that sets up the *ultimate conclusion*: All who are against us are against God. Once the cultist is thus deceived, he becomes willing to do almost anything to protect the group from the enemy.

Persecution Complex:

"The world is against us because we have the truth."

One does not have to look far to find plenty of examples of the cultic-persecution complex. David Koresh, "the wacko in

Waco," carried a Glock 9-mm pistol and kept an arsenal of deadly weapons at his disposal because he believed the "agents of Satan" were about to attack him and launch the final Battle of Armageddon.[37] Expecting a soon-to-come apocalypse, Koresh's Branch Davidians fortified their Mount Carmel complex outside Waco, Texas, to prepare for the end of the world.

Sheik Oman Abdel-Rahman told his Muslim followers to "kill the enemies of God in every spot to rid it of the descendants of apes and pigs fed at the tables of zionism, communism and imperialism."[38] Like a true cult leader, Abdel-Rahman assumes that his enemies are God's enemies as well.

There is little difference in the attitude of many of the more traditional or institutionalized cults. Down deep, they know they are different or out of step with traditional beliefs, so they expect to be rejected. Think of the abuse and rejection Mormons and Jehovah's Witnesses must experience as they go door to door to peddle their beliefs. "Jesus warned us that we would be persecuted," they assume, almost inviting more persecution.

Institutionalized cults may have been started by fanatics, but as they grew, their leadership diversified and with time came to develop theological explantions for why they are persecuted. But in today's extremist cults, where the leader has a small but radical following, any rejection of the leader may result in direct hostility.

A nomadic cult founded by Jimmie T. Roberts of Kentucky has no name and wanders from place to place, often eating out of garbage cans. Nicknamed "the garbage eaters," they have left in their wake a trail of broken homes, battered women, and abused children.[39] Believing that children are too young to know God, they assume little ones are "ruled by Satan." This mentality then assumes that unruly children are agents of the devil and need to have the devil beaten out of them!

Jim Jones was so paranoid because of his sinful lifestyle and unlawful activities that he knew intuitively that he was in trouble. So he devised a scheme of moving around the country to avoid police investigators. Finally, when he wanted to avoid the federal government, he moved his flock to Guyana. There in the sticky South American jungles, he armed his men with guns, laced his Kool-Aid with cyanide, and prepared for an inevitable confrontation with the outside world—a confrontation that cost the lives of more than 900 people.

The Moonies are so prepared for persecution that they have developed the concept of "Heavenly Deception" to handle it. When all else fails, they actually encourage lying. Ex-Moonie Christopher Edwards tells of his shock during his first flower-selling assignment. The workers were to solicit funds by asking, "Buy some flowers for a Christian youth group . . . to help some needy children?" When he questioned these statements by his team leader, Edwards was told, "It's for his soul and the glory of Heaven. Look, wouldn't you deceive a little to save the man's soul? It's called Heavenly Deception. It's turning Satan's kingdom against himself, using Satan's money to build the Heavenly Kingdom."[40]

Spiritual deception is a gradual, subtle process. The Great Deceiver convinces the cult leader that he has found the truth that no one else has ever discovered. Armed with this egotistical ammunition, the cultist begins to weave a web of religious deception. He first falls victim to it himself. Then he convinces others that he is right and manipulates their resources to further spread his message. In time, this leads to oppressive organizational controls to ensure this process continues.

Over a period of time, various followers contribute time, service, talents, intellect, and money to further the cause of the cult. While various factors may contribute to this process, much of it develops by chance. Adventists started out trying to explain why Jesus did not return in 1844. The Saturday Sabbath wasn't on their agenda until later, when they were influenced by Seventh-day Baptists. Mormons were convinced that Nauvoo, Illinois, was the promised land until Joseph Smith was killed. Then it was Independence, Missouri—until Brigham Young led a contingent to the Salt Lake Basin.

The great danger in spiritual deception is that once the process falls into theological cement, it locks people into an institutionalized belief system that is very difficult to penetrate. The cultist is so sure that he is right that he is out to convert you to his point of view at all costs. In some cases that may mean surrendering your money, your material possessions, your spouse and children, and even your life!

4

Apostles of Error

Erroneous Doctrines of Christian-based Cults

Jan grew up in a typical evangelical church. She had heard the gospel since childhood. Sunday school classes, youth group activities, and church musicals were a part of her life. But she struggled with the transition from childhood to adolescence. It was as though she really wasn't ready to grow up yet. But the demands of her peers thrust her into the uncharted waters of young adulthood.

Jan had difficulty making decisions. Her more dependent personality seemed to keep her from reaching out to others. She kept waiting for someone to reach out to her, but it never happened. By the time she graduated from high school she was lonely, confused, and sometimes depressed. She began doubting her faith and dreaded having to move on to college life. Yet, somehow, she hoped to find a new life for herself at college.

Away from family and friends, Jan was vulnerable to attention and acceptance. She soon met a sophomore girl who invited her to a Bible study at a storefront in the community. There she met several young people. They were happy and excited about God. They also showed her lots of attention and acceptance. Soon she found herself totally involved with life in the group. Her interest in school, parents, and home began to fade.

The openness of her newfound friends helped Jan open up about her own struggles. Public confessions of sinful thoughts and actions seemed to have a cleansing effect and create a bond among group members. Wrong attitudes, jealousies, and sexual fantasies were openly acknowledged. Soon Jan found herself opening up more and more in public meetings.

"It all seemed so helpful at first," she later admitted. "I had no idea that I had been lured into a Bible-based cult."[1] The Church of Bible Understanding, also known as the "Forever Family," had won her heart and soul. Stewart Traill, the cult leader, seemed like the greatest speaker and Bible teacher she had ever heard. Others members considered him to be God's primary spokesman for the last days. Some even considered him an incarnation of Elijah.

As incredible as it may sound, thousands of Christians are lured unknowingly into spiritual deception every year by cults that have a close affinity to biblical Christianity. In many ways, these Christian-based cults are the most deceptive and dangerous of all. Unlike New Agers, Moonies, and Hare Krishnas, the members of Christian-based cults look, talk, and behave like legitimate Christians.

So Close, Yet So Far

Religious cults that arise from within orthodox and evangelical Christianity have all the outward appearances of being Christian. They talk about God, the Bible, Jesus, salvation, and heaven. In most cases, they claim to have a better knowledge of the Bible, a closer walk with God, and a more disciplined Christian lifestyle. But as close as they are to the truth, their deviations from orthodox beliefs are heretical, dangerous, and divisive.

"When they asked us to sign over the deed to our home, something snapped inside of me," Laura said. "I just gave up my own identity and succumbed to the identity of the group. Leaving was out of the question at that point. Where would we go?"

Dale and Laura gave up their home, sold their furniture, and moved into the group's headquarters—Mount Carmel, near Waco, Texas. They had no real idea what Seventh-day Adventism was all about or why the Branch Davidians had split away from them. All they knew was that the group had taken over their lives and possessions. With nowhere to go and little contact with the outside world, they succumbed to life at Mount Carmel, where David Koresh claimed he was building the House of David by having sex with everyone else's wife.[2]

More traditional cults may not be so extreme because they have gone through institutionalization over a period of many years. Their organizational structure has replaced the dominance of their founder. But underneath all the rhetoric there is still a strong sense of control from the top. Cult members are not always held captive against their wills. But many are held captive by threats of rejection, punishment, and even eternal damnation.

"If you marry a nonchurch member," the Mormon bishop warned, "you will not inherit eternal exaltation."[3] Ashley struggled with her decision to leave the Mormon Church because she felt she was denying the Holy Spirit and condemning herself to hell. She had been taught all her life that the Church of Jesus Christ of Latter-day Saints was the only true church. "All others are false," she had heard them say so many times.

Satan's greatest deception is to present error in such a manner that it is so close to the truth that it appears to be the truth. The better the counterfeit, the greater the deception. Anyone can detect the difference between Monopoly play money and a real dollar bill. But it takes an expert to discern a good counterfeit. The same principle is true in discerning the theological errors of Christian-based cults. They may sound evangelical, but they don't mean what you think they mean.

Wrongly Dividing the Word

Deviation from biblical truth will always lead to wrong ideas and a false destination. One cult may be theologically off a little and another a lot, but both are deceived into thinking they are right when they are wrong. Deviation from the truth always leads to error, and error always leads to confusion.

Jesus rebuked the religious leaders of His own day, reminding them, "You are in error because you do not know the Scriptures or the power of God" (Matthew 22:29 NIV). The basic cultic deviation is first theological, then experiential. Once theological error is entertained and accepted, it conditions the manner in which cultists practice their beliefs in their private and public lives.

A Corner on the Truth:

*"We have found the truth
no one else has discovered."*

Spiritually deceived people are always convinced they have discovered some biblical truth that no one else knows. This generally leads to the claim that they alone can properly interpret Scripture and that historic Christian beliefs which appear to differ with their views are wrong. This kind of reasoning quickly leads to spiritual pride and arrogance.

Herbert W. Armstrong, founder of the Worldwide Church of God and publisher of *The Plain Truth* magazine, exemplifies this attitude of spiritual superiority when he states, "I found that the popular church teachings and practices were not based on the Bible. They originated in paganism. The amazing, unbelievable truth was, the sources of these popular beliefs and practices of professing Christianity were quite largely paganism and human reasoning, not the Bible!"[4]

Mormons are convinced that their founder, Joseph Smith, discovered certain golden plates in his backyard with a special message from God, called *The Book of Mormon.* Christian Scientists believe that Mary Baker Eddy's *Science and Health* is the key to unlocking the healing powers of the Scriptures. Seventh-day Adventists recognize Ellen G. White as a prophetess of God whose revelations prove the 1844 date of Christ's entrance into the heavenly Holy of Holies and His demand that the Saturday Sabbath be reinstituted for the true church.

In every Bible-based cult there exists a basic deviation from the biblical doctrine of revelation. Evangelical Christians believe the Bible is the inspired revelation of God's truth to mankind. We believe it is complete, authoritative, infallible, and inerrant. Cultists, on the other hand, will profess to believe the Bible, but will always want to add some other source of spiritual truth.

The basic mentality of Christian cults is the leader/founder's belief that he or she is right and all others are wrong. This is just as true of R.B. Thieme as it is of Garner Ted Armstrong. Thieme openly attacks other Christian ministries as being erroneous in their doctrines and methods, calling them "hypocrites, jerks and self-righteous snobs."[5]

Thieme's booklets show him in full military regalia, laud his knowledge of biblical languages, and emphasize his worldwide fame for his isogogical, categorical, and exegetical teaching of the Bible. As to his attitude about other believers, Thieme claims, "About 95 per cent of all born-again believers are living a pseudo, abnormal life. They are not only missing the boat, but they have found some satanic substitute or gimmick"[6]

Yet it is Thieme himself who superimposes nonbiblical terminology (e.g., heart "lobes," "grace apparatus perception," and "faith rest technique") on the Scriptures, denies the efficacy of the blood of Christ, and believes man exists to resolve the millions-of-years-old conflict between good and evil angels.[7]

Ronald Enroth of Westmont College in Santa Barbara, California, observes that authoritarian leadership based upon an exclusivistic elitism is a crucial dimension in all religious cults. He observes, "Related to the oppositional character of cults is their elitism and exclusionism. The group is the only one which possesses the truth; and therefore to leave the group is to endanger one's salvation."[8]

It is this very attitude of exclusivity which causes so many cults to develop strict and legalistic guidelines for their members. Enroth notes several examples:[9]

The Christ Family believes that killing animals and eating meat is wrong. Therefore, they require even visitors to take off their belts and shoes before entering one of their camps.

The Church Universal and Triumphant, an occult/psychic group, believes that hair carries the records of the past. Therefore, they require both men and women at their Summit University to have short hair as a sign of their new birth.

The Unification Church (Moonies) believes that sleepy demons attack believers during the night. Therefore, they jump up out of bed in the morning in a way that will shake off all the demons from the night before.

Oppositional Stance:

"All other religions are wrong but ours."

Once a religious cult is convinced that it has a corner on the truth, all other religious groups are judged to be in error. The cult becomes its own standard of "orthodoxy" and all others are viewed as heretics. Christian-based cults are especially critical of other Christian denominations in this regard.

Victor Paul Wierwille, founder of The Way International, believes that biblical truth has been lost since the first century A.D. and that he alone has taught the Word correctly since that time. By contrast, all other Christian bodies are viewed as being in error.

R.B. Thieme of the Berachah Church believes that the concept of the atonement by the blood of Christ has "traditionally been misunderstood." He adds further that: "the majority of hymns which have been written about the blood are totally confusing."[10] By inference, he implies that the traditional evangelical view of the blood atonement is wrong.

Jehovah's Witnesses believe that Christendom is the "chief spokesman of Satan on earth." Non-Witnesses are viewed as the "Great Whore of Babylon." They are to be "hated in the truest sense" as haters of God and unfit to live on the earth. They even go so far as to plead Jehovah's wrath and anger upon those who profess to be Christians.[11]

From the time of Joseph Smith's "first vision," Mormons have condemned all other churches as false. They view their church as the "only true and living church upon the face of the whole earth."[12] They believe salvation cannot be found apart from the Mormon Church because "all other churches are entirely destitute of all authority from God."[13] A recent Mormon theologian, Bruce McConkie, declared, "Mormons . . . have the only pure and perfect Christianity now on earth. . . . All other systems of religion are false."[14]

One of the most outspoken cults is the Church of Scientology. They believe they are being persecuted and attacked by the federal government. Therefore, they are constantly engaged in legal conflicts with government agencies. In fact, the Scientology Code calls upon L. Ron Hubbard's followers to "punish to the fullest extent of my power anyone misusing or degrading Scientology to harmful ends."[15]

The Unification Church (Moonies) believes it is in a spiritual struggle for the souls of young people. Reverend Moon's visits to the United States have been described as Father's (Moon's) attempt to pull American young people to the side of God in a great spiritual "tug of war."[16] The enemy is not only secularism but American Christianity, which is viewed as having a false view of the importance of Jesus, whom Moon claims to have conquered in the spirit world. When Moon was indicted on federal tax-evasion charges in 1981, he told his followers that he was declaring war on the "real enemies of America"—the U.S. government.

Doctrinal Ambiguity:
"Truth doesn't have to make sense."

Most cults arise from the aberrational teachings of a single leader who has given little thought to the doctrinal implications of his or her teaching. Once the basic teachings of that leader are examined by other theologians, doctrinal discrepancies begin to emerge. This usually puts the cult on the defensive. Doctrinal "theologizing" becomes necessary in order to defend the leader's views.

It is this defensive posture that often leads to doctrinal ambiguity and even secrecy. Cult theology becomes what Enroth calls "split-level religion." It has both an *inner* truth (the cult's real belief system) and an *outer* truth (the appealing public face put on controversial beliefs). For example, Moonies will not hesitate to represent themselves as a "Christian youth group," knowing all along that they believe Jesus failed in His earthly mission.

One writer puts it this way: Split-level cultic religion "accepts the appropriateness (and practical necessity) of a deliberately created gap between the picture that is projected to the general public and the inner reality known to initiates."[17] For example, members of the Church Universal and Triumphant who reach the level of instructional tapes called "Keepers of the Flame" are required to sign a pledge of confidentiality and promise to share this information with no one. The tapes are to be returned or destroyed!

Most religious cults thrive on an appeal to the devotee's emotions. In many cases, that appeal is very subjective—even anti-intellectual. "Follow your feelings" is the message of Indian guru Bhagwan Shree Rajneesh. Former devotees of guru Maharaj Ji and the Divine Light Mission describe a similar appeal to "blissful feelings . . . closing your mind to your past . . . opening up to new experiences."[18]

Even long-standing cults like the Seventh-day Adventists, Mormons, and Jehovah's Witnesses fall back on the "leap of faith" argument. "Just believe it and God will take care of the rest," a Mormon once told me (Ed). "It doesn't have to make sense to be true," he added.

Unfortunately, some evangelicals resort to this same kind of anti-intellectual appeal. That is totally unscriptural. The biblical writers constantly appealed to scriptural statements, historical evidence, and eyewitness accounts to verify their teachings. In defending the fact of the resurrection of Christ, the apostle Paul said, "He appeared to Peter, and then to the Twelve. After that, he appeared to more than five hundred of the brothers at the same time, most of whom are still living [in Paul's day], though some have fallen asleep. Then he appeared to James, then to all the apostles, and last of all he appeared to me also" (1 Corinthians 15:5-7 NIV).

"Just believe!" may sound like good advice. But when faith is detached from the facts, it becomes a purely erroneous experience. Tragically, there is little difference between a cultist claiming to have seen an angel, translated a golden tablet, been baptized by John the Baptist, and commissioned to be an apostle and a cancer victim claiming to have been healed only to die of cancer some months later.

Denial of the Trinity:
*"A three-headed god
comes right from ancient paganism."*

Virtually every cult, except the Seventh-day Adventists, denies the Christian doctrine of the Trinity. The biblical view of the divine equality of the Father, Son, and Holy Spirit as a tri-unity is sternly rejected by most cults. Some deny God the Father (Jesus-only Pentecostals); some deny the deity of Christ (Mormons and Jehovah's Witnesses); some deny the personality of the Holy Spirit (Jehovah's Witnesses and Christian Scientists).

Jehovah's Witnesses teach that Jesus was a created being and that the Holy Spirit is the invisible force of God, not a person of the godhead. Jehovah God (Father) is the only divine being. Christ is "a god," but He is not God. In regard to the Trinity, Watchtower literature clearly states, "Such doctrine is not of God.... Satan is the originator of the trinity doctrine ... of a freakish-looking three-headed God."[19]

Mormons believe that God was once man (in fact, Adam) and that he became an exalted man who eventually was enthroned as God. Joseph Smith said, "God was once as we are now."[20] Brigham Young said, "When our father Adam came into the Garden of Eden, he came into it with a celestial body and brought Eve, one of his celestial wives with him.... He is our father and our God and the only God with whom we have to do."[21] Lorenzo Snow, former president of the Mormon Church, said, "As man is, God once was; as God is, man may become."[22]

Christian Science founder Mary Baker Eddy said, "The theory of three persons in one God suggests heathen gods."[23] She believed the Jehovah of the Old Testament was a tribal god, not the Divine Principle of Love, whom she worshiped. Ultimately, she taught that "the soul, or mind, of the spiritual man is God, the Divine Principle of all being."[24]

Worldwide Church of God founder Herbert W. Armstrong also denied the biblical doctrine of the Trinity. Armstrong taught that Jesus was not divine, but a human being who was the first person ever saved by God. "Millions are deceived," Armstrong proclaimed, "by the Satan-inspired doctrine of the deity of Christ."[25] Armstrong's followers believe that each individual has the potential to become God. In the pamphlet *Why Were You Born?* Armstrong says, "The purpose of your being alive is that finally you be born into the Kingdom of God, when you will actually *be* God ... you are training to become God."[26]

In occult and New Age circles, the doctrine of the Trinity is vehemently denied. Theosophist Helena Blavatsky said,

"We reject the idea of a personal God. . . . Jesus Christ was no man but the divine principle in every human being."[27] Swedenborgians also reject the Trinity as a "false tenet . . . a perversion of the Christian Church." God is viewed as the impersonal Divine Essence. [28] Reincarnationists like Edgar Cayce or Shirley MacLaine view God as an ever-expanding pantheistic impersonal force. To them, God is Universal Mind, Energy, or Force. Every individual is involved in a series of reincarnations attempting to merge upward into becoming God.

Defective Christology:
"Jesus died for our sins, but . . ."

Who is the real Jesus? Why did He come to earth? What did He come to do? The answers to these questions make up the segment of theology generally known as Christology, or the doctrine of Christ. This doctrine is the great dividing point between the cults and Christian denominations. It is over the person and work of Christ that the cults produce their greatest errors. In his popular book *The Real Jesus,* Garner Ted Armstrong states, "Jesus did not come to save the world some two thousand years ago, He has not been trying to save it since, and He is not trying to save it today."[29]

Christian Science founder Mary Baker Eddy claimed that Jesus was a spiritual, not physical, being born of the virgin Mary's "spiritual thoughts." His death was an illusion showing us how to triumph over the physical realm of existence. Eddy taught that His atonement and resurrection were only spiritual. "The material blood of Jesus," she wrote, "is no more efficacious to cleanse from sin when it was shed upon the accursed tree than when it was flowing in his veins."[30]

Jehovah's Witnesses, following the teachings of Charles Russell, believe Jesus was a "human son of God" created by

Jehovah. He was "a god," but "he was not God."[31] They also believe that the human Jesus was not raised from the dead, but that He was raised spiritually and He has returned (in 1914) spiritually (or as a spirit). The denial of the deity of Christ and His bodily resurrection and return are the major pillars of Jehovah's Witness theology.

Mormons, following Brigham Young, believe that Jesus was conceived by Adam-God, the "same character who was in the Garden of Eden and who is our father in heaven."[32] Mormons deny the spirituality of God, teaching that He was previously the man Adam. They also teach that there are many gods. Joseph Smith said, "The doctrine of the plurality of gods is as prominent in the Bible as any other doctrine."[33] Mormons also believe that mortal men can, by obedience to the Mormon Church, become gods themselves. Jesus is viewed as the first son of the physical union of Adam-God and Mary. According to Mormon doctrine, Christ is no more uniquely divine in His essence than is any human being. Mormons, therefore, deny His essential deity by elevating all men to the level of deity.

Mormons also teach that at the wedding at Cana, Jesus married Mary, Martha, and the "other Mary" so that He could have eternal offspring in the life to come. Otherwise, He would be limited to being an angel and not a god in the eternal state, (Mormons teach that one must be married in this life to be married in the next life). While Mormons teach the concept of Christ's atonement, they believe His death on the cross only guarantees one's resurrection, not one's salvation.

Seventh-day Adventists clearly affirm the deity of Christ. Yet they tend to favor the idea that Jesus had an inherited tendency to sin, and thus deny or question the doctrine of impeccability. But it is in regard to their view of the atonement of Christ that Adventists face their greatest challenges. They do not believe the atonement was finished on the cross but is only now, since 1844, being accomplished in the heavenly Holy of Holies. Prior to October 22, 1844, Christ only forgave sins, but since then He has removed them by the process of the "investigative judgment."

Sun Myung Moon of the Unification Church teaches that Jesus was a man who is now a spirit being. Moon states, "It is plain that Jesus is not God himself."[34] He also adds that Christ's death on the cross was unable to establish the kingdom of heaven on earth because Jesus came to rule, not to die. Thus, He failed in His earthly mission. Now, Moon believes, it is his turn to fulfill the messianic calling.

The apostle Paul said to not be led astray "if someone comes to you and preaches a Jesus other than the Jesus we preached, or if you receive a different spirit from the one you received, or a different gospel from the one you accepted" (2 Corinthians 11:4). He was even stronger when he said, "Even if we or an angel from heaven should preach a gospel other than the one we preached to you, let him be eternally condemned!" (Galatians 1:8).

The great problem with the cults is that they teach another Jesus who is less than the divine Son of God. The Jesus of the cults is not the Jesus of the Bible. Therefore, the Jesus they present must be rejected as a lie and a perversion of the biblical Jesus. The Bible warns us, "Every spirit that acknowledges that Jesus Christ has come in the flesh is from God, but every spirit that does not acknowledge Jesus is not from God. This is the spirit of the antichrist, which you have heard is coming and even now is already in the world" (1 John 4:2,3).

Salvation by Works:

*"It is one thing to believe,
but you've got to work at it too."*

Every religion in the world says you must work your way to God. Only biblical Christianity says God has worked His way to you. This is the final watershed between biblical Christianity and cultic confusion. The cults are never satisfied with the doctrine of grace. They always want to add something to the idea of salvation by faith alone.

Christian Science teaches that salvation comes only when one's mind can overcome the physical illusions of sin and death. Mrs. Eddy said, "Man as God's idea is *already* saved with an everlasting salvation."[35] How does one realize this salvation that is already provided? By practicing the principles of Divine Science as elucidated by Mrs. Eddy. These principles are intended to release a person from false beliefs about sin, sickness, death, hell, judgment, and condemnation. They involve personal repentance and the need to stop sinning in order to overcome the illusion of sin.

Jehovah's Witnesses teach that salvation will come only for those who have faith in Jehovah God and dedicate themselves to do God's will by being His faithful witnesses on earth. Thus, the concept of "salvation by witnessing" is essential to Jehovah's Witness theology. But the "anointed class" (144,000) and the "other sheep" are saved by their faith and dedication to God. Thus, Jehovah's Witnesses add dedication to faith as an ingredient in salvation. Further, they insist such dedication can only be demonstrated by baptism by their leadership. Ultimately, they split the church into two bodies with two separate future hopes: one earthly and one heavenly.

Mormons present an even more complicated view of salvation. They vigorously reject the doctrine of justification by faith, calling it a "pernicious doctrine."[36] Instead, Mormons teach that obedience to the laws and ordinances of God is essential for eternal salvation, which cannot be obtained apart from the Mormon Church. One must be baptized in, married in, and a member of the Mormon Church to live in the celestial realm. Salvation not only guarantees eternal life but also exaltation to become a god, live in celestial marriage with one's wives, and to continue producing children for all eternity.

Seventh-day Adventists deny that they teach salvation by works, but their doctrines of the investigative judgment and Sabbath-keeping do just that. Adventists believe the command to keep the Saturday Sabbath is binding on the church today. All who fail to observe it prove they are lost and under the mark of the Beast. Hoekema observes, "In the last analysis, the Adventists teach that it is not the work of Christ done once for all on the cross, but their faithful keeping of God's commandments and their faithful confession of every sin that determines whether they are saved or lost."[37]

Other examples of salvation by works are almost endless:

Hare Krishnas must keep repeating their prayers to Krishna.

Moonies continue selling flowers and raising money as the devoted "heavenly children" of Reverend Moon.

Devotees of Rajneesh must continue on the path of enlightenment until they become Buddhas themselves.

Followers of Maharishi Mahesh Yogi, the originator of Transcendental Meditation, must continue to meditate until their souls merge with the absolute being of everything around them.

The Way International founder Paul Wierwille teaches that "the only visible and audible proof that a man has been born again and filled with the Holy Spirit is *always* that he speaks in a tongue or tongues."[38]

The Church Universal and Triumphant teaches that one must reach the level of the "I AM" Ascended Masters and enter the realm of the Violet Consuming Flame in order to find true salvation.

The Church of the Living Word (or The Walk) teaches that salvation is a continuing process administered by the church and resulting in the deification of its members. Thus, salvation is in stages and is based upon personal effort rather than the grace of God.[39]

Legalistic Structure:
"We don't dress or act that way."

The ultimate mechanism of control in the cult is the use of sanctions, discipline, intimidation, or excommunication. This approach to controlling behavior is a lot like the practice of "shunning" in the Amish communities. Those who fail to or refuse to conform are ostracized by the rest of the group. This creates a mentality of conformity to avoid rejection. Enroth observes,

> Cults require conformity to established practices and beliefs and readily exercise sanctions against the wayward. Those who fail to demonstrate proper allegiance, who raise too many questions, disobey the rules or openly rebel are punished, formally excommunicated or asked to leave the group.[40]

Public confessions, emotional humiliation, and in some cases even corporal discipline are used to control cult members. This will vary greatly from one group to another. The intensity of control will also vary from small, tightly controlled groups to larger and more loosely structured groups. Mormons hold people by promises of celestial marriage and eternal families. They intimidate by threatening to withhold eternal blessings. But they don't hold people by force against their wills, like Jim Jones did. The same is true of Jehovah's Witnesses. They promise to get you through the Battle of Armageddon, but they don't hold anyone captive by force.

The real strings are attached to the cult members in the preaching and teaching of each group. For example, Mormon missionaries always look clean-cut, ride a bicycle, and wear white shirts with ties. Hare Krishnas shave their heads and sell flowers and magazines. Moonies also tend to look clean-cut, but Branch Davidians look like rejects from a rock group. Each cult has its own "look" and "vocabulary."

The longer one is in a particular cult, the more familiar he or she becomes with the terminology and lifestyle of the group. Strange terms like "temple marriage," "heavenly family," "flirty fishing," "pre-clear," "auras," "channeling," and "mind science" don't seem so strange anymore. Even the unconventional dress or look of the group becomes so familiar that it seems ordinary.

Rules, regulations, and restrictions help to keep the cult followers in line. Conformity to the lifestyle of the group becomes the everyday reality of the devotee. Thoughts of violating that conformity are viewed as rebellion against God Himself. Therefore, sincere cultists will often allow themselves to be subjected to ridiculous and excessive restrictions in order to maintain their acceptance by the group or to avoid exclusion.

Certainly there is a place for discipline, self-denial, and self-restraint in true Christianity. But when group-imposed restrictions become the tests of spirituality or the basis for membership, acceptance, or rejection from fellowship, then the group has overstepped proper biblical guidelines. Harold Bussell, chaplain at Gordon College, puts it this way, "We start creating unhealthy dependence on *our* word, rather than on God's Word."[41] When that occurs, the cult member accepts the legalistic views of the group as gospel truth and he or she is locked into a lifetime of self-imposed spiritual seduction.

Riders of the Cosmic Circuit

Eastern Mysticism and Hindu-based Cults

He is God in human form," the New Delhi girl announced to Tal Brooke. *Newsweek* called him, "India's first *Avatar* since Krishna" in a story of how he had turned water into gasoline for his car. He is Sai Baba, India's god-man incarnate, complete with undeniable miracles and healing powers.

"The moment I had long awaited and the very reason I had come to India was to find One who had crossed the gulf of eternity and peered into the heart and secrets of all existence," Brooke explains. "If you will, a Rider of the cosmic Circuit—one who has mastered the cosmos."[1]

Tal Brooke continues,

> "Bhagavan (God) is bringing you into his presence," the driver assured me. In the small town of Andhra Pradesh, I soon stood among Baba's elect devotees waiting for the arrival of his limousine. The hush spreads over the crowd. I am in the inner

courtyard, where few are permitted. It has been over a month since I first got the news of Baba in Delhi.

Then a limousine glides into the gate through awed silence. Two dazzling eyes pierce the windshield. Baba emerges, as people stand at a respectful distance. He looks off into mountains and at the sky. His hands weave the air in cryptic gestures. The earth seems to stand still.

Sai Baba glows red in the coral-amber penumbra of South India's equatorial sunset. The door of his limousine is closed behind him. Before me undoubtedly stands the most magnetic human form I have ever seen in my life. The eyes remind me of a searching lighthouse.

Then my mood suddenly repolarizes by Baba's force, as I feel the contradiction that comes from being head-on with a presence superhumanly great. I am dwarfed. I feel hope and I feel the abyss. I am a clear-glass tumbler standing before an all-seeing-eye.

A Telegram from the Supernatural

There was an immediately obvious non-human quality about Baba, but I was not sure I could define it. Only a "full master" could transcend the human condition. As Baba proceeded from person to person, he seemed to act in absolute spontaneity, suggesting the busy impersonality of a bee vibrating pollen out of a flower. And this rebounding from person to person made me ponder a key idea of Vedanta—Baba's instant, spontaneous access to people's thoughts could be explained by the concept of "thoughtless-all-knowing." Only an enlightened person without the limiting ego could harbor the infinite impersonal mind of God, as the mystics explain it. And this implied to me that Baba was like a walking doorway into the Absolute.

Baba suddenly spun away from the people he was talking to and came straight over to me. Baba's English was practically baby-talk, while his black eyes told an entirely different story, radiating vibrant awareness. He did not seem to assess me, because he already knew me. "Hello, Rowdeeee," he chimed with taunting playfulness. Then looking concerned he asked,

"What's wrong, some sickness in the stomach?"

Baba was right. I had dysentery. I made a signal with my eyes to his hand as though to ask what he had been materializing. Baba anticipated the question.

"Oh yes . . . called *vibhuti*, divine ash."

Again Baba's hand began rotating in wide circles for at least the fourth time in five minutes. In an instant he had a handful of grey powder sitting in his hand, which he immediately poured into mine saying,

"Eat, eat, it is good for the health."

I stood there stunned eating the ash out of my hand. What I wanted to do, far from eating the ash, was to enshrine it in a glass case in the British Museum or take it to the Lawrence Berkeley radiation labs for analysis. I had seen a miracle! I was now eating that miracle! Yet I had in my hand the very evidence that would cut through the foundational philosophies that my culture was now so enamored with—the materialism, scientific pre-suppositions, indeed the empty logical positivism of our day and our institutions. There it was in my hand, a supernatural statement against all this empty-headed presumption. A telegram from the supernatural.

Before a silent crowd of onlookers, Baba looked me up and down. He patted me on the back.

"I have been waiting for you. It was I who made you come to India."[2]

The Journey into Inner Space

Brooke was quickly identified as an "Adept," one having great potential to become spiritually advanced. He soon was promoted into the inner circle of Sai Baba's followers in India. As a Westerner he experienced the inner life of the cult like few others ever had. But in time he would write, "What had at first looked like the gates of Heaven, when I first entered Baba's Kingdom, had suddenly one day become the gates of Hell."[3]

Baba claimed to be the world's only living *avatar* (a god willing his own incarnation). Hindus believe that an avatar, like Krishna, breaks out of the ocean of Brahman to come to earth to change one age into another age. Indian mystics believe this is the Kali Yuga, the age of iron and wickedness. They also believe that Vishnu will appear soon as Kalki, the final avatar, and inaugurate a new age of peace.

Sai Baba has claimed since childhood that he is the Kalki avatar, as well as the returned Christ. Countless miracles are attributed to him and his followers number in excess of twenty million devotees. Sai Baba is the only Indian god-man to have temples built to him during his own lifetime. Born on November 23, 1926, during an astrological convergence of great importance, Baba was raised in the remote town of Puttaparthi in the Penukunda District of India. The area is known for its religious devotion and occult phenomenon. Born as Sathyanarayana Raju, he began materializing objects not found in his region even as a young child.

In March of 1940, Raju screamed violently, went into convulsions, and was unconscious for several days. When he awoke, he evidenced a total transformation of personality. His family was shocked and feared he was demon-possessed. On May 23, 1940, three months after he had first fallen unconscious, the 13-year-old announced that he was Sai Baba, a reincarnation of one of India's most powerful god-men, Sai Baba of Shirdi.

Claims of healing miracles, personal "appearances," levitation, manifestations, and even a transfiguration (blinding light radiating from his head) spread all over India. One of his early converts was India's outstanding nuclear physicist, Dr. Bhagavantam, a graduate of Cambridge University. The skeptical physicist argued with Baba about the subatomic source of energy. Baba told him that ultimate energy is pure consciousness from God. Asking the doctor to pour sand through his hands, Baba purportedly materialized a copy of the sacred *Bhagavad Gita* into the scientist's hands, and he became a convert for life!

"I am the embodiment of truth," Baba proclaims. "The moment you came into my presence, all your sins are forgiven. . . . My power is limitless and divine. . . . I can give you full self-realization, and take you back to the eternal, limitless God-consciousness."[4] By meditation on and worship of Baba, one hopes to experience possession by the "inner Baba," who works the miraculous transformation of the soul.

Hindu-Based Cults

Hinduism originated in India 3,000 to 4,000 years ago and is probably the oldest false religion still widely practiced in the world today. Bob Larson has called it "religious anarchy in action."[5] It has no official ecclesiastical hierarchy or structure. Doug Groothuis notes, "Hinduism is a religion of diverse faces—some polytheistic, some theistic, and some pantheistic."[6]

At the heart of Hinduism is the concept of *monism* ("oneness with all"). It has been called the "great discovery" of India's sages. It is the idea that man is one with the universe. The ultimate reality beyond the phenomenal universe is consciousness, called *Brahman*. It is viewed as the eternal nature of all that is—humans, animals, and even the rocks and dirt.

Like Buddhism, Hinduism shares the Eastern tradition of an all-encompassing oneness. The comprehension of that oneness releases the soul from the illusion of death and the vicious cycle of reincarnation. The ignorance of that oneness is a problem of mental perception, not mortal sin. When men fail to understand this they are doomed to repeat various reincarnations until they finally come to true enlightenment.

In Hinduism, the experience of oneness with the One is called *moksha, satchidananda,* or *satori.* According to the late and controversial guru Bhagwan Shree Rajneesh, "*moksha* is not freedom *of* the self, but freedom *from* the self."[7] Through the process of meditation, he promises that "you will be tuned to the infinite, then you will be tuned to the cosmic—then you will be one with the whole."[8]

The Hindu scriptures, *Upanishads*, call this merger of the self with divine consciousness, "That art Thou."[9] The Hindu texts go on to promise: "He who has realized eternal Truth does not see death, nor illness, nor pain; he sees everything as the Self, and obtains all."[10] This is pantheistic monism: all is god; all is one; therefore, I am god. In this belief system there is no ultimate distinction between humanity and deity. Groothuis explains, "The spirit of oriental religion differs substantially from Christianity in that it blurs or obliterates the distinction between Creator and the creation."[11]

To accomplish oneness with the divine is to plug into the spiritual power line of the cosmic circuit. Whether one calls this practice self-discovery, meditation, yoga, or something else, it is an absolute imperative in Eastern religions. Western spirituality of faith, prayer, and obedience to an external God is replaced with experimental meditation on the god within oneself. Eastern meditative practices emphasize emptying the mind of the illusion of separation from the divine and the regaining of unity with the divine. To accomplish this, holy words (*mantras*) are often repeated to change one's conscious state. Special postures (*yoga*, meaning "union with God") may also be employed to gain spiritual unity with all things.

God's Cosmic Game

The goal of the Eastern mystics is to find god within one's self. The god of Eastern religions is beyond rationality. He cannot be objectified or quantified. He is neither good nor evil. One cannot have a personal relationship with this god because this god is not a person. God is viewed, rather, as the great cosmic Force. He is the collective consciousness of all humanity, which has both a dark side and a light side. If this sounds familiar, it was woven into the fabric of George Lucas's *Star Wars* trilogy. "May the Force be with you," was more than harmless wishful thinking—it is the heart and soul of Eastern mysticism!

If God is viewed as an impersonal cosmic Force, then the world is but an illusion in God's great cosmic game. Thus, Hinduism sweeps away the reality of sin, pain, suffering, and death as illusions of the mind. In the sacred *Bhagavad Gita* ("Song of God"), Lord Krishna, the manifestation of God on earth, advises, "That reality that pervades the universe is indestructible. No one has the power to change the changeless. Bodies are said to die, but That which possesses the body is eternal. It cannot be limited or destroyed."[12]

To the devout Hindu, it does not matter what happens (or from their viewpoint, *appears* to happen) in this life. Since all that is material is illusion, it does not matter whether one is rich or poor, educated or uneducated, clean or filthy, good or bad. Each individual must rise above his circumstances through a series of reincarnations until he or she has become one with the Infinite. To accomplish this, the sacred *Upanishads* teach that meditation is the best way to purify the heart through an unbroken stream of thought focused on an object. By this process, the mind is able to attain perfect calmness and pursue the path of salvation (called "Enlightenment") by contemplations. When God-realization is achieved, enlightenment occurs and the individual's soul is released into the Cosmic Force.

The teaching of the *Bhagavad Gita*, also called the "Song Celestial of Lord Krishna," teaches three essential elements of theology:

1. *Man is immortal.* He has always existed as an expression of godhead and he will always exist and shall never cease to be. Therefore, he cannot really die or cease to exist.
2. *Man is part of the infinite.* He is eternally part of the Absolute Reality (*Brahman*). But he

must come to the realization of this truth in order to attain it.

3. *Reincarnation* (transmigration of the soul) and *karma* (the law of cause and effect) *explain life on earth.* Man must pass through many successive reincarnations in order to escape his karma and be united with the Eternal Force.

Within the Hindu religious system is a reverence given to teachers (gurus) as essential guides along the spiritual path to Enlightenment. Their teachings are transmitted through men who have realized deity. Irvine Robertson observes,

> The "gurus" of today consistently refer to their teachers from whom they received enlightenment. Thus the Guru Maharaj Ji acknowledges his father, Shri Hans Ji Maharaj, as his Satguru; Guru Maharishi Mahesh Yogi learned the technique of transcendental meditation (TM) from his teacher, Guru Dev; His Divine Grace A.C. Bhaktivendanta Swami Prabhupada teaches the supremacy of the Lord Krishna as he learned from his guru, Bhakti Siddhanta Sarasvanti; and so on. None of the present "swamis" claim originality, although each indicates that his is *the* way for the present time.[13]

Some gurus have gone so far as to claim to be avatars, incarnations of God on the earth. Krishna is generally recognized as the last true avatar. But current mystics have also claimed to be God incarnate. Maharaj Ji is hailed as "Lord of the Universe . . . the greatest incarnation of God that ever trod the face of this planet."[14] Swami Prabhupada is honored as "one who knows the Absolute Truth." He is recognized as Supreme and Mighty Lord because he is "God's most confidential servitor."[15] Meher Baba claimed to be the final incarnation of the godhead in the lineage of Zoroaster, Krishna, Rama, Buddha, Jesus, and Muhammad. Today, Sai Baba claims to be the reincarnate Christ, the only true avatar on earth.

The Great Excuse

The key to Eastern mysticism is its denial of reality. It is a very convenient religion for people who have been constantly invaded and defeated over the centuries. To them, there is no victory or defeat. It is all an illusion. There is also no life or death. These are also illusions. The *Upanishads*, meaning "secret doctrines," reveal the knowledge by which one can escape the harsh realities of life—by denying those realities exist!

The term *Hindu* was originated by the Persians from the Sanskrit name for the Indus River. Hindus themselves refer to their religion as the "eternal system" (*sanatana dharma*). It encompasses various and diverse sects, beliefs, and practices that are all considered part of the one eternal system. Thus Hinduism is like a great tree that has gradually grown and enlarged, rather than a building that was erected by some specific plan.

The divisions of Hinduism are generally based upon devotion to one's favorite deity. A kind of Hindu trinity is represented by *Brahma* the creator, *Vishnu* the preserver, and *Shiva* the destroyer. Beyond them are countless other deities. *Vishnu* is considered to have ten incarnations (e.g., Rama, Krishna, Buddha Kalki [who has yet to appear], and so on). *Vishnu* is symbolically represented by a seven-headed cobra (the symbol chosen by the Symbionese Liberation Army, which abducted Patty Hearst in the sixties). *Shiva* is depicted in highly sexual connotations as a god of terror who wanders about naked, overindulging on drugs, and encouraging sexual orgies and self-mutilation. His female consort, *Shakti*, leads the practice of temple prostitution. The innermost sanctuaries of Shiva Temples always contain a *lingam* stone (a stylized erect phallus) like the one Indiana Jones sought in the movie *Temple of Doom*.

The Dravidians were the earliest settlers of the Indian peninsula. Their religion was animistic and resembled witchcraft. This accounts for the wide acceptance of localized deities and demon worship. Eventually Aryan peoples from the European continent conquered India and introduced their own gods, such as Soma, deity of the hallucinogenic soma plant. This led to the acceptance of mind-expanding drugs. During this period the *Vedas* ("wise sayings") were transferred orally from generation to generation. By 1000 B.C. they were written down in the form of hymns and prayers. During this period the social caste system developed: *Brahmins* were priests and scholars, *Kshatriyas* were rulers and soldiers, *Vaishyas* were farmers and merchants, and *Sudras* were peasants and servants. Eventually, 3,000 subcastes developed, with the "untouchables" at the very bottom of the social structure. Bob Larson notes, "In later centuries, this class division was presumed to be a justification for the doctrines of *Karma* and reincarnation."[16]

By 600 B.C. the culture of India was dramatically impacted by the *Upanishads'* which reformed Hinduism from an animistic religion of exorcism and spell-casting into a more philosophic religion that emphasized disciples "sitting at the feet" of wise master teachers (gurus). Life was viewed as an endless cycle (a great wheel) in the soul's transmigration through a series of reincarnations. Escaping the retributive law of karma could occur only when an individual soul was absorbed by the universal soul (*Brahman*).

The final era in Hinduism's historic development came right after the beginning of the Christian period, when the Vedantic literature became India's dominant scriptures. During this time the concept of *maya* was developed. It taught that all matter is illusionary. Reality is, in fact, unreality. Therefore, the message of the *Bhagavad Gita* is one of indifference to desire, pleasure, or pain.

It is the concept of *maya* that becomes the great excuse in Hindu religions. The suffering millions of India suffer only because of wrong thinking. Their plight is only an illusion. Since man is ultimately god, sin is also an illusion. Moral guilt and social justice are viewed as virtually unnecessary. Whatever doesn't get resolved in this life will be taken care of in the next, and the next, and the next.

Karma is the inexorable law of retributive justice and acts independent of the gods. Every act of this life influences one's next incarnation. The healthy and wealthy are viewed as having accumulated good karma in their past life (or lives) and the poor and sickly are viewed as having their just reward for their past sins in another life.

The theological and philosophical concepts of Hinduism leave one with the ultimate conclusion of fatalism. One is resigned to his or her fate in this life as a victim of cosmic chance. There is no loving Savior to forgive your sins or set you free from your karma. Your only hope is to do better this time so you can reincarnate better next time. In the meantime, all of the universe is *lila*, God's cosmic game. Pain and pleasure are only illusions. Suffering is not real and need not be alleviated. To do so interferes with the laws of karma.

Left to its logical conclusions, Hinduism produces a society that worships sacred cows, snakes, and rats as reincarnated people, while allowing real people to live in filth and squalor on the excuse that it is all an illusion! In such a culture, "holy men" charm snakes, sit on beds of nails, walk on hot coals of fire, and eat cow manure and broken glass!

Yet it is the above-stated concepts that give Hindu-based cults their great appeal. Nearly ten thousand Westerners flock to India every year in search of spiritual truth. Thousands more are attracted to Hindu-based cults at home. All of them are seeking the "great escape" from the harsh realities of life.

Getting Back to God

Back to Godhead, the colorful magazine of the Hare Krishna movement, promises it is "the only magazine in the

Western world to present the authorized transcendental science of God-realization known only to the saints of India's unbroken disciplic succession."[17] Popularly known as Hare Krishna, the movement is officially called the International Society for Krishna Consciousness (ISKCON). It promotes chanting the name of the Supreme Personality of the Godhead, Lord Krishna, as the way back to the blissful state of personal deity.

Hindus consider Krishna to have been one of the nine incarnations of the god Vishnu. However, ISKCON teaches that "Krishna is the Supreme Personality of the Godhead and the supreme authority on the Gita."[18] Following the pantheistic concepts of Hinduism, Krishna devotees believe Krishna is the essence of all existence and that one's knowledge of him must be relearned. Thus, Krishna-consciousness is viewed as the "perfect process for solving all the problems of life because it can at once end our illusionary separation from Krishna, the Supreme Lord."[19]

Krishna devotees all use the same *mantra*, called *Mahamantra* ("the great mantra"):

> Hare Krishna, Hare Krishna
> Krishna, Krishna, Hare, Hare,
> Hare Rama, Hare Rama
> Rama, Rama, Hare, Hare.

The founder and guru of the modern Krishna movement was His Divine Grace A.C. Bhaktivedanta Swami Prabhupada whose picture adorns most ISKCON literature. He claimed to be the self-realized "representative of Krishna" and is honored as Supreme and Almighty Lord by his devotees. His death in 1978 had no measurable effect on his followers. Interestingly, he followed the dualistic school of Hindu thought rather than the monistic. Nevertheless, the swami taught absorption into godhead as the ultimate goal of Krishna devotees.

ISKCON is a modern adaptation of *bhakti yoga*, which was originally developed by Caitanya Mahaprabu (A.D. 1486-1534). He emphasized liberation (*mukti*) through constant devotional service to Krishna as the ultimate personal god. Caitanya introduced *sankirtana*, the ecstatic chanting and dancing that is at the heart of the Hare Krishna movement today. A.C. Bhaktivedanta was born in Calcutta, India, in 1896 as Abhay Charan De. He was introduced to *bhakti yoga* in 1933, changed his name in 1947, and in 1954 he renounced his wife and family to become a monk.

Swami Bhaktivedanta came to New York in 1965 and founded ISKCON in 1966. He eventually published 30 books, founded the *Back to Godhead* magazine, and established 100 temples in North America. It is within the rigid structure of temple life that devotees are pressured to conform. Women are viewed as inferior to men and are not allowed to make decisions. Children are taken away from their parents at age five and sent to the ISKCON school to be educated in Krishna-consciousness so they will not have to be reincarnated again.

Dedication to Krishna must be total. The devotee is asked to give up all personal desires to the Supreme Lord. Men shave their heads except for the *chutiya*, a small tuft or ponytail on the back of the head. Women wear the modest Indian saris. Sex is forbidden except for the purpose of having children in marriage. Eating is strictly limited to a vegetarian diet. And communal life is rigidly regulated. Devotees are awakened at 3:30 A.M. by chanting "Hare Krishna." Worshiping deities and "feeding" and bathing of idols follows at 4:00 A.M. This is followed by breakfast, ecstatic group chanting and dancing (*sankirtan*), and six or seven hours of literature distribution to those poor souls who have forgotten Krishna.

When a new temple was opened in the Haight-Ashbury district of San Francisco, it created an immediate sensation— an alternative to the drug culture. George Harrison's song about Krishna, "My Sweet Lord," hit the top of the music charts and the movement took off like a rocket.

The missionary zeal of Hare Krishna devotees is incredible. They virtually give up their lives to promote their faith in Krishna. Ken Boa observes,

> The soul goes through the fourfold misery of birth, disease, old age and death with every incarnation. Thus, there is a need for liberation from *samsara*, the cycle of repeated incarnations. One who attains Krishna consciousness achieves this liberation and receives an eternal, spiritual body. He then dwells in eternity, bliss and knowledge with Krishna in his residence, Krishna-loka. This is the soul's journey back to Godhead.[20]

It is the excessive devotion to the constantly repeated *mantra* and the rigid control of the devotee's personal life that concern pastors, parents, and psychologists alike. The endless repetition of chanting throws the devotee into a trance. Personalities change. Outward displays of emotion disappear. Ritual replaces responsibility. The end result is a kind of self-hypnosis that leaves the devotee with no will, no life, and no purpose of his own—all in the name of coming back to God.

Spirit of Antichrist

There can be no doubt that Satan himself and his demonic hordes fill the void of consciousness that is so essential to the Hindu concept of Enlightenment. The search within the inner recess of the human soul that is devoid of Jesus Christ eventually leads to the evil one! It is in this sense that the apostle John warned, "The spirit of the antichrist . . . even now is already in the world" (1 John 4:3).

That evil spirit takes many forms: Sai Baba, with his claim to be the final incarnation of God (the Kalki avatar), the reincarnated Christ, comes complete with incontestable miracles. Meher Baba, also of Poona, India, who claimed to be the incarnation of Christ, stopped speaking from 1925 until he "dropped his body" (died) in 1969. "You have had enough of my words, now is the time to live by them," he announced before his self-imposed silence. Peter Townshend of the rock group The Who worshipped Baba as the Christ, as do all "Baba lovers." Baba Muktanda of Mangalore, India, claims 100,000 followers from the United States who have experienced *shaktipat*, or instantaneous enlightenment, for only $100 a day. "God is within you. Honor and worship your inner being," Muktanda declares. His get-to-godhead-quick-approach is especially appealing to American audiences.

The great tragedy of Eastern mysticism is that it does not deliver what it promises. One needs only to examine the plight of India's people for evidence. Mysticism leaves people either devoid of reality or desperately depressed by their human struggle to become god. The appeal is simply a repackaging of Satan's oldest lie: "You shall be like God." It is also the spiritual self-deception that Satan himself concocted when he aspired to be God and fell from his exalted state. Trying to become their own gods, sinful people fall victim to the father of all lies—Satan himself.

The New Age Rage

New Age Cults
and Their Popular Appeal

I first met Orin in 1977," Sanaya Roman explains of her first encounter with her spirit guide. "Orin came through the Ouija Board, announcing that he was a master teacher and that we would be hearing more from him as I grew more able to receive him."[1]

Sanaya was a college graduate pursuing a business career in marketing. She had read several books by Jane Roberts, the self-proclaimed "channel" of Seth. After Sanaya talked about the books with her friends, they decided to get a Ouija board and contact some guides on their own. When they began to get messages, they asked for the highest guide available.

Sanaya Roman goes on to say that once she met Orin, she put away the Ouija board and began channeling his messages directly while in a deep trance. She later met Duane Packer, who channeled DaBen. They found that their guides knew one another, so Sanaya and Duane began channeling together. Today they write books and teach seminars called "How to Channel Your Spirit Guide."

In the first chapter of their book *Opening to Channel*, they introduce the reader to a welcome message from Orin and

DaBen. This message announces channeling as an evolutionary leap upward into spiritual unfoldment and conscious
transformation. Channeling, according to Orin and DaBen,
builds a bridge to a loving, meaningful higher consciousness
known as the All-That-Is (or the Universal Mind).

Roman and Packer promise several benefits from channeling via the message of Orin and DaBen:

- Channeling will give you the wise teacher you
  seek—from within yourself.
- Your guide will be a friend who is always there
  to support you.
- Channeling will help you learn to love yourself
  more.
- Spirit guides will help you achieve new levels
  of personal power and spiritual growth.
- All you have to do is ask for a guide and one will
  come to you.

The authors go on to explain that there are basically two
types of spirit guides:

1) *High-level guides.* These spirits deal with the larger
issues of life. Some are former earth-dwellers, like Christ or
Buddha. Others are angels or extraterrestrial beings from
other galaxies. Some appear as American-Indian medicine
men, some as Chinese sages, and some as East-Indian gurus.
The great masters, like Saint Germain, are from the "fourth
dimension" outside the galaxies of stars.

2) *Personal guides.* These are "guardian angels" assigned
to each one of us for our lifetime. These personal guides act as
links between you and your high-level guide. We are also told
not to worry about the source of the guides; we need only to
follow those who look out for our good.

Orin and DaBen inform us that guides work through the
soul to pass along information to your consciousness. Trans-
mission is able to take place once you align your energy field
with theirs.

Open to What?

Mixing a little bit of scientific information about electro-magnetic fields together with self-help psychology and occult spiritism, the seeker is left wide open to buy into the demonic realm of the spirit world. Opening your soul to channeling the psychologically induced impressions of one's so-called spirit guide plays right into the hand of Satan. Such a subjective and self-centered approach to truth leaves one the victim of "the father of lies" (John 8:44).

C.S. Lewis, in his masterpiece *The Screwtape Letters*, warns against producing a vaguely devotional mood of prayer that has no real concentration of the will or intelligence and bears only a superficial resemblance to true prayer. "That is exactly the sort of prayer we want," Screwtape advises Worm-wood. The demonic uncle goes on to advise his nephew that the best way to nullify human prayer is to get people to "turn their gaze away from Him (God) towards themselves."[2]

This is precisely the danger in the New Age cults. The objective focus is shifted away from God toward self and results in some of the most incredible self-deception ever perpetrated on the general public: channeling, visualization, astral projection, altered consciousness, reincarnation, and even time travel!

In her book *Creative Visualization*, Shakti Gawain advises her reader to relax into "a deep, quiet, meditative state of mind" in order to visualize the reality that you want to create for yourself. "It is not necessary to have faith in any power outside yourself," she adds.[3] Following New Age physics, Gawain suggests that the world is pure energy, rather than material substance, and that things only appear to be real or solid. They can be changed by the positive affirmations of pure energy. She does admit, however, that things like rocks are denser in form and "slower to change and more difficult to affect."[4] No kidding!

To help her readers find the power of positive affirmation, Gawain suggests the following:[5]

- Every day in every way I'm getting better and better.
- My life is blossoming in total perfection.
- Everything I need is already within me.
- I am the master of my life.
- It's okay for me to have everything I want!

Then she explains, "Affirmations are often most powerful and inspiring when they include references to spiritual sources. Mention of God, Christ, Buddha, or any great master adds spiritual energy to your affirmation."[6] She closes with the following examples:

- My higher self is guiding me in everything I do.
- The power of God flows through me.
- Divine love is working through me.
- I am one with my higher nature and I have infinite creative power.
- Wherever I am, God is, and all is well!

The New Theology

New Age "theology" represents a do-it-yourself form of religion. One can pick and choose whatever ideas, beliefs, concepts, and concerns happen to appeal to himself personally. The rest can merely be set aside; they need not be rejected.

The bottom line is obvious. New Age theology rests upon pantheism:

> All is God,
> God is all,
> Man is part of all,
> Therefore, man is God.

The only thing separating man from God is his own consciousness, not his sin. Thus, New Agers propose finding God within oneself by altering one's consciousness through meditation, chanting, channeling, sensory expansion, ecstatic dancing, and even fire-walking! The New Age approach to spirituality is more a matter of experience than belief. Altered conscience leads to self-realization, which results in personal transformation (the New Ager's "salvation"). In this process, personal experience becomes the final authority to define one's spiritual journey. It works like this:

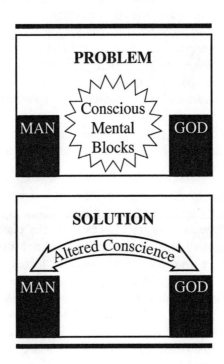

New Age Network

In his very helpful book *A Crash Course on the New Age Movement*, Elliot Miller defines the New Age movement as an informal network of individuals and organizations bound together by *common values* (mysticism and monism) and a *common vision* (coming new age of Aquarius).[7] Within the

New Age network are several separate strands that intercon-
nect:

1. *Consciousness movement:* those advocating the expansion of human consciousness by altered mental
   states, resulting in the expansion of human awareness
2. *Holistic health:* those encouraging better food and
   diet for better mental and spiritual development
3. *Human potential:* the self-help psychology of self-
   awareness, self-actualization, and self-improvement
4. *Eastern mysticism:* various gurus advocating Transcendental Meditation, astral projection, reincarnation,
   and various Hindu doctrines that view the material
   world as illusionary
5. *Occultism:* pseudoscientific return to witchcraft,
   satanism, shamans, mediums, palm readers, and
   Tarot cards

The blend of these various elements varies with every
individual and every subgroup within the New Age network.
Some lean toward *ecological* issues (save the planet); others
lean toward *global peace* issues (make love, not war); and still
others prefer a *mystical* orientation that mixes meditation,
yoga, est, and astrology with a strong belief in reincarnation.
The combinations of any of these elements are like fingers of
an intellectual hand reaching out to potential followers.

Miller states, "New Agers tend to be eclectic: they draw
what they think is the best from many sources. Long-term
exclusive devotion to a single teacher, teaching, or technique is
not the norm. They move from one approach to another in their
spiritual quests."[8] Thus, the subjective guides of experience
and intuition are the final authorities for New Age thinkers.
The Bible and the gospel message are vehemently rejected.
Because there is no objective truth, the New Ager creates his
or her own subjective truth. Therefore, the uniqueness of the
gospel of salvation through Jesus Christ can be easily rejected
with, "That's *your* truth, but it's not for me."

Scientific Mysticism

Modern man has reached the point where he does not want to face the logical consequences of a secular world without God. But instead of repenting of his rebellion against God, he has now turned to a kind of scientific mysticism that has been popularized as the New Age movement.[9] Modern New Age mysticism is a combination of transcendentalism, spiritualism, Oriental mysticism, and transpersonal psychology. It rests upon the humanist psychology of Abraham Maslow, Fritz Perls, Carl Rogers, and Rollo May, all of whom emphasized the elevation of personal growth as the highest good and placed the transcendent at the top of the list of man's hierarchical needs.

The New Psychology, as it came to be called, developed a trend in therapy toward deification of the isolated self and the rejection of traditional morality as moral blindness in favor of holistic psychic health. Thus, it developed hand-in-hand with the whole Human Potential movement. Key elements of New Age thought include restructuring the mind through meditation, sensory deprivation (for example, flotation therapy), and the self-tuning of the mind and body to become receptors and transmitters of cosmic forces. Psychic therapies claim to manipulate "life energies" to provide inner healing of individuals and to promote human relationships in harmony with cosmic forces.[10]

Dave Hunt is certainly correct in his observation that the whole of New Age mysticism is based upon Teilhard de Chardin's concept of the evolution of the soul.[11] Teilhard was a French Catholic priest, paleontologist, and theologian who attempted to "Christianize" evolution with a theistic view in which the soul emerged as the driving force of evolution. This evolution would lead to a collective superconsciousness of humanity, which in turn would result in a new age of life on earth.[12]

Teilhard's mysticism is expressed most clearly in his now popular *Hymn of the Universe*, in which he advocated the concept of centrism, or the tendency of things to converge and move to the center, resulting in the totalization of all phenomena.[13] This end result of spiritual evolution will be realized in a collectivism of all reality, by which everything will become a part of a new organic whole. Present human consciousness (*noosphere*) will culminate in a *theosphere* when converging human spirits transcend matter and space in a mystical union called the *omega point*.

It is this merging of scientific mysticism with a rejection of materialistic secularism that has resulted in New Age thinking. This thinking then couples with the Human Potential movement, which offers a number of techniques for advancing one's metaphysical evolution. Since all ideas have political consequences, we should not be surprised to discover that the political agenda of New Age thinking includes ecological concerns, sexual equality, and the unification of the world order by the transformation of the current political order through a "planetary consciousness."

The New Age transformationalists seek the total transformation of society along ideological lines consistent with their own beliefs. By challenging the "myths" of matter, time, space, and death, New Agers believe they will release our untapped human potential to create a new and better world.

The End of the Intellectual Rope

Twentieth-century man has come to the ultimate conclusion that he needs hope beyond himself to solve the problems of life. His choices are relatively few indeed. He can turn to God, himself, others, nature, or a mystic collective consciousness, but in reality he has only two choices: himself or God. Ironically, man's rationalism has driven him to irrationality. Either he must accept the logical consequences of living in a world without God or he must turn to God. All other options are merely wishful thinking.

Modern Americans, however, usually find it difficult to throw God away altogether. We always seem to rely on some popular myth that Superman (or someone like him) is going to come from outer space to save the world. Unfortunately, our own scientific rationality ought to tell us that this isn't so.

The great danger in New Age thinking is its unwillingness to face the facts. There is no scientific proof for the mystical claims of reincarnation, spirit guides, astral projection, time travel, or a dozen other ideas popularized at New Age psychic fairs. When the process of mystification is complete, it leaves man dangling at the end of his own intellectual rope—with nowhere to turn!

The spiritual void caused by the rejection of Christianity has left modern man desperately looking for a spiritual reality beyond himself. New Agers argue that our overemphasis on rationality has caused us to lose our intuitive awareness. Like the old Jedi warrior in *Star Wars*, New Agers advise people to let their feelings guide them. The collective "force" of humanity (past and present) will guide you better than following mere objective facts.

In the end, objectivity is thrown out the window by New Agers. In turn, they want to blame the rest of the world for its collective intellectual blindness. This leads to the great *paradigm shift*, or new way of thinking about old problems. Leading the vanguard of New Age thinkers is Fritjof Capra, who argues that the old mechanistic perspective of the world must be replaced by the view that sees the world as one indivisible, dynamic whole whose parts are interrelated in the cosmic process.[14]

Following the earlier ideas of Austrian Ludwig von Bertalanffy and South African Jan Smuts, Capra promotes a holistic approach to solving social problems based upon the General Systems Theory (GST), which calls for the unification of the physical and social sciences to produce a great global society.

Selling It to the Public

In order to intellectually promote the idea of a New World Order, New Agers turn to mysticism as an ally to the systems movement. Synthesis replaces analysis of scientific data. The intuitive ability to recognize "wholes" replaces the need to analyze all the "parts." Capra clearly states, "The systems view of life is spiritual in its deepest essence and thus consistent with many ideas held in mystical traditions."[15]

New Agers tie their concepts of an emerging world order to the concept of purposeful and creative evolution. Following the ideas of German philosopher G.W.F. Hegel, they view God as a *process* rather than a person. Thus, for New Agers, evolution is "God in process." Elliot Miller observes, "Without such faith in evolution, New Agers would be incapable of maintaining their distinctive optimism."[16]

Consequently, New Agers believe in the evolutionary emergence of a new collective consciousness that will result in a new humanity. They will solve the threats of nuclear war, ecological disaster, and economic collapse by an intuitive and mystical approach to life. New Age thinker Donald Keys put it like this: "A new kind of world—the world into which we are already moving—requires a new kind of person, a person with a planetary perspective."[17]

To make this hopeful human improvement work, New Agers propose a "quantum leap" forward in evolution. John White says, "We are witnessing the final phase of homo sapiens and the simultaneous emergence of what I have named Homo Noeticus, a more advanced form of humanity. . . . As we pass from the Age of Ego to the Age of God, civilization will be transformed from top to bottom. A society founded on love and wisdom will emerge."[18]

All of this may seem like intellectual wishful thinking in light of the human tragedies of crime, war, drought, and starvation. But to the New Agers, it is a religion—with faith in evolution as the process and the worship of the planet as God. Teilhard himself, though a Jesuit Catholic paleontologist and philosopher, suggested that the planet earth was itself a living thing. Today it is called "Gaia" or "Terra," the mother-earth goddess of ancient mythology. It is further suggested that the mind of Gaia, in turn, must participate in some universal or cosmic mind. On this basis, New Agers call upon everyone to surrender their personal agendas to the ecological well-being of the living Earth—Gaia. "Save the planet" is the evangelistic cry of the New Age movement.

A Return to Paganism

The New Age worship of the earth and the deification of the planet represents a return to primitive paganism. According to Margot Adler, a practicing witch and coven priestess, "the modern pagan resurgence includes the new feminist goddess worshipping groups, certain new religions based on the visions of science fiction writers and attempts to revive the surviving tribal religions."[19] Judeo-Christian patriarchal religions with a Father-God figure are vehemently rejected in favor of goddess religions and witchcraft (or Wicca), which promote a spirituality of ecological wholeness and human pleasures.

While goddess religion has gained popularity because of its alignment with feminism, shamanism has exploded in popularity with men. Blending animism (spirit contact through natural objects; e.g., sacred trees or mountains) with pantheism (belief that all is God), shamans try to harmonize the natural and spiritual worlds. Following American-Indian tradition, shamans view themselves as spiritual masters rather than mere medicine men.

Shaman is a term adopted by anthropologists who studied the Tungus people of Siberia. It is equivalent to "witch," "witch doctor," "medicine man," "sorcerer," "wizard," and so on. Shamanism is the most ancient system of mind-body healing known to humanity. It represents false religion that is under the influence of "the god of this world"—Satan!

Dave Hunt expresses a strong concern that modern shamanism is creeping into today's churches under the guise of psychological terms and labels.[20] The techniques of visualization, guided imagery, and inner healing have all been practiced in shamanism for thousands of years. But today they have been redefined as a part of the New Age language of transpersonal psychology. Some like Morton Kelsey have gone so far as to suggest that Jesus was the "greatest of all shamans."[21] He equates clairvoyance, telepathy, out-of-body experiences, est, and psychokinesis with manifestations of the power of God.

It is this kind of mental gymnastics that enables New Agers to redefine the terms and concepts of spirituality. They are ready to accept the earth or the self as God. They believe in the existence of departed spirits, ghosts, time travelers, extraterrestrial beings, angels, demons, witches, and wizards. Their influence can be seen in movies like *Star Wars*, *Ghost*, *Field of Dreams*, *E.T.*, *Jewel of the Nile*, and *Dances with Wolves*. They see great spirituality in Indian medicine men, Hindu gurus, Tibetan lamas, Sufi mystics, Zen teachers, and Oriental hermits. But they are united in their rejection of God the Father, the deity of Christ, and the personality of the Holy Spirit.

The Counterfeit Christ

While New Age thinkers buy into Eastern mysticism, they clothe it in Christian terminology. Growing up in the Western world makes it difficult for some people to totally shed their religious heritage. So they repackage it to make it more acceptable to the Western mind. Douglas Groothuis of Probe Ministries notes that:

> New Age spirituality takes on a distinctive Western identity. Because the West still remembers its Christian heritage, traffics in Christian images and bandies about Christian words, Christian symbols serve as a good medium for advancing the cause. The semantic rail system has already been laid by hundreds of years of Christian tradition, and the message is now steaming full speed ahead.[22]

The Christ of the Bible is totally reinterpreted and repackaged as the New Age Jesus. New Agers separate the historical *Jesus* of Nazareth from the *Christ* consciousness which He came to attain. Jesus is not the way, the truth, and the life; He is a way-shower. He is one of the Ascended Masters who realized oneness with God. But He is not viewed as the unique and divine Son of God. To New Agers, Christ is one of the monistic masters in a whole pantheon of deities.

Actress Shirley MacLaine, a prominent New Age promoter, has said Jesus "became an adept yogi and mastered complete control over His body and the physical world around Him. . . . [He] tried to teach people that they would do the same things if they got in touch with their spiritual selves and their own potential power."[23]

New Agers like MacLaine leap to this conclusion by suggesting that Jesus traveled to India during His silent years before His public ministry. There He supposedly came under the teachings of the Hindu masters—teachings which He unsuccessfully attempted to communicate to the Jewish community when He returned to Israel.

The counterfeit Christ of the New Age movement is being repackaged as a tolerant, broad-minded, nonjudgmental teacher. He is a way-shower who points men toward the God within themselves. As the cosmic Christ, He is now one of the Ascended Masters who continues to reveal Himself as an emissary of the kingdom of light.

In his very thorough study *The Counterfeit Christ of the New Age Movement*, Ron Rhodes of the Christian Research Institute points out that orthodox Christian beliefs are explained away by New Agers in one of three ways:[24]

1. Supposed discoveries of hidden writings about Christ (e.g., *Gnostic Gospels*)
2. New revelations of truth about Jesus from psychics and channelers
3. Esoteric interpretations (deeper meanings) of Scripture

The details about Jesus may vary from one New Age teacher to the next.[25] David Spangler believed Jesus merely "attuned" to Christ and became His channel. Edgar Cayce taught that Jesus became the Christ in His thirtieth reincarnation. Levi Dowling believed Jesus became the Christ through ancient Egyptian initiation rites. Elizabeth Clare Prophet believes Jesus traveled to India as a child and eventually ascended to Christhood and returned to His homeland.

However the particular details may vary, all New Age thinkers agree that Christ is only one of many Ascended Masters who may serve as guides to the truth. New Age Christology is drawn from a vast array of existing religious and philosophical concepts that are eclectic and syncretistic to the extreme. In a do-it-yourself religion, one ought not be surprised to find a make-your-own Jesus!

Voices from the Dark Side

New Age Spiritism

New Age thinking is rooted in the hippie counterculture of the sixties and seventies. Though the hippie movement died out after the Vietnam War, its ideas remained behind. Elliot Miller observes that New Agers are primarily baby-boomers (born shortly after World War II) who have recycled, but not rejected, the ideals of the hippie counterculture:[1]

1. Antimaterialism
2. Utopianism
3. Exaltation of nature
4. Rejection of traditional morality
5. Fascination with the occult

The New Age movement is not a passing fad. It has been gaining momentum for three decades. It represents a cultural revolt against the spiritual void of secularism. It was not until the late eighties that the general public became aware of the popular appeal of New Age thinking. Actress Shirley Mac-Laine's autobiography *Out on a Limb* and several subsequent books openly promoted New Age ideals: "I am God," reincarnation, seances, crystals, and pyramid power. In August 1987, 20,000 New Agers gathered at various "sacred sites" around the world for the "Harmonic Convergence," a supposed cosmic event of great significance. By December 7, 1987, the New Age movement had made the cover of *Time* magazine.

Miller refers to the New Age subculture as "another America" existing alongside the secular and religious establishments and competing with them for cultural dominance.[2] He characterizes New Agers as sincere, intelligent, optimistic, and humanitarian. Unlike traditional Eastern mystics, New Agers are positive about life and their involvement in the world. They embrace the future while promoting the ideals of global peace, economic prosperity, political unification, and ecological balance.

New Agers have been variously described as "Western mystics," "hippies come of age," "secular prosperity theologians," and "secularized spiritualists." But it is their combination of subjective spirituality and secular morality that leaves them so vulnerable to astrological and occultic influences.

Age of Aquarius

New Agers hitchhike much of their ideology on the concepts of astrology, especially the idea of the "Age of Aquarius." New Agers believe that a spiritual age is now upon us in which many people are evolving into advanced stages of spiritual consciousness. They further believe that *personal* transformation must precede *planetary* transformation. This means that New Agers are committed to the proselytization of new "converts" to their cause. They are out to win over people to what some, like Marilyn Ferguson, have called "the Aquarian conspiracy."[3]

Astrologers believe that human evolution is progressing in cycles corresponding to the signs of the zodiac. Each cycle allegedly lasts about 2,000 years. Following the beliefs of astrologers, New Agers believe man is now moving from the Piscean (intellectual) Age into the Aquarian (spiritual) Age.

On April 25, 1982, millions of people in 20 major cities around the world were stunned by a large, full-page newspaper ad boldly proclaiming:

THE WORLD HAS HAD ENOUGH...
OF HUNGER, INJUSTICE, WAR.
IN ANSWER TO OUR CALL FOR HELP,
AS WORLD TEACHER
FOR ALL HUMANITY.
THE CHRIST IS NOW HERE.[4]

The advertisement went on to announce that since July 1977, the Christ has been "emerging as a spokesman" for the world community. "Throughout history," the notice continued, "humanity's evolution has been guided by a group of enlightened men, the masters of wisdom." The public notice went on to announce that the world teacher who stands at the center of this great spiritual hierarchy is Lord Maitreya, known to Christians as the Christ. Christians await the return of Christ, Jews await the coming of the Messiah, Buddhists look for the Fifth Buddha, Hindus expect the Lord Krishna, and Moslems await the Imam Mahdi. "These are all names for one individual," the notice proclaimed, assuring the readers of a New World Order of peace and prosperity.[5]

The "Christ Is Now Here" ad campaign was engineered by New Ager Benjamin Creme, an English esotericist who was a disciple of Theosophy's Helena Blavatsky and Alice Bailey. Miller notes that if Blavatsky was the "grandmother" of the New Age movement, Alice Bailey would be its "mother."[6] She, more than any other individual, took the ideas of spiritualism and repackaged them into the basic tenets of the New Age movement. Creme, in turn, hit the road like an evangelist to promote these concepts on a nonstop, worldwide tour.

Constance Cumbey, a Christian attorney from Detroit, Michigan, first alerted the evangelical community to what she called *The Hidden Dangers of the Rainbow* in her 1983 book. While many feel she overreacted to the conspiracy threat from the New Age movement, no one can doubt her sincerity in attempting to alert the Christian public to what she discovered in New Age books, seminars, and lectures. Even Elliot Miller admits, "There is an 'Aquarian Conspiracy'—a conscious effort by a broad-based movement to subvert our cultural establishment so that we might enter a 'New Age' based on mysticism and occultism."[7]

New Age Activism

Since the publication of Mark Satin's *New Age Politics* in 1978, it has been clear that New Age activists intend to continue promoting a political agenda for a united global community under the control of a one-world government. In order to convince society of the need for this New World Order, New Agers have adopted several promotional techniques:

> *Psychic healing*: Using man's inner psychic energy to heal his emotional conflicts and distress
>
> *Holistic health*: Combining diet and inner dynamic force to produce a healthy and productive life
>
> *Transpersonal education*: Also called holistic education, it targets public education as the medium to combine humanistic and mystical approaches to learning
>
> *Values clarification*: An educational technique that emphasizes that one's values emerge from within himself and not from external codes, such as the Ten Commandments.
>
> *Human Potential*: Thought-reform techniques promoting the use of guided imagery and visualization through organization development (O.D.) and organization transformation (O.T.) seminars. Used to bring humanistic psychology and Eastern mysticism into the workplace.

New Agers promote the basic human values as 1) survival, 2) interdependence, 3) autonomy, 4) humanness. This leaves little or no place for biblical Christianity. In fact, the occult connection with New Age thinking is essentially antichristian. A New World Order based upon New Age ideology would likely view evangelical Christianity as bigoted, divisive, and sectarian. This could easily set the stage for justified persecution of Christians as rebels against the Aquarian regime. Elliot Miller warns, "Christian dogmatism could easily be viewed (in fact, already is) as antirevolutionary: a threat to the global unity necessary for racial survival. And when survival dominates over all other values, the elimination of any perceived threat to it could easily be 'justified.' "[8]

New Age Spiritism

The gasoline that drives the New Age engine is *spiritism* which is the practice of communicating with departed human spirits or extrahuman intelligences through a human medium by the process of channeling. In his recent book *Channeling*, Jon Klimo claims that channeling involves a human being who is possessed by an external force, power, or personality.[9] This entity exercises control over the perceptual, cognitive, and self-reflective capacities of the person who has relinquished himself to the external force.

The Bible clearly warns against involvement with witchcraft, seances, and mediums. Deuteronomy 18:10-12, commands, "Let no one be found among you . . . a medium or a spiritist or one who consults the dead. Anyone who does these things is detestable to the LORD." The prophet Isaiah warned, "When men tell you to consult mediums and spiritists, who whisper and mutter, should not a people inquire of their God? Why consult the dead on behalf of the living?" (8:19,20).

Scripture acknowledges the reality of demonic spirits and their attempts to communicate through human mediums (*see* 1 Samuel 28:6-14; Acts 16:16-19). It always presents them as evil, deceptive, and malevolent. They are channels to Satan's lies, not to God's truth. Laura Cameron Fraser, the Pacific Northwest's first ordained woman Episcopalian priest, resigned her parish in Issaquah, Washington, rather than renounce her belief in her channeled entity named "Jonah."[10]

Much of the spiritist bent of New Agers comes from the nineteenth-century spiritualist movement. In the early 1800s Henry David Thoreau and Ralph Waldo Emerson became transcendentalism's leading lights. Influenced by English translations of Oriental scriptures, transcendentalists began to open the Western mind to occult images. In 1848, the Fox sisters claimed to hear rappings in the walls of their Hydesville, New York, house. These were allegedly communicated by the spirit of a murdered peddler who lay beneath the house. R.J. Burrows observes, "The rappings at Hydesville marked the birth of spiritualism, that branch of occultism that communicates with departed spirits."[11] Spiritualism emphasized the reality of the existence of departed spirits. New Thought gave a framework to the system. Emanuel Swedenborg (1688-1772) opened the door to receiving telepathic images. Anton Mesmer (1734-1815) taught people to use hypnotic trances (mesmerism) to discover deeper thoughts and to heal physical illnesses.

In time, American psychic healer Phineas Quimby modified Mesmer's ideas to emphasize the power of mind over matter. Christian Science founder Mary Baker Eddy was profoundly influenced by Quimby's ideas, as was the modern priestess of prosperity, Terry Cole-Whittaker, who claims, "You can have exactly what you want, when you want it, all the time."[12]

An eccentric Russian noblewoman, Helena Blavatsky, founded the Theosophical Society in 1875 in America during the height of the spiritualist "revival." She went beyond communicating with the dead spirits of departed relatives and claimed to channel the spirits of the Ascended Masters. Blending Oriental traditions, Hindu reincarnation, Darwinian evolution, and Christian terminology, Blavatsky sold her spiritistic vision with enthusiasm. To her, man was evolving from apehood to godhood. Peace and prosperity were just around the corner—but so were World Wars I and II!

Tune In and Beam Up

Popular channels in the modern New Age movement vary from those receiving *telepathic messages* (Alice Bailey and Helen Schucman), *full-trance* channels (Kevin Ryerson and Jack Pursel), and *incarnational channels* (J.Z. Knight and Penny Tores). Each in his or her own way claims to be communicating a message from someone or something beyond this present earthly experience. They are in essence claiming supernatural revelations of truth.

Jane Roberts: "Seth"

In September 1963, at age 34, Jane Roberts claimed to have an out-of-body experience. This led to an interest in psychic phenomenon. By late 1963, she and her husband Rob were experimenting with a Ouija board that sent them messages through an entity called "Seth."

She wrote,

> Neither Rob nor I had any psychic background, and when I began to anticipate the board's replies, I took it for granted they were coming from my subconscious. Not long after, however, I felt impelled to say the words aloud, and within a month I was speaking for Seth in a trance state.[13]

Rob took verbatim shorthand whenever Jane went into a trance. Portions of this material were organized into several books and attracted a readership of millions who were drawn to Jane's simple and unpretentious style. Seth's basic message was, "You create your own reality."

The success of the sales of the "Seth material" popularized the idea of receiving spiritual instruction direct from the "Other Side" without a human guru or teacher. Soon, channeling was viewed not as an elitist experience but a natural human potential that could be cultivated by anyone, and dozens of "channels" came on the scene. Since Roberts's death in 1983, Tom Massari, Jean Loomis, and a host of other channels have claimed to be "Seth."

J.Z. Knight: "Ramtha"

The most famous entity currently is "Ramtha," who is channeled by former Baptist J.Z. Knight of Yelm, Washington. An attractive blonde with a very winsome personality, J.Z. is totally "transformed" by the 35,000-year-old Lemurian warrior-king. The fragile Knight suddenly takes on decidedly masculine qualities, total voice and speech pattern changes, and speaks with humor and intensity.

Ms. Knight claims that in February 1977, while she and her second husband (she has now been divorced a third time) were experimenting with pyramid power to preserve food, a bold, warriorlike man nearly seven feet tall appeared to her and announced, "I am Ramtha, the Enlightened One." In time, she claims, she came to "know, trust and love him immensely."[14]

Ramtha became an instant success. His followers number over 50,000 and include prominent actors and actresses like Shirley MacLaine, Linda Evans, Burt Reynolds, and Phillip Michael Thomas. As time has passed, Ramtha has claimed to be "God," "the supreme cause," and "the divine source." He has even predicted natural disasters that failed to come to pass. One of his predictions made Linda Evans several weeks late for the filming of "Dynasty."

Jack Pursel: "Lazaris"

Pursel was an insurance salesman in Florida with little interest in "spiritual" things. But his wife Penny, who has since left him and remarried, was into metaphysics. She got him to practice meditation and noticed that he spoke with a different voice while in a trance. Pursel himself could never remember these experiences after he awoke, so Penny tape-recorded them. At first he was shocked and upset by what he heard. "I was scared," he admits. "I did not understand. I cried for a while. Then, somehow, it became all right."[15]

Purcel named the entity "Lazaris" (with emphasis on the middle syllable). Soon he was channeling full-time, speaking with a British/Scandinavian accent. His relaxed, amiable manner and practical approach to solving life's problems have gained increasing popularity over the years.

Kevin Ryerson: Several Entities

Kevin grew up in Sandusky, Ohio, experimenting with meditation, ESP, and Zen Buddhism. At age 22, he joined a meditation group that promoted the ideas of Edgar Cayce, who was famous for his psychic diagnoses of medical problems. Soon Ryerson was doing the same through a series of entities he called "Spirit" or his "Higher Self."

Rather than public lectures, Ryerson prefers private consultations on "readings." One of these was recreated in the January 1987 ABC television miniseries "Out on a Limb." It featured his conversation on a California beach with Shirley MacLaine. It was this meeting that became instrumental in her "conversion" to the New Age movement. Ryerson also had a profound effect upon actress/singer Bette Midler, whose popular songs "The Wind Beneath My Wings" and "From a Distance" have put the New Age message to music.

Penny Tores Rubin: "Mafu"

In what appears to be the Los Angeles housewife's version of Ramtha, Mafu claims to be a member of the "Brotherhood of Light" in the "seventh dimension," last reincarnated as a leper in first-century Pompeii. Rubin, a former Catholic who divorced and remarried since she became a channel, claims that Mafu first spoke to her in June 1986.

Today Rubin has a host of devoted followers, gets lots of media attention, and holds audiences with prominent actors, doctors, educators, and even world leaders. Radio and television appearances, lectures, and private readings have vaulted Rubin into the public eye and to great popularity in New Age circles.

Other entities channeled by various people include, "Dr. Peebles," a nineteenth-century physician, "Indira Latari," a nineteenth-century Hindu woman, "Chief White Eagle," a Cherokee medicine man, "Bashar," an extraterrestrial from the planet "Essassani," "Saint Germain," an Ascended Master from the "seventh dimension," "Leah" from Venus, "Matea," a 35,000-year-old black female spice trader, "Merlin the Magician," deceased rock star John Lennon (channeled by Linda Deer Domnitz), and "Spectra," an extraterrestrial higher intelligence from the future.

The channeling craze is "like having a telephone to God," Ryerson told Shirley MacLaine. It has caught on because it short-circuits real prayer. It involves little or no disciplined study. And it promises instant answers, inspired advice, quick solutions, and easy access to spiritual information not readily available to others.

The Ultimate Seduction

Elliot Miller observes that the varied messages of the channels are ultimately the same: We are gods; we don't need a savior other than ourselves; there is no sin or death; we create our own reality. New Agers imply there is no objective truth, only subjective "truth." Since we create our own truth, we create our own reality. Miller writes, "Once the New Ager accepts this premise, an almost insurmountable barrier to Christian penetration is erected."[16] No matter what appeal the Christian makes, the New Ager will tend to dismiss it as irrelevant to his own personal "reality."

Desperately seeking answers to the great human problems of inner spirituality, personal growth, true peace, and security, the New Ager turns to himself, the planet, the forces of nature, and the spirit world for help. In all this quest, he misses the true Christ, the real source of the peace, security, and stability he seeks.

In the meantime, New Agers are left hoping for some great cosmic deliverer to rescue the world and preserve its peace. Constance Cumbey is right when she says, "For the first time in history there is a viable movement—the New Age movement—that truly meets all the scriptural requirements for the antichrist and the political movement that will bring him on the world scene."[17]

We agree the stage has certainly been set for a New World Order based upon a subjective view of reality. It will only be a matter of time until the objective standards of truth will be totally eroded in the modern world. We are getting closer, and the only real question left is this: How much time do we still have until it's too late?

Satan and His Angels

Satanism and Demon Possession

Belief in the existence of Satan and his demonic hordes has been challenged long before our present time. In 1678, Benjamin Camfield wrote in his *Theological Discourse of Angels* that this was an "atheistical and degenerate age, wherein the general disbelief of spirits (angelic and diabolical) may well be thought the ground and introduction of all irreligion and profanity, which naturally follows upon it."[1]

What could be expressed modestly by Camfield in the seventeenth century can certainly be shouted from the rooftops today! In fact, we have now come to a strange turn of events in modern society. Belief in spiritual things has been so extinguished by secularism that the void has been replaced by worship of the satanic and the demonic. We have kicked God out of our schools and the devil has rushed in to fill the void!

Young people are turning on to the satanic and the demonic at rates unparalleled since medieval times. "It is cool to believe in the Devil," one teen announced recently to one of our youth ministers. "There is a lot more excitement and thrill in the occult than there is in the church," added another.

Today people are experimenting with astrology, witch-craft, Ouija boards, divination, channeling, Tarot cards, fortune-tellers, mediums, crystals, and shamans. Mankind has come to the final conclusion of disbelief in God and has turned to belief in the very opposite! Satan has cleverly convinced the modern mind that he is not to be taken seriously until all other spiritual options are exhausted. Then, when empty souls turn to him in desperation, he can take them over completely and totally.

C.S. Lewis wrote in *The Screwtape Letters*, "There are two equal and opposite errors into which our race can fall about the devils. One is to disbelieve in their existence. The other is to believe, and to feel an excessive and unhealthy interest in them. They themselves are equally pleased by both errors."[2]

A Personal Encounter

I (Richard) remember my first encounter with a demon-possessed person. Her name was Caia. She had called the church where I was pastoring at the time and asked to see me.

I began talking to Caia about dating, her parents, and her college career. But when I asked her why she had *really* come, she closed her eyes and sat in absolute silence. Her facial expression began to change. Her mouth distorted into a snarl and perspiration began to drip down both sides of her face.

Then suddenly, without saying a word, her eyes popped open, she stood up abruptly, and walked over toward the window air conditioner. She stood with her back to me, her long hair blowing behind her from the air conditioner unit.

Then, without warning, came the most frightening voice I have ever heard. It was a deep and gravelly voice with intense vibrato. It sounded like the voice of a man in torment speaking from deep within a cavern.

"I'll tell you why I've come. I know who you are. I've come to stop you!" the voice announced.

Caia still had her back to me. I could not imagine that it was she who was speaking. Her innocent female voice had turned into the most masculine voice I had ever heard. I slid back into my chair, speechless, as chills went up and down my spine.

Then she whirled around and came toward me. She still had that awful snarl on her face. Sweat was still dripping from her brow. Her eyes seemed to be aflame with rage. The voice—that evil voice—was talking nonstop as she walked toward me. She placed her hands on the front of the desk.

I pushed my chair back up against the wall. Blood rushed to my head. I tried to regain my composure.

"I know you," the voice within her kept repeating. Then she began to recount about half a dozen events from my life that had occurred when I was a child, teenager, or young adult. Each time, the demonic voice would reveal something that this girl could not possibly have known on her own.

I was startled by this supernatural display of knowledge. It struck a note of terror within my heart as I realized I was not dealing with an ordinary human being.

Suddenly she came around the desk, grabbed a letter opener, and pointed the sharp end against my throat.

"I am going to destroy you," the voice blurted out. "I'm going to destroy you *now*!"

I had remained silent throughout this incredible display of demonic power and influence. As she pushed closer with the letter opener, I began to repeat the name of Jesus out loud. Over and over I said His name. The demon continued talking, but I could no longer understand what it was saying.

I continued to repeat, "Jesus, Jesus, Jesus."

The voice ceased. Caia laid down the letter opener, turned, and walked away. As she reached the door, her feminine voice and girlish smile returned.

"Thank you, Pastor Lee," she said sweetly. "I'll see you again."

She opened the door, walked past my secretary Dot, got in her car, and drove away.

Dot could see that I was visibly shaken and asked me what was wrong. I told her not to schedule Caia for another appointment—ever. That afternoon I told my wife, Judy, about the incident and we prayed together for God's protection over our lives.

During the next few weeks our telephone would ring between 2:00 and 4:00 A.M. When I would answer, I would hear growling, like an animal, at the other end. I was sure that it was Caia. Soon we stopped answering the phone after midnight and eventually the calls ceased.

In the meantime, Caia called the church frequently, wanting an appointment. But Dot refused. Then, one Saturday afternoon I went up to my office to use my study. As I was leaving, I opened the door to the darkened hallway and there stood Caia!

She said she was sorry if she had frightened me. I backed up into Dot's empty office and Caia stood in the doorway. She began to plead with me for help. She told me her parents had been involved in the occult and were Satan worshipers. She explained that they had named her Caia after Caiaphas, the high priest who had helped plot the arrest and crucifixion of Jesus.

She claimed that as a child she had seen animal sacrifices and human sexual orgies. She also said that she had been physically and emotionally abused, and simply wanted someone to help her.

I explained that I would be willing to help her but because the building was empty, this was not the time for us to be talking together. Feeling put off, she became angry and turned to walk away. But when she looked back, that same angry snarl appeared on her face.

"I'm going to tear up your church!" the demonic voice announced. Then she turned and walked out, slammed the door, and drove away.

That weekend I searched the Scriptures about dealing with the devil and demonic powers. I had never faced anything like this before. I knew I could not handle this alone and called upon God for His help and grace.

The weekend passed without incident. But on Monday morning, Dot called me frantically. "Come quickly!" she said. "The auditorium is a mess!" I rushed over to the church to find that the first three pews had been ripped from the floor bolts and tossed over the pews in the back of the auditorium. The pulpit had been thrown back into the choir loft, and chairs were scattered across the platform.

"What could have done this?" Dot asked, bewildered by this awesome display of force.

We could only speculate. I wondered if it was Caia who had done this. But how? She was frail. Only some superhuman force could have enabled her to do this.

Weeks passed. I continued to search the Scriptures as the intensity of an impending crisis seemed near. About a month later, while I was preaching on a Sunday night, Caia walked into the auditorium. She came down the center aisle and sat in the second row.

During the message, she sat expressionless. But as time went on she began making groans and growling sounds. The people around her became distracted by the noises. But she made it through the sermon. Then, during the invitation, she left her seat, came forward to the altar, and knelt to pray. At the same time, her growling became more severe.

I quickly dismissed the service and motioned to my wife Judy, my assistant pastor, and one of my deacons and his wife to assist me. After everyone else left, I knelt beside Caia and asked her what was wrong.

Instantly she whirled around, thrust her fingernails into my cheeks, and began babbling in that low, evil voice: "I'm going to destroy you. You can't stop me. You have no power over me," it began to say.

"Who are you?" I blurted out.

"You could call me Legion," the voice responded. "We've been called that before."

I began repeating the scriptures I had been memorizing during these unusual weeks. I closed my eyes and said them aloud again and again.

Then Caia abruptly jumped up and ran toward the inside brick wall of the church and began beating her head against it. Before anyone could reach her, she fell to the floor and began thrashing around. She also began to foam at the mouth as her twisting gyrations continued. Then she stopped and she lay motionless on the floor.

"Leave her alone," I told the others. She laid there for about ten minutes. It seemed like an eternity. The foam turned to saliva. She eventually recovered and sat up. Within a few more seconds she stood up and started walking toward the back of the church.

Approaching the door, she turned, looked at me, and said in her own voice, "When the time comes, no matter when it is, I'll know and I'll be back!" Then out she walked into the night.

There is no doubt in my mind Caia was demon-possessed. She had displayed supernatural intelligence and power and spoke in another voice that was obviously not her own. Like many who have experimented with the occult, she was a disturbed and tormented soul.

A Pilgrimage into Darkness

Youth specialist Jerry Johnston tells the compelling story of Sean Sellers's tragic pilgrimage into the occult:[3]

Sean'[s] parents were long-haul truckers when the family lived in Greeley, Colorado. Sean filled the empty hours when both parents were on the road with the occult. He excelled in a local kids' Dungeons and Dragons fantasy role-playing group, so he was made Dungeon Master. The responsibility prompted the junior higher to pore through every book he could find on witchcraft, satanism, sorcery, wizards and black magic. . . .

He found his way into a self-styled satanic coven. "We used to have baptism ceremonies," he remembers. "The leaders would dress in black robes, but the new person would be in a white robe. . . . They made the new person strip, kneel before the altar; then we'd cut his hand and let the blood drip into the chalice. Then we would pass the cup around, drinking the blood and dedicating ourselves to Satan."

During Sean's 1984 sophomore year the Sellers moved to Oklahoma.... Before his altar, black candle burning, Sean intoned the prayer (to the devil) and, in his words, "Something happened. I felt a power there. The temperature of the room dropped.... I felt my blood pressure go up. There was an erotic sensation, a lifting sensation in my whole body.... I opened my eyes and saw bright spots dancing around the room.... I saw demons flying. And there was this voice. A whisper. It said, 'I love you.'"

As his sophomore year progressed, Sean formed a club called "Elimination" to recruit new followers to Satan.... As usual in satanic recruitment technique, the beginners were to know nothing about the satanic belief system until they were gradually pulled into the camaraderie and loyalty of the group....

Sean knew he was getting into deep trouble his junior year; he mentioned to several adults that he thought he might be going crazy.... Just after school started in 1985, Sean played out his prediction. It was time for a sacrifice to Satan.

Sean sneaked his dad's .44 pistol and with his buddy Richard, drove late to the convenience store.... The murder was slow-motion.... The clerk is behind the counter. Richard begins walking from the rest room. Sean raises the pistol; the clerk shrinks back to open the cash register. Sean fires and misses. The clerk runs for the back of the store but is stopped by Richard. Sean fires again and the clerk goes down. He fires again. And again.

The police never solved the homicide; and six months later Sean was deeper still into his own Hell. He called himself Ezurate after the name of the demon he was sure possessed him. Sean prayed at his bedroom altar to Satan . . . and pulled out the .44. In the middle of the night, he stepped down the hall to his parents' room. It was so dark [he] could scarcely make out the two forms sleeping on the waterbed. He aimed at the first form's head and fired. His mother raised up on the other side of the bed. . . . He fired.

Sean Sellers's attorney tried to explain his demon-possession to the jury, but they sentenced Sean, not Ezurate, to die by lethal injection for murdering three people. Today, he is on death row in McAlester, Oklahoma. "Harmless curiosity," some will say about dabbling in the occult. But don't try to tell that to Sean Sellers. It is a nightmare he lives every day of his life.

The Occult Explosion

Despite tragic stories like Sean's, kids are turning on to Satan in record numbers. "He is the ultimate high," said a teenager in Denver. "I can't wait until I can be just like him," said another in Atlanta. "I was just curious at first," admitted a girl in Miami, "but now I'm hooked!"

The current fad of satanism and satanic cults is reaching epidemic proportions in the United States and Europe. Award-winning investigative reporter Maury Terry warns, "There is compelling evidence of the existence of a nationwide network of satanic cults."[4] Acclaimed novelist Arthur Lyons said, "The United States probably harbors the fastest growing and most highly-organized body of satanists in the world."[5] Theologian Merrill Unger said, "The scope and power of modern occultism staggers the imagination."[6] Apologists John Ankerberg and John Weldon add,

> Unfortunately, Satanism, witchcraft, santeria, voodoo, and other "hard core" forms of the occult are only the proverbial tip of the iceberg.[7]

They go on to list mediums, mystics, clairvoyants, psychics, channelers, spiritists, gurus, shamans, Ouija boards, Tarot cards, and a "thousand other" occultic practices that dot the face of the modern American landscape.

Ankerberg and Weldon also observe the crucial link between the occult and the New Age movement. The revival of occultism in the sixties paved the way for the success of New Age ideas in the seventies and eighties. New Age acceptance of occult and psychic practices defies modern logic. But that acceptance is at the heart and core of New Age thinking. The message of the channelers is always the same: "You can save yourself"; "You can be like God"; "You will never die." These are the very same lies Satan told Eve in the Garden of Eden (Genesis 3:4,5).

New Age occultism is the exact opposite of biblical truth. Elliot Miller observes, "The repeated teaching that we are perfect, autonomous and totally self-sufficient gods conditions New Agers to vehemently reject the basic gospel message that we are sinners, accountable to God for our sin and incapable of saving ourselves."[8]

Psychic predictions and prophetic devices such as the I Ching (an ancient Chinese divinatory device), Tarot cards, astrology, runes (Viking symbols), tea-leaf reading, palm reading, water-witching, and the writings of Nostradamus (a sixteenth-century French occultist whose prophecies greatly influenced Adolph Hitler), have become commonplace today. Bob Larson observes that these have become symbols of certitude in a restless and uncertain age. "In spite of the capriciousness of such artifices," he writes, "many who have rejected organized religion have turned to exotic occult instruments to direct their lives and offer advice about their futures."[9]

Nostradamus is enormously popular today. His *Centuries* (100 verses) can be found in virtually every secular bookstore in America. While many consider his writing to be meaningless jumble, others believe it contains predictions of the rise of Hitler, the assassinations of John and Robert Kennedy, the development of modern aircraft, an invasion from outer space in 1999, and the final end of the world in 3797. However, modern readers often fail to observe that today's English translations of this complex and nearly indecipherable sixteenth-century document are heavily editorialized by the modern translator's own views. Nevertheless, the popular acceptance of such gibberish points to the desperation of modern man to find the truth about the future anywhere but in the Bible.

Defining the Devil

The term *occult* comes from the Latin word *occultus*, meaning "to cover, hide, or conceal." It implies secret knowledge that can be obtained only by mystical or magical powers. This knowledge may be gained solely through contact with the unseen spirit world. Dr. Ronald Enroth, professor of sociology at Westmont College (California), observes that the phenomena collectively known as "the occult" have three distinct characteristics: [10]

1. The communication of information unavailable through the human senses
2. Contact with supernatural powers, paranormal energies or demonic forces
3. The acquisition of these powers to manipulate human actions

By contrast, the Bible warns us that "in later times some will abandon the faith and follow deceiving spirits and things taught by demons" (1 Timothy 4:1). The next verse warns that such deception will be taught by "hypocritical liars" who will seduce an entire generation away from the truth. The Bible further calls them "godless men, who change the grace of our God into a license for immorality and deny Jesus Christ our only Sovereign and Lord" (Jude 4). They will appear in the "last times" following their own "ungodly desires" because they do not have the Spirit of God (Jude 18,19).

The Bible also identifies the unseen spirit world as being under the control of Satan and his demons. Satan (which means "accuser") is called "the god of this age" who blinds the minds of unbelievers and keeps them from the truth (2 Corinthians 4:4). He is the "ruler of the kingdom of the air" who controls "those who are disobedient" (Ephesians 2:2). Jesus called him the "prince of this world" whose judgment is coming (John 12:31). The Scripture reminds us "the whole world is under the control of the evil one" (1 John 5:19).

Satan, originally called Lucifer, appears to have been an archangel who was endowed with wisdom and power. Yet his very excellence inspired the pride that led to his downfall. At the heart of his rebellion was the desire to be as God and to take control of the universe.

The prophet Ezekiel said of Satan:

> You were the model of perfection,
>   full of wisdom and perfect in beauty.
> You were in Eden,
>   the garden of God. . . .
> You were anointed as a guardian cherub,
>   for so I ordained you. . . .
> Your heart became proud
>   on account of your beauty,
> And you corrupted your wisdom
>   because of your splendor.[11]

The apostle John describes Satan as the one who has been "sinning from the beginning" (1 John 3:8). He calls him the "evil one" who inspires lies and murders (verse 12). The apostle Peter warns us, "Your enemy the devil prowls around like a roaring lion looking for someone to devour" (1 Peter 5:8). But the apostle James adds, "Resist the devil, and he will flee from you" (James 4:7).

Satan is described in the Bible as the ruler of the kingdom of spiritual darkness, which is in opposition to the kingdom of Christ (Matthew 16:18). He is depicted as residing in a defensive fortress, behind the "gates of Hades," desperately trying to hold onto his kingdom. He rules the realm of demons and evil spirits (Matthew 9:34), and opposes the people of God (2 Corinthians 2:11). He is an apostate angel who fell from his heavenly position through willful and deliberate rebellion (Luke 10:18).

Also called the devil, Satan is the one who blinds the minds of unbelievers (Acts 26:18); sows seeds of error and false doctrine in the church (Matthew 13:39); possesses unbelievers (John 13:27) and persecutes believers (2 Corinthians 12:7). He has great power, subtilty, and treacherous devices (Ephesians 6:11). He is the enemy of Christ, His gospel, His church, and His eternal kingdom.

Ankerberg and Weldon observe that Satan and his demons are the reality behind occult practices, idolatry, and false religion. "The reason is simple," they state. "Satan has as his purpose the denigration of God through the moral defilement and spiritual destruction of man, God's creation. . . . The only thing a man will ever receive from a demon is deception about what is important spiritually."[12] Despite faking love and concern for their victims, the actions of demons are always selfish, cruel, and destructive. They ultimately attempt to destroy what they possess.

Emanuel Swedenborg, himself an occult medium, warned that the "spirits" (demons) were liars and seducers who could not be trusted.[13] Thus, one should not be surprised that the demonic, so-called spirit guides uniformly hate Jesus Christ, deny His deity, pervert the gospel, endorse false religion, promote immorality, and destroy those whom they possess. The current claims about these spirits as kind, wise, and loving beings is all part of their seduction to ensnare modern people. Under the pretense of love, they promote the lies of the devil himself.

Playing with Fire

Occult Practices and Astrology

Dabbling in occult fads, symbols, or practices is the first step toward serious trouble for many curiosity seekers. *The Satanic Bible* has sold nearly 700,000 copies! While some may read it initially as a joke, others become hooked on its diabolical message. And it isn't long until they are plunging in deeper and deeper.

Jerry Johnston defines four categories of satanic or occultic practices common today:[1]

1. *Teenage dabblers*. This group is made up of kids who begin experimenting with games, Ouija boards, symbols, jewelry, chants, incantations, and satanic rituals.

2. *Undercover groups*. These are self-styled covens, usually run by adults. Teens are often told they are joining a secret club or they are videotaped taking drugs or having sex and then blackmailed into cooperation.

3. *Public religious satanists*. True converts or theatrical shysters, these Church of Satan

promoters (for example, Anton LaVey and Michael Aquino) are making a fortune off their enterprise. Selling books, videos, and tapes and conducting endless speaking tours, they are the Satan-sellers of today.

4. *Hardcore satanic cults.* These are the well-organized, highly secretive satanists who practice animal and human sacrifice. Crime experts estimate that as many as 50,000 human beings are killed by them in ritualistic sacrifices every year.

Today's occult practices include a variety of activities:

witchcraft	satanism
voodoo	spiritism
astrology	shamanism
divination	hypnotism
visualization	clairvoyance

Within these activities are numerous phenomena—some real, some imaginary:

telepathy	altered consciousness
seances	psychic healing
astral travel	pyramidology
crystal-gazing	telekinesis

Ankerberg and Weldon note that today, many occult practices and phenomena have been redefined, relabeled, and repackaged as psychological practices. They note, "It is this masking of fundamentally occultic realities as either human or divine which entices many people into entering a domain they would otherwise never think of entering."[2]

It is the psychologized packaging of occultism that has made it more acceptable to modern Americans and Europeans.

The hook is in the appeal that it will "help" the experimenter. So after a period of raw secularism, many people find themselves turning on to shamans, satanists, witches, mediums, channelers, psychic healers, and parapsychologists of all types. But behind all these practitioners looms the actual spirit-power that is the source of their supernatural knowledge, power, and strength.

Michael Harner, visiting professor at Columbia and Yale and a practicing shaman, notes, "Whatever it is called . . . the fundamental source of power for the shaman [is] . . . a guardian spirit."[3] Without this spiritual power source, the shaman, spiritist, or satanist is helpless. He has no power within himself. It must come from an external spiritual entity.

Because of satanic and demonic influences, there is no such thing as harmless dabbling in occult practices. Most people have forgotten that mass-murderer Charles Manson started out trifling with the occult and totally flipped out. So did Jim Morrison (of The Doors rock group) and Janis Joplin, both of whom committed suicide.

But when people pick up slick magazines like *Conscious Connection*, it all seems rather glamorous. Advertisements promote psychic seminars, cassette tapes, videos, and personal consultations. Prices range from $18 to $250. "Tune in to Your Inner Voice," "Meditate like a Monk," and "Supercharge Your Brain" the ads read. Psychic paraphernalia for sale includes a do-it-yourself fortune-telling kit for $24.95. Astral octave-tuning forks are $27.50 each.

Experimentation with the occult is like experimenting with drugs Once you get started it is hard to quit. "I got in deeper than I ever imagined," one teen told our youth minister recently. "I thought I could quit at any time, but I couldn't," she confessed. A college student admits he got involved by reading *The Satanic Bible* and *The Witches' Bible* as a joke. "But it is no joke now!" he adds. "I got into a lot more than I ever bargained for."

Rosicrucian Initiation

Occult organizations are many and varied. One of the oldest is the Ancient and Mystical Order of Rosae Crucis (or Rosicrucian, from "rose cross").[4] In the seventeenth century, a pamphlet entitled *Fama Fraternitis* by Johann Valentin Andrea (1586-1654) circulated in Germany. Johann was a Lutheran pastor who claimed to write about the discoveries of one Christian Rosencreutz who had traveled to Egypt in the fifteenth century. There he supposedly discovered the mystery of the "rose cross." Rosicrucian societies flourished in seventeenth- and eighteenth-century Europe. Freemasonry includes a Rosicrucian degree, and the two groups may have been interconnected at one time.

Rosicrucians came to the United States in 1694 under the leadership of Grand Master Kelpius from Europe. But its popular appeal did not come until H. Spencer Lewis was initiated by leaders of the French Rosicrucian Order in 1909. By 1915, he founded the Ancient and Mystical Order of Rosae Crucis (AMORC) with ceremonies that blended Judeo-Christian concepts with pagan mythology and occult practices. AMORC mixes the beliefs of Egyptian mythology, pseudo-scientific alchemy, and paranormal experiences.

Claiming that their principles go back to the "mystery schools" of pharaohs Thutmose III and Amenhotep IV (1500 B.C.), Rosicrucians place a great deal of emphasis on the mystical powers of ancient Egyptian religion. Special interest is placed in the power of the mind to move objects. Rosicrucian literature claims the ancient pyramid blocks (which weighed two to four tons each) were "moved" into place by mental telepathy. The pharaoh's chief advisers and architects were adept at the secret powers of the intellect and used their minds to move the blocks.

Like many who dabbled in Egyptology prior to the twentieth century, early Rosicrucians made several historical errors. For one, the pyramids were built around 2500 B.C., long before Thutmose III and Amenhotep IV (who were the pharaohs of the oppression and exodus of the Jews). Rosicrucian literature never historically validates its claims and never mentions the possibility that the blocks of stone were moved into place by ropes, rollers, dirt ramps, and muscle power (a method that has now been clearly demonstrated).

The Rosicrucians define God as the "Supreme Intelligence" or the "First Cause." He is an impersonal form of "pure energy." Borrowing from its Egyptian interests, AMORC literature recognized Amen-Ra, the Egyptian sun god, as the principle god of the universe. Jesus is viewed as a Rosicrucian initiate (during His childhood years in Egypt). The Old Testament is viewed as poetic and the New Testament is viewed as missing the "secret teachings" of Jesus. Larson notes, "Bible beliefs are replaced with a concoction of teachings about the lost continent of Atlantis and a race of Negroes called Lemurians."[5]

Secret, sealed instructions called *mandamus* encourage initiates to construct an altar (*telesterion*) in their homes with idols of Egyptian deities, black candles, incense, and the life symbol (*ankh*) which is popular with satanists. The packet includes a copy of the "confession to Maat" (Egyptian god of truth). Members are encouraged to contact departed spirit masters who are part of the "universal soul." Initiates are encouraged to seek possession by these "personalities" who are in need of physical expression.

Rosicrucians use the symbol of a rose in the center of the cross to represent the reincarnation of the human soul as well as various Egyptian geometric and hieroglyphic symbols. They teach reincarnation, encourage contact with spirits, and even promote possession by those spirits. While not a large group, they have been very influential in occult circles for the last 300 years.

Theosophy

Helena Petrovna Blavatsky was born into Russian nobility in 1831. As a child she exhibited psychic tendencies. Later she dabbled in Hinduism and spiritism. Her first marriage, to czarist General Blavatsky, 53 years her senior, lasted three months and her second marriage lasted only one day! Her teenage husband was declared to have gone insane during their honeymoon and the marriage was annulled.

After her marital failures, young Helena embarked upon a worldwide search for "truth," traveling to India, Tibet, Egypt, Europe, and eventually to America. In 1875, she founded the Theosophical Society in New York City. The key to her search for truth lay in her claim to be possessed by the spirits of the great *mahatmas* ("masters") she allegedly met in the Himalaya Mountains of Tibet. She eventually became a channel or medium through which these spirits spoke their messages.

A large and imposing woman with dark, piercing eyes, Madame Blavatsky became the matriarch of the occult movement in the nineteenth century. Her 6,000-page, multivolume work *The Secret Doctrine* set forth her views on reincarnation, absorption with the world soul, contact with departed spirits, the formation of a world brotherhood, and the coming of a great teacher to usher in a New Age of Understanding and a new political order. Her early "converts" included George Bernard Shaw and Thomas Edison. Her writings were also prized by Adolph Hitler and Sirhan Sirhan (who assassinated Robert Kennedy).

Theosophists consider Jesus Christ to be a reincarnation of Lord Krishna. They worship a being called "Lord of the World," as well as a variety of light rays and emanating spirits, including Master Morya. The atonement of Christ is dismissed as a "pernicious doctrine." The virgin birth, bodily resurrection, and literal second coming of Christ are denied. Salvation is secured through a process of esoteric divine wisdom (Greek, *theosophia*) which can be obtained only by mediums from the higher spirit (or "masters").[6]

The Theosophical Society, headquartered in Wheaton, Illinois, is relatively small, claiming 100,000 followers at most. But its influence is widespread. Many of Blavatsky's ideas are at the heart and core of the New Age movement today.

Spiritism

Also known as spiritualism, *spiritism* is the practice of contacting departed spirits. It can be traced all the way back to biblical times (1 Samuel 28). American spiritists trace their heritage back to the residence of John Fox in Hydesville, New York, where strange "rappings" were heard in the walls of the house in 1848. The Fox's daughters, aged twelve and fifteen, claimed they were communicating with the departed spirit of Charles Roena, a peddler who had been murdered in the house some years earlier. Soon seances were set up to communicate with the departed spirit, who later identified himself as "Split-foot"![7]

Newspapers picked up the story and it was widely circulated as fact. Mediums from Europe flocked to America and began conducting seances. Lights flickered, furniture moved, ghosts appeared, and spirits took over the mediums and spoke with other voices. How much was trickery and how much was demonic one can only guess. Some of the strange experiences that were widely reported and substantiated may have been tied to the extraordinary psychic abilities of the mediums, but some experiences also included the communication of knowledge and information that was beyond the normal range of human concoction.

The National Association of Spiritualist Churches was formed in 1893 and headquartered in Washington, D.C. While outwardly resembling traditional churches, the spiritualist churches feature "spirit greetings": sermons delivered while in a trance and psychic readings in place of Scripture. Most of the devotees are former Roman Catholics, though Episcopalian bishop James Pike attracted national attention when Arthur Ford's seances to contact the bishop's departed son were televised.

Spiritualists emphasize the Fatherhood of God, the brotherhood of man, the endless progression of human existence, and communication with angels and spirits. They promote the so-called "Aquarian Gospel" and a pseudo-Christ who is little more than a medium who used mass hypnosis. One spiritist called the Day of Pentecost (Acts 2) the greatest seance ever conducted.

The Bible clearly condemns witches, wizards, sorcerers, fortune-tellers, mediums, and soothsayers (Exodus 22:18; Leviticus 19:26; Deuteronomy 18:9-14; Acts 16:16-18). Leviticus 19:31 warns, "Do not turn to mediums or seek out spiritists, for you will be defiled by them. I am the LORD your God." Such people were to be stoned to death in the Old Testament era (Leviticus 20:27). The New Testament also warns, "Do not believe every spirit, but test the spirits to see whether they are from God, because many false prophets have gone out into the world" (1 John 4:1-3).

Astara

Robert and Earlyne Chaney publish the monthly magazine *The Voice of Astara* in Upland, California, claiming that Astara is the "Light Bearer" for this century. *Astara* means "place of light" and is derived from Ashtar or Ishtar, the Greek goddess of divine justice. The cult's teachings combine spiritism, theosophy, Rosicrucianism, lama yoga, and the utterances of Kut-Hu-Mi, whom Earlyne Chaney claims has communicated with clairvoyantly since she was a child.

In the movement's main text, *Astara's Book of Life*, the reader is promised a revelation of the "inner mysteries of life and immortality."[8] A series of correspondence courses leads the devotee through four degrees of twenty lessons each, revealing the Astarian sign, word, and secret handshake.

Astarians also claim their teachings are rooted in the ancient concepts of Mermes Trismegistus, an Egyptian magician who founded the first of the "mystery schools." The departed Egyptian spirit Zoser is the Chaneys' current spirit guide and is said to bring healing to those who call upon his name.

Astarians claim that Jesus traveled to India, Egypt, and Tibet to be initiated into the "mystery schools." They claim to confess Christ as the "light of the world." But it is an impersonal, cosmic Christ they portray. They deny His deity and the exclusivity of the gospel. They teach, rather, that there are many paths that lead to God.

Astrology

Astrology is one of the most primitive of all cults. The ancient Babylonians believed the sun, moon, and stars ruled the lives of men like celestial deities. They thought if they could predict the movement of these heavenly bodies, they could then predict human behavior. During the Persian conquest of the Middle East, the idea of birth horoscopes emerged within astrology. During the Greek or Hellenistic period in the second century A.D. the Alexandrian astronomer Ptolemy developed astrology into its present form.

Believing the earth was at the center of the universe and that the sun, moon, and planets revolved around it, Ptolemy devised the current form of the twelve signs of the zodiac: Aries, Taurus, Gemini, Cancer, Leo, Virgo, Libra, Scorpio, Sagittarius, Capricorn, Aquarius, and Pisces. Despite being based on an incorrect view of the universe, astrology remains popular in both practical and intellectual circles. Hitler dabbled in it; so did Nancy Reagan. Occult psychotherapist Carl Jung was involved in it. Jeane Dixon, the notorious false prophet, promotes it. So did Edgar Cayce. And most New Agers are into it.

Basically, astrologers attempt to compute the exact moment and place of one's birth and correlate it with the position of the stars and planets as they appeared to the earth at that moment. Astrologers believe that a permanent heavenly imprint is made upon each person at the moment of birth—an imprint that corresponds to the eventual experiences of one's life. It is upon this basis that astrologers attempt to predict the events of people's lives.

Research scientist Geoffrey Dean estimates that there are as many astrologers as there are psychologists in the Western world today.[9] The growing popularity of astrology even lures many professing Christians. It is not uncommon to mention your birthday to people at church these days and have someone identify your astrological sign: "Oh, you must be a _____!" Such was unheard of in Christian circles ten or twenty years ago.

Practicing witch Sybil Leek said, "Astrology is my science, witchcraft is my religion."[10] Helena Blavatsky (Theosophy), Alice Bailey (Lucius Trust), and Edgar Cayce (Association for Enlightenment) were modern mediums, all of whom spoke highly of astrology and claimed it was the gateway to the spirit world.

Astrologers also believe the world is moving in an evolutionary cycle toward the fulfillment of its cosmic destiny. Human freedom is an illusion in light of the impersonal fatalistic destiny of people, nations, and civilizations that rise or fall according to the stars. Astrological concepts such as "planetary vibrations" and "electromagnetic attractions" have never been scientifically verified. In fact, astronomers point out that the constellations (as viewed from earth) have shifted 30 degrees in the last 2,000 years. This alone invalidates the entire zodiac system established by Ptolemy. It is now off by one month since his time. Today's Virgo is really a Leo!

Astrology is clearly condemned in Scripture. In Deuteronomy 18:9 (KJV), the Israelites were warned against "observer[s] of the time" (astrologers). The prophet Jeremiah said, "Learn not the way of the heathen, and be not dismayed at the signs of heaven" (10:2 KJV). In both Daniel 2 and 4, the young Hebrew prophet seeks the wisdom of God to confound the astrologers, magicians, and wise men of Nebuchadnezzar's court. The prophet Isaiah clearly makes fun of the way the Babylonians trusted in the zodiac: "Let your astrologers come forward, those stargazers who make predictions month by month, let them save you" (47:13).

No Christian needs to dabble in astrology. It is God who rules from the heavens, not the stars. The great sign that will appear in heaven is the coming Christ (Matthew 24:30). It is His will that influences our lives, not the planets. And it is His Spirit who guides us, not horoscope imprints.

Witchcraft and Satanism

Satanic circles, ritual dances, incantations to the devil, human and animal sacrifices, and the drinking of blood have all been part of satanic worship for centuries. These practices can be found from primitive tribes to modern educated circles. In every case, the black arts are practiced and the spirits (demons) or the devil himself are called upon in some manifestation of destructive power.

Ken Boa observes, "Witchcraft, sorcery, divination and magic are ancient and universal. Every culture, primitive or civilized, East or West, had its share of magicians, sorcerers, and witches."[11] The Bible treats such individuals as real and serious threats. The pharaoh's sorcerers were able to duplicate some of Moses' miracles (Exodus 8:11,12). Simon Magus (Acts 8:9-11), Elymas the magician (Acts 13:8,10), and the medium at Philippi (Acts 16:16-18) seemed to have certain powers that went beyond normal human ability or chicanery.

Several Bible passages clearly condemn witchcraft and demonism: Exodus 22:18 says, "Do not allow a sorceress to live." Leviticus 19:26 tells us, "Ye shall not eat any thing with the blood; neither shall ye use enchantment [witchcraft] nor observe times" (kjv). First Samuel 15:23 adds, "For rebellion is as the sin of witchcraft" (kjv). And the apostle Paul wrote in Galatians 5:19-21, "The acts of the sinful nature are obvious: sexual immorality ımpurity and debauchery; idolatry and witchcraft. . . . Those who live like this will not inherit the kingdom of God." In Revelation 21:8 and 22:15, sorcerers, murderers, and idolaters are pictured as being excluded from heaven and cast into the lake of fire.

The apostle Paul's admonition in Ephesians 6:12,13 is perhaps the most sobering warning in the New Testament:

> For our struggle is not against flesh and
> blood, but against the rulers, against the authori-
> ties, against the powers of this dark world and
> against the spiritual forces of evil in the heavenly
> realms. Therefore put on the full armor of God,
> so that when the day of evil comes, you may be
> able to stand your ground.

This is the only possible explanation for the existence of evil in the world today. What possesses an Adolph Hitler to exterminate six million Jews? What provokes a Saddam Hussein to assassinate his own officers? What compels a Charles Manson to murder innocent people? What disturbing influence causes a Jeffrey Dahmer to rape, kill, and cannibalize his victims? Is it not Satan and his demonic hordes?

What is it that tempts men into thinking they are gods? What sinister force would dare to denounce the existence of the Almighty, deny the deity of Christ, despise the power of His blood atonement, and deprecate the reality of His resurrection and return? What spirit of error would reject the grace of God and renounce the glories of heaven?

Is it not Satan and his angels of deceit?

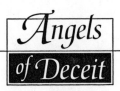
Angels
of Deceit

PART TWO

The Masters of Deception

But there were also false prophets among the people, just as there will be false teachers among you. They will secretly introduce destructive heresies. . . . In their greed these teachers will will exploit you with stories they have made up.

—2 Peter 2:1-3

A Guide
to False Prophets

Biblical Tests for
False Prophets

Spiritual deception by false prophets is not a new phenomenon. False prophecies have been around as long as there have been legitimate prophets of God. Moses raised the question to the children of Israel, "How can we know when a message has not been spoken by the LORD?" His answer was, "If what a prophet proclaims in the name of the LORD does not take place or come true, that is a message the LORD has not spoken. That prophet has spoken presumptuously. Do not be afraid of him" (Deuteronomy 18:21,22).

The threefold biblical test of a true prophet of God is listed in Deuteronomy 18:20-22:

1. He must speak in the name of the Lord, not some other god.
2. His message must be in accord with God's revealed truth in Scripture.
3. His predictions of future events must come true exactly as predicted.

One of the most scathing denunciations of false prophets in all of Scripture is delivered by the prophet Jeremiah. In his time, Jeremiah had to deal constantly with false prophets who opposed his ministry, contradicted his message, and even conspired to have him killed. They kept telling the leaders of Jerusalem that the people had nothing to fear from the Babylonian invaders, but Jeremiah knew differently. Jerusalem was on the verge of destruction and the people were about to be taken into captivity for 70 years.

"My heart is broken within me," Jeremiah confesses of his agony over these false prophets, who "follow an evil course and use their power unjustly" (23:9,10). "Both prophet and priest are godless," the Lord responds (23:11). Then He tells Jeremiah His opinion of these false prophets:

> Do not listen to what the prophets are prophesy-
>   ing to you;
>   they fill you with false hopes.
> They speak visions from their own minds,
>   not from the mouth of the LORD (verse 16).
>
> I did not send these prophets,
>   yet they have run with their message;
> I did not speak to them,
>   yet they have prophesied (verse 21).

> I have heard what the prophets say who prophesy lies in my name. They say, "I had a dream! I had a dream!" How long will this continue in the hearts of these lying prophets, who prophesy the delusions of their own minds? (verse 25).
>
> Yes...I am against the prophets who wag their own tongues.... Indeed, I am against those who prophesy false dreams...because every man's own word becomes his oracle and so you distort the words of the living God, the LORD Almighty (verses 31,32,36).

Jeremiah could not make his complaint any clearer, nor his case any stronger. God is against those false prophets whose spiritual delusion causes them to invent their own message apart from God's truth. The Bible presents them in seven categories:

1. *Self-deceived.* Some false teachers may be sincere, but they are still wrong. They have deceived themselves into believing their messages are true. As Jeremiah points out, their messages come psychologically from within their own minds and are not from God.

2. *Liars.* Some false prophets are deliberate liars who have no intention of telling the truth. The apostle John says, "Who is the liar? It is the man who denies that Jesus is the Christ. Such a man is the antichrist—he denies the Father and the Son" (1 John 2:22).

3. *Heretics.* These are those who preach heresy (false doctrine) and divide the church. Of them John said, "They went out from us, but they did not really belong to us" (1 John 2:19). The apostle Peter said, "There will be false teachers among you. They will secretly introduce destructive heresies. . . . These men blaspheme in matters they do not understand" (2 Peter 2:1,12).

4. *Scoffers.* There are some who do not necessarily promote false teaching so much as they outright reject the truth of God. Of them the Bible warns, "In the last days scoffers will come, scoffing and following their own evil desires" (2 Peter 3:3). The apostle Paul calls them "lovers of themselves . . . boastful, proud . . . conceited" (2 Timothy 3:2,3). Jude calls them "grumblers and faultfinders" (verse 16).

5. *Blasphemers.* Those who speak evil of God, Christ, the Holy Spirit, the people of God, the kingdom of God, and the attributes of God are called blasphemers. Jude calls them "godless men . . . [who] speak abusively against whatever they do not understand. . . . They are clouds without rain . . . trees, without fruit. . . . wild waves of the sea . . . wandering stars" (Jude 4,10,12,13). The apostle Paul says that he himself was a blasphemer before his conversion to Christ (1 Timothy 1:13).

6. *Seducers.* Jesus warned that some false prophets will appear with miraculous signs and wonders to "seduce" (KJV) or

"deceive" (NIV) the very elect, "if that were possible" (Mark 13:22). Our Lord's implication is that spiritual seduction is a very real threat even to believers. This would account for the fact that a few genuine, but deceived, believers may be found among the cults.

7. *Reprobates.* This term means "disapproved," "depraved," or "rejected." Paul refers to those who have rejected the truth of God and turned to spiritual darkness. Consequently, God has given them over to a "reprobate mind" (Romans 1:28 KJV). They have so deliberately rejected God that they have become "filled with every kind of wickedness" (verse 29). As a result, they are "God-haters" (verse 30), whose behavior is "senseless, faithless, heartless, ruthless" (verse 31). These people are so far gone spiritually that they know it and don't care!

In Jesus' own prophetic message, the Olivet Discourse, He warned, "Watch out that no one deceives you.... Many will turn away from the faith...and many false prophets will appear and deceive many people.... For false Christs and false prophets will appear and perform great signs and miracles" (Matthew 24:4,10,11,24). Our Lord warned His disciples of the possibility of spiritual seduction by false prophets and teachers, especially as we approach the end of the age.

The following guide to false prophets (chapters 11–25) is provided to acquaint you with some of the more popular or influential false teachers of our time. (This list of false prophets appears in alphabetical order.) Each teacher is set in his or her historical context, the origin of his or her beliefs is examined, and the doctrines he or she taught as well as personal views are analyzed in the light of biblical teaching. While some followers may not adhere consistently to all of their founder's ideas, these teachers are presented as representative of the groups they helped organize and influence.

This critique does not intend to imply that *all* the teachings of a given cult leader are biblically wrong or heretical. For example, Mormons generally hold to high moral standards in their family lives; Seventh-day Adventists offer excellent critiques of scientific evolution; and Jehovah's Witnesses are committed to personal evangelism. But within each of these systems are biblical and doctrinal errors that destroy or distort God's truth.

Worldwide
Church of God

Herbert W. Armstrong

The first Sunday of 1934 was the first time the true gospel of Jesus Christ was preached since A.D. 69! That is the boast of the late Herbert W. Armstrong (1892-1986), founder of the Worldwide Church of God headquartered in Pasadena, California. Armstrong is probably best known as the founder of *The Plain Truth* magazine, *The World Tomorrow* telecast, and Ambassador College.

Born in Des Moines, Iowa, in 1892, Armstrong had little

interest in spiritual matters until his wife, Loma, became "converted" through the efforts of an Adventist friend who convinced her that other churches were wrong about the matter of the Saturday Sabbath. After several arguments and months of intense study, Herbert concluded that his wife was right. She had convinced him that obedience to the Ten Commandments and various Old Testament laws were essential to salvation. In time, he came to believe that *all* other churches were deceived but his own.

Mrs. Armstrong had been proselytized by a neighbor lady who belonged to the Church of God (Adventist), a splinter group off the Seventh-day Adventists headquartered in Stanbury, Missouri. Armstrong eventually joined this church body then later departed in a dispute over Anglo-Israelism (the belief that Anglo-Saxons are the descendants of the ten lost tribes of Israel).

Much of Armstrong's early teaching paralleled Adventist doctrine:

1. Saturday Sabbath worship
2. Observance of Old Testament feasts
3. Abstinence from "unclean" foods
4. Denial of eternal punishment

Convinced that he had been misled by the traditional churches, Armstrong became their avowed enemy. In his autobiography he writes, "I found that popular church teachings and practices were not based on the Bible. They originated . . . in paganism."[1] Convinced that he alone was right, Armstrong organized the Radio Church of God, later named the Worldwide Church of God, in 1934 in Eugene, Oregon. From that first broadcast on a little 100-watt radio station, Armstrong launched what would become a multimillion-dollar enterprise with daily broadcasts on 400 radio and television stations; a magazine with a circulation of two million copies a month; college campuses in California, Texas, and England; and an annual budget of $40 million.

Recovering the Lost Gospel

Herbert W. Armstrong actually believed the true gospel was lost after A.D. 69 when the Romans conquered Jerusalem and destroyed the Temple. He further believed it remained lost until 1934, when he began preaching on the radio. Armstrong claims, "No other work on earth is proclaiming this true gospel of Christ to the whole world."[2] *The Plain Truth* magazine declared, "There is only ONE CHURCH on earth today which understands and is proclaiming that exact order of events, doing the work of God in preaching his message to the world as a last witness."[3]

Armstrong believed that God worked in 19-year cycles. The first two of these ran from Pentecost (A.D. 31) until the destruction of Jerusalem (A.D. 69). At that point, he said, the Roman Empire corrupted the original commandment-keeping church and blunted its message. The true church was driven into the "wilderness" for 1,260 years (from the "1,260 days" of Revelation 12:6). Attempts during the Reformation then failed to liberate the true gospel, and finally in 1934, Armstrong himself became the fulfillment of Jesus' prophecy (Matthew 24:14) that the gospel of the kingdom would be preached in all the world before His return. Initially, Armstrong allotted two more 19-year cycles to accomplish this task (1934-1972). He actually believed he was a modern-day John the Baptist called to prepare the way for Christ's coming.

Armstrong himself said, "For eighteen and one half centuries that Gospel was not preached. The world was deceived into accepting a false gospel." But then he raised the reader's hopes: "Today Christ has raised up His work and once again allotted two 19-year time cycles for proclaiming His same Gospel, preparatory to His Second Coming." In 1967, Armstrong predicted millions would die in the next four or five years from drought, famine, and disease epidemics.[4]

Believing time was running out in 1970, Herbert commissioned his son, Garner Ted Armstrong, to go on a highly publicized national speaking tour to proclaim the soon return of Christ. The May-June 1970 issue of *Tomorrow's World* features a five-page article announcing that God's 6,000-year allotment of self-rule to man was about to end: "But time is now almost up! The new order—the happy world tomorrow—will soon be here. . . . In less than 15 years all nations are going to live in this utopia . . . a Millennium of abundant and happy living."[5]

These erroneous attempts to date the second coming and the beginning of the millennium ought to be enough to identify Armstrong as a false prophet. But his other teachings are just as erroneous. In the February 1972 issue of *Tomorrow's World*, Armstrong acknowledged the "whole question of chronology is in confusion, and no one can be positively sure of dates."[6]

During 1972, Garner Ted Armstrong, who by now was the popular national speaker on the *World Tomorrow* telecast and vice-chancellor of Ambassador College, was dismissed by his father for disciplinary reasons involving several alleged sexual affairs. He was recalled briefly in 1978, and dismissed again. Not to be outdone, Garner Ted moved to Tyler, Texas, and founded the Church of God International and his own telecast, all the while still promoting the same beliefs.

Herbert died in 1986 at age 94, leaving Joseph Tkach to head the Worldwide Church of God.

Armstrong's Theology

The unorthodox beliefs of the Armstrong cult are as follows:

1. *The divinity of man.* God is in the process of recreating Himself. Upon conversion we are *begotten* (or "conceived"), but *not born* of God. Armstrong says, "The purpose of you being alive is that finally you be *born* into the Kingdom of God, when you will actually *be* God."[7]

2. *Denial of the deity of Christ.* Jesus is viewed as a human creation of God who is the first and thus far only person to be saved by achieving perfect human character through obeying the Law. The deity of Christ is called a "Satan-inspired doctrine . . . about which millions are deceived."[8]

3. *Rejection of the Trinity.* "God is not a single person... but a *family* of persons."[9] Presently, Armstrongists believe only Christ and the Father are part of the godhead. They reject the personality of the Holy Spirit. "God's spirit... is not a distinct person as is the Father or Christ."[10] However, the godhead is not limited. At the resurrection, believers will be "born of God" and "we then shall be God."[11]

4. *Salvation by works.* Salvation is viewed as a process beginning in this life and culminating at the resurrection. Thus, no one is already saved, except Jesus. Armstrong wrote, "People have been falsely taught that Christ 'completed the plan of salvation on the cross'—when actually it was only begun there. The popular denominations have taught... 'believe on the Lord Jesus Christ, and you are that instant saved!' That teaching is false!"[12] He believed that water baptism was required for salvation as well as Saturday Sabbath-keeping. "Sunday observance," he wrote, "is the Mark of the Beast."[13] Yet, long before Constantine (A.D. 325), Ignatius of Antioch and Justin Martyr (second century A.D.) wrote that Christians were no longer living according to the Jewish law nor observing the sabbath because they have "received grace."[14]

5. *Belief in Anglo-Israelism.* This nonbiblical theory teaches that Anglo-Saxons are the ten lost tribes of Israel. Therefore, Britain (Ephraim) and America (Manasseh) are heirs to the covenant blessings of biblical Israel. To prove this, Armstrong relies on the dubious and unscholarly arguments of nineteenth-century Anglo-Israelism. The lost tribe of Dan is believed to have migrated across Europe, leaving behind the tribal name: *Dan*zig, *Dan*ube, *Dn*ieper. The name *Saxon* is claimed to be derived from *Isaac-son,* and *Brit*ain comes from the Hebrew word for covenant (*berith*). However, Armstrong did not study Hebrew, Greek, or any other language! He took these assertions based on a mangled understanding of Hebrew linguistics from non-scholarly, secular sources and assumed they were correct. Following his assumption that Great Britain is Israel, he further assumes the throne of England is David's throne.

The June 1953 issue of *The Plain Truth* states, "Elizabeth II actually sits on the throne of King David of Israel—that she is a direct descendent, continuing David's dynasty—the *very throne* on which Christ shall sit after His return."[15] *The Plain Truth* (June 1953) claims the stone in the base of the throne was the stone Jacob used for his pillow (Genesis 28:11,18). It is said that later the stone came under the care of Jeremiah the prophet, who then took it to England, where it eventually became the coronation stone of the Davidic dynasty of British kings. This kind of speculation alone ought to discredit the Armstrong cult from any further serious consideration.

Children of God

David Berg

During the height of the Jesus Movement, David Berg (born 1919) vaulted into national prominence with his Teens for Christ coffeehouse known as The Light Club in Huntington Beach, California. Bob Larson notes, "It was there that his radicalized, anti-establishment gospel took root among religiously zealous hippies."[1]

Disenchanted with the Christian and Missionary Alliance Church by whom he had been ordained, Berg left to establish

155

himself in the parachurch coffeehouse ministry. David was deeply influenced by his mother, Virginia, a radio evangelist, and an extremist televangelist named Fred Jordan. Under their influence, Berg turned against the established church and found a ready-made audience among the hippies of Southern California in the late sixties.

In 1968, Berg, his wife Jane, and their four children moved to California to open the Christian coffeehouse to reach disillusioned teenagers. In time, hundreds of long-haired, sandal-clad, "freaks" were "turning on" to God at The Light Club. They flocked into the crowded facility to study the Bible with David Berg. When *Time* magazine ran a cover story on the Jesus Movement, they chose Berg's ministry as a typical example of the avant-garde Christians who were reaching out to troubled youth.[2]

Berg became an instant celebrity. Writers flocked to him for interviews. Kids showed up by the hundreds. But within two years, Berg began to show cultic tendencies. He departed from biblical orthodoxy and introduced deviant practices among his followers. Converts began adopting Bible names as a symbol of their spiritual new birth. Berg himself took the name Moses, or "Mo." He began signing his letters Moses David; these letters came to be known as "Mo Letters" to his followers.

In 1969, Berg predicted that California would be hit by an incredible earthquake and slide into the ocean. So he took his family and 50 followers to Arizona. The group of 75 people then wandered across the United States and Canada, disrupting church services and holding demonstrations along the way. While they were in Tucson, Arizona, Berg met Maria, a church secretary who left her family to become his mistress. Berg's wife Jane, called "Mother Eve" by cult members, remained with her husband until 1980, accepting Maria as a part of their marriage. Later, Jane Berg left her husband and ran off with another cult member.

Children of God

By 1970, Berg began calling his group the Children of God (COG). He renamed his own children with biblical names. Linda, his oldest daughter, whom he renamed Deborah, would later write a devastating exposé of her father's illicit sexual exploits.[3] When charges of kidnapping and brainwashing surfaced, Fred Jordan evicted the group from his Texas "Soul Clinic" ranch. Berg then divided the followers into 12 groups, analogous to the 12 tribes of Israel, and sent them off in different directions to sing, preach, and raise money.

During this time, I (Ed) encountered one of the groups (comprised of Linda Davis's children) in San Francisco. My wife, Donna, and I had just finished eating at Fisherman's Wharf when a car sped up to the curb and a troupe of kids jumped out, began singing to the fascinated crowd, handed out literature (which I still have), took up a collection, jumped back into the car, and sped away. The children were so cute and they sang so well that the crowd shelled out lots of money in appreciation.

I can still recall standing there watching them, thinking, "Something isn't right here. This just isn't normal. Who are these people?" Soon parents all over America were asking the same questions. In time, a group called FREE COG was formed by parents who claimed their teenage children were being held against their will and constantly moved from place to place to keep them away from their families.

The Children of God claimed over 10,000 converts. Berg isolated himself to what he now called the "Royal Family" or the "House of David," practicing incest with his daughters, adultery with Maria and other COG members, and still granting sexual "visiting rights" to his wife, Jane.

During a trek to Montreal, Canada, to witness at the "Expo 70" World's Fair, Berg issued the first of his infamous "Mo Letters." He announced he was divorcing his wife, who represented the old dispensation, and marrying Maria, who represented the new dispensation. Maria, his new wife, was to represent the church that was to reign with Christ in the new Israel of the new dispensation.

The "Mo" Letters

From 1970 onward, Berg began to denigrate the Bible as being no longer relevant under the new dispensation. It was to be replaced by the "Mo Letters" as God's Word to the new Israel. At that time, Berg predicted God's judgment would soon fall upon America and he left with the "Royal Family" for Europe.

The letters began to take on exotic and bizarre tones as Berg became free with his constant sexual references and overtones. Berg's letters often began, "Hear, O Israel, the words of thy King!"[4] Viewing himself as God's end-time prophet, Berg moved further and further from his orthodox roots. By 1972 the "Royal Family" was lodged at an estate in Bromley, Kent, a suburb of London. Berg elevated his daughter, Deborah (Linda), to be "Queen of God's New Nation" and promptly attempted incest with her. When she refused, she was deposed as Queen of the Family.

Berg began saying the traditional churches had gone astray in their puritanical teachings about sex. "To the pure all things are pure," he would argue. On October 28, 1972, he issued his famous "one wife" letter, which would become the basis of all his future pronouncements about sex. "The private family is the basis of the selfish capitalistic private enterprise system and all its selfish evils," he wrote. "God is the greatest destroyer of home and family of anybody. We are Revolutionary! We are . . . not hesitating to destroy marriages that don't glorify God and put Him and His work first!"[5]

Raised in a family of religious extremists, Berg had come to believe they were "God's exceptions"—special people, anointed prophets, God's own children. With that mind-set, anything could be justified as an exception to the rules if it advanced the cause of God. It was on this basis that Berg tried to justify his incestuous relationships with his daughters, sexual adultery with other women, and his so-called marriage to Maria.

"My mother was forced to accept his argumentation," Deborah later explained. If she resisted such counsel, she felt she would be resisting the very counsel of God. It was this kind of evil genius that enabled my father to engineer a multinational cult."[6]

Using biblical terminology to justify his actions, Berg renamed the group the Family of Love, portrayed the Holy Spirit as the "Holy Queen of Love," and began to promote fornication, polygamy, incest, and adultery as free expressions of God's love. In a "Mo Letter" entitled, "Come on Ma! Burn Your Bra!" Berg described communion with "sexy naked God" in a wild orgy with the Holy Spirit, His totally surrendered Bride. Berg also promotes religious prostitution, which he calls "flirty fishing," urging his female converts to be "hookers for Jesus." Illegitimate pregnancies result in "Jesus babies," conceived for the cause of evangelism.

Berg's daughter, Deborah Davis, made this observation: "My father's involvement in sexual immorality (beginning when he was a boy) caused him to reexamine the laws of God as revealed in Scripture and twist and interpret them to satisfy his own moral condition."[7] In 1980, Berg wrote, "No, I don't have to keep the ten commandments! All I have to do is love and do whatever I do in love!"[8]

Believing the Children of God are latter-day Israel and thus heir to all God's promises, Berg guarantees they will survive the Battle of Armageddon, which he predicts will take place in 1993. He also claims now to be in contact with unseen spirits, including Abrahim, a departed gypsy king. And he professes to have had sexual intercourse with spirit beings whom he calls goddesses. Viewing himself as God's King David, Berg excuses all sexual license in the name of religion.

The Bible views such people as abandoned by God. Romans 1:24 says, "Therefore God gave them over in the sinful desires of their hearts to sexual impurity for the degrading of their bodies with one another."

Association for Research and Enlightenment

Edgar Cayce

All healing comes from God," Edgar Cayce (1877-1945) said frequently. Referred to as the "Sleeping Prophet," Cayce (pronounced *Kay-cee*) gave thousands of "readings" while under self-hypnosis. Claiming his only desire was to help people find God, Cayce was able to diagnose illnesses and prescribe proper medical treatment while in a trance state.

Born and reared in Hopkinsville, Kentucky, Edgar dropped

out of school in the eighth grade to work on the family farm. Raised in the Disciples of Christ Church, he claimed to believe in Christian orthodoxy and even taught Sunday school at one time. But his encounters with the occult began early in life. His father, he claimed, could make tables move and brooms dance.[1] His grandfather was a famous water witch. An elderly black woman prescribed unusual treatments for his illnesses when he was a baby. In later childhood he claimed that invisible playmates materialized around him, but disappeared when others came into the room.

At age 13, Cayce claimed a "Shining Lady" appeared in his room and told him he could have whatever he desired. He responded that he would like to be able to help the sick. Later in life he would give lengthy and detailed medical advice to thousands of people while in a trance. He even shared some of his psychic experiences with evangelist D.L. Moody, who warned him to beware of evil spirits.

Cayce himself believed he was the prophet described in Numbers 12:6. In his early twenties, he lost his voice. Doctors were unable to help him, so he turned to a hypnotist named Al Layne. He was able to restore Cayce's voice through self-induced hypnosis. Layne eventually encouraged him to take hypnotic readings on other people's illnesses. Cayce was soon an instant success. He was able to correctly diagnose people's illnesses and prescribe successful treatments. Viewing his clairvoyant abilities as a "gift" from God, he began to give readings on a regular basis without charging for his services.

Despite his limited education, Edgar Cayce was able to use technical terms from biology, physiology, and pharmacology while in his self-induced trances. In time, his fame spread. The October 9, 1910, issue of the *New York Times* declared, "Illiterate man becomes a Doctor when hypnotized." Despite his unique abilities, his wife urged him to abandon these practices. But every time he did, he lost his voice, and was forced to slip back into self-hypnosis in order to recover.

In 1923, Cayce met Arthur Lammers, a student of metaphysics, the occult, and Theosophy. He encouraged Cayce to talk about the future while in a trance and let him record the reading. During this time, the hypnotized Cayce claimed the world was a pantheistic manifestation of God, that reincarnation was the path to salvation, and that Jesus was the thirtieth reincarnation of Adam, Enoch, Melchizedek, and others. He claimed later "psychic revelation" that indicated Jesus was an Essene, that He was initiated in the "mystery societies" of Egypt and India, and that He used astrology and occult divination.[2]

During his lifetime, Edgar Cayce gave over 15,000 readings, of which 14,246 were stenographically recorded and indexed. They are preserved in fireproof vaults at the headquarters of the Association for Research and Enlightenment (A.R.E.), which was founded by Cayce in 1931 at Virginia Beach, Virginia. He chose this because he had "prophesied" it would be safe from future natural disasters (which he had also predicted).

Approximately two-thirds of Cayce's readings involved diagnoses of physical ailments. While some were amazingly accurate, others were not. He told cancer victims to eat three almonds (a source of laetrile) a day and suggested smoking was harmless if held to six to eight cigarettes a day. Both of these prescriptions have since been discredited.

Despite the fact that Edgar Cayce was sincere, charitable, read the Bible, and taught Sunday school, his readings were anything but biblically sound. A.R.E. literature calls his readings the "most impressive record of psychic prescriptions ever to emanate from a single individual."[3] But despite his high percentage of accuracy, Cayce made numerous false "prophecies" regarding Hitler, World War II, the submerging of New York City in the 1970s, the rise of Atlantis in the twentieth century, and even the prediction of his own miraculous healing on New Year's Day, 1945. He died three days later!

Larson notes, "Cayce's undocumented revelations of historical events, erroneous prophecies of geological alterations, and unsubstantiated tales of lost empires, should cause serious students of history and the Bible to question his credibility."[4]

Yet there are over 400 physicians who are A.R.E. members and utilize Cayce's readings as part of holistic health cures. The A.R.E. headquarters at Virginia Beach houses a large occult/metaphysical library, endorses and attracts numerous occult and New Age practitioners, and is part of the mainstream of occultic interest and practice in the world today.

In contrast to Cayce's revelations stands the warning of Scripture: "In the latter times some shall depart from the faith, giving heed to seducing spirits, and doctrines of devils" (1 Timothy 4:1). Edgar Cayce's apparent "sincerity" does not excuse his making himself available to demonic spirits, nor does it legitimatize the false doctrine he disseminated while in self-hypnotic trances.

Predictor of Future Events

Jeane Dixon

Like Edgar Cayce, Jeane Dixon (born 1918) had humble beginnings. She was born in Medford, Wisconsin, to German immigrants. Her family, the Pinckerts, later moved to Santa Rosa, California, and became very prosperous. When Jeane was only eight years old, she attended a private party with her parents at the estate of naturalist Luther Burbank, a family friend. A gypsy fortune-teller had been hired to "entertain" the guests. When she saw Jeane's hands, she gasped and told her parents she would become a famous prophet who could foresee the future.[1]

"Never have I seen such lines!" the gypsy proclaimed, saying that the palm lines on Jeane's right hand formed a perfect six-point star of David. Alan Streett points out that the gypsy was so impressed that she gave Jeane a real crystal ball and a deck of fortune-telling cards, urging the little girl to develop her psychic powers.

Later, as a teenager, Jeane was introduced to a Jesuit priest named Father Henry. He taught her how to read and forecast astrological charts. Today, she writes a popular news column predicting future events and offering astrological advice. She uses a combination of crystal balls, Tarot cards, and horoscopes to make her predictions. She also receives some prophecies through visions and dreams.

Dixon herself acknowledges that the source of her prophetic visions began on July 14, 1952, when she saw a vision of a large python snake coiling itself around her body during a sleepless night. The serpent looked her in the eyes and then looked eastward as if to imply that all wisdom comes from the East. Since that vision, Dixon has developed a habit of rising, facing east, and praying.

Christians immediately recognize the serpent as symbolic of the devil, not wisdom. It is also interesting to note that *python* is the Greek word for "divination." Later visions would deal with a worldwide church, minus the pope, and a world government ruled by a child born on February 5, 1962. Earlier predictions included the fall of China to the Communists, and the deaths of Franklin Roosevelt, Winston Churchill, John Kennedy, and Marilyn Monroe.

Jeane Pinckert married James Dixon at age 21 and moved to Washington, D.C., where they had a prosperous real-estate business. A Roman Catholic, Jeane Dixon, like Edgar Cayce, never repudiated her church. But she allows for psychic and occult experiences as valid and legitimate expressions of God's truth. In 1964 she founded Children to Children, which operates homes for troubled and orphaned youth.

Despite her religious background and personal philanthropy, Jeane Dixon follows many unscriptural practices. She enthusiastically endorses astrology, which the Bible resoundly condemns. Deuteronomy 18:10 says, "Let no one be found among you who . . . practices divination, or sorcery [or] interprets omens." The prophet Isaiah condemns the "astrologers" and "stargazers" who "make predictions month by month" as false prophets (Isaiah 47:13).

Mrs. Dixon also endorses the use of enchantments. She combines crystal balls, horoscopes, and fortune-telling cards to make her predictions. Yet the Bible condemns such practices. In Acts 19:19 we read of a host of converted psychics, mystics, and occultists who "openly confessed their evil deeds" and burned their occult books (i.e., scrolls) to the glory of God and the gospel of Jesus Christ.

Jeane Dixon has also made several false prophecies. She incorrectly predicted that World War III would begin in 1958; that the Russians would be the first to land a man on the moon; that Lyndon Johnson would win re-election to the presidency; and that Lansing, Michigan, would be buried in a blizzard in 1966. It has been estimated that less than 10 percent (10%) of her predictions ever come true. This fact alone disqualifies her from being a true prophet of God. The Bible condemns such false prophets as speaking from the "deceit of their heart" (Jeremiah 14:14 KJV).

Three of Jeane Dixon's major prophecies have to do with future events.[2] While kneeling in prayer at the Catholic Cathedral in Washington, D.C., in 1958, she claims the Virgin Mary, robed in purple, revealed to her that the Roman Catholic Church would unite all the nations under one world church. Later that same year Dixon saw the Virgin again. This time the Cathedral was illuminated with rays from Mary's body, spelling *Fatima*, and revealing the empty throne of the pope. She took this to mean that the world church would grow without the aid of a human papal leader and that he must be pointing the way to another. Dixon also claimed to have a vision at 7:00 A.M. (EST) on February 5, 1962, of a child being born who would revolutionize the world and unite all mankind under one church without the aid of the pope.

Allan Streett points out that Jeane Dixon is a lot like the demon-possessed girl with the spirit of divination in Acts 16:16-18. She too could predict the future. She too made a religious profession acknowledging Paul and his companions as the servants of God. Yet Paul rebuked her and commanded the demon to leave her. She lost her "prophetic" abilities, but she found Jesus Christ as her Savior and Lord.

Jeane Dixon claims to receive her "prophecies" by mental telepathy. But she also uses a crystal ball, fortune-telling cards, palmistry, astrology, and numerology to predict the future. These are the kinds of occult artifacts condemned in Scripture. Acts 19:18-19 describes those converts to Christ who had practiced magic and divination; they came forward to discard their books and artifacts and burned them up in testimony to God's saving grace.

Christian Science

Mary Baker Eddy

Mary Baker (1821-1910) was born into a strict Congregationalist family in Bow, New Hampshire. A semi-invalid most of her childhood and teenage years, Mary missed a great deal of school and was virtually self-educated. Throughout most of her life, Mary was preoccupied with her own health problems.

In 1843, at age 22, Mary married the first of her three husbands, Colonel George Glover, who had amassed a fortune as a slave trader. Several years her senior, he died of yellow fever just six months later in 1844 while they were living in Charleston, South Carolina. Mary was pregnant with their unborn child and returned to New England where she bore George, Jr., in 1845. Traumatized by her husband's death, she sent the child off to live with relatives. He died at age four. During those years her health continued to deteriorate.

In 1853, Mary Glover married her second husband, Daniel Patterson, an itinerant dentist. It was an unhappy marriage from the start. Patterson was reported to have other women in his life, and stayed away much of the time.[1] After 13 years of marriage, Dr. Patterson left her. Seven years later, in 1873, Mary secured a legal divorce from him.

The Quimby Connection

But it was during the time she was Mrs. Patterson that several key events occurred in her life. In 1862, she went to Portland, Maine, to be treated by Dr. Phineas Quimby, who had developed a system of mental healing which he called "the Science of Health." It was Quimby's ideas that would later become the foundational concepts of Christian Science. After being treated by Quimby, Mrs. Patterson claimed to be cured of her lifelong spinal illness and began lecturing on his spiritual science, which she found quite fascinating. Later evidence revealed that she copied extensively from his writings. In fact, the published *Quimby Manuscripts* verified that he actually used the term *Christian Science* as early as February 1863.[2]

Then in January 1866, Phineas Quimby suddenly died. Two weeks later, Mary Patterson fell on icy pavement and was seriously injured. Years later, she said doctors had proclaimed the injury was fatal and that she had only a few days to live. On the third day after her fall, Mary read Jesus' words, "Get up, take your mat and go" (Matthew 9:6). Taking heart from this text, she claimed an instantaneous and miraculous healing.

Though the doctor who attended to her later swore under oath that he never said her injury was fatal, it was the turning point of her life. As Quimby's disciple, she had learned the concepts of "inner healing" or "mind science." The basic principles she learned from Quimby were these:

1. *God is good.* Therefore, all is good. Sin was viewed as an illusion of the mind. The entire material world, including the physical body, is an illusion. The only reality is the spiritual realm.

2. *God is spirit.* Therefore the spiritual can overcome the physical. True healing comes when the mind overcomes the body. The illusions of sin, pain, and death are conquered by the mind of Christ.

3. *All healing is spiritual.* Since the mind can heal the body, doctors and medicine are unnecessary. Thus, Christian Science licenses its own "practitioners," who take the place of regular doctors.

The Rise of Christian Science

For the next several years, Mrs. Patterson traveled and lectured extensively on the principles of inner healing, which she called "Christian Science." In reality, she was peddling a "christianized" version of mystical pantheism repackaged for the nineteenth-century Western mind. By 1870, she was charging people $300 for a dozen lessons in the healing sciences. In 1875, she finished compiling her ideas in writing and published them under the title *Science and Health with Key to the Scriptures.* The first edition was produced privately and a hall was rented in Lynn, Massachusetts, where Mary preached her doctrines on Sunday.

In 1877, Mary Baker Glover Patterson married Asa G. Eddy. He became her first student to be licensed as a "Christian Science Practitioner." In 1879, the Church of Christ (Scientist) was officially organized and chartered in Boston. In 1881, Mrs. Eddy founded the Massachusetts Metaphysical College in Lynn, and later moved it to Boston. Then in 1882, Asa Eddy died from organic heart disease. Mary Baker Eddy, however, announced to the press that he had been murdered with arsenic "mentally administered" by their family's enemies!

Toward the end of her life, Mary had to wear glasses, purchase dentures, and once again suffered declining health. On her deathbed she asked Adam Dickey, one of her closest associates, "If I should ever leave here, will you promise me that you will say that I was mentally murdered?" On December 3, 1910, Mary Baker Eddy, who taught that death was an illusion, succumbed to that illusion and died!

Theologically, Mary Baker Eddy believed she had received the "final revelation" of God in her discovery of the divine principle of scientific mental healing.[3] She referred to her discovery as Christian Science and believed her *Science and Health* to be the "voice of Truth to this age" and that it was "revealed Truth uncontaminated by human hypotheses."[4] To this day, her text is read in Christian Science churches by the First Reader, while the Bible (which she alleged was full of errors) is read by the Second Reader.

Theology of Christian Science

Mary Baker Eddy's unorthodox views include the following:

1. *Matter is an illusion.* Mrs. Eddy said, "All is infinite mind and its infinite manifestation, for God is all-in-all. Spirit is immortal Truth; matter is mortal error. Spirit is the real and eternal; matter is the unreal and temporal."[5]

2. *Sin, sickness, and death are illusions.* She said, "The only reality of sin, sickness, or death is the awful fact that unrealities seem real to human, erring belief, until God strips off their disguise."[6] Death is defined as "an illusion...the unreal and untrue."

3. *God is the Divine Principle.* He is not viewed as a person, but as the universal mind or spirit, called the "Divine Principle," thus, the Christian Science schools are called "Principia." The Christian doctrine of the Trinity is totally rejected. She separated the Gods of the Bible between the *Elohim* (Spirit

God) and *Jehovah* (the materialistic, vengeful Jewish tribal God). She also made a distinction between *Jesus* (a limited human being) and *Christ* (a spiritual idea). The only Trinity she would accept was the trinity of "life, Truth and Love."[7]

4. *The incarnation, virgin birth, blood atonement, and bodily resurrection of Christ are all illusions.* Believing that anything physical or material was an illusion of the mind, Mrs. Eddy was logically forced to strip away the human reality from the person and work of Christ. Her views totally contradict the Bible, which says, "Every spirit that acknowledges that Jesus Christ has come in the flesh is from God, but every spirit that does not acknowledge Jesus is not from God" (1 John 4:2,3).

5. *Denial of heaven, hell, and the final resurrection.* Believing salvation to consist of mental illumination, Mrs. Eddy viewed hell as an illusion, heaven as a state of mind, and the resurrection as unnecessary.[8] As to the second coming of Christ, Mrs. Eddy believed it occurred in 1866 with her "recovery" of the spiritual ideas of "Christian Science."[9]

The real tragedy of Christian Science is that it holds out the false hope of spiritual healing and escape from the reality of death. Many Christian Science devotees have died tragically by refusing medical assistance in the name of their faith. To them, calling for a doctor is giving in to the illusion that one is really sick. Since such would be an act of disbelief, one must overcome his or her illness by the principles of so-called Christian Science, which in reality is neither Christian nor scientific!

Church of Scientology

L. Ron Hubbard

The Church of Scientology was founded in 1955 in Washington, D.C., by L. Ron Hubbard (1911-1986), a science-fiction writer who developed Dianetics as a cure for mental health. He wrote over 800 books and articles that sold over 90 million copies in 31 different languages. He was awarded the gold medal by the French Academy of Arts, Sciences and Letters and the Italian Latina Literary Award for his works. Several of his books have reached the number-one spot on the national bestseller lists.[1]

Over 600 Churches of Scientology proclaim Hubbard's gospel of Dianetics, claiming to be "dedicated to helping individuals lead happier and more productive lives."[2] The term *Scientology* is derived from the Latin word *scio* ("knowing") and the Greek word *logos* ("study of"). Together these terms mean "knowing how to know." Thus, Scientology promises to unlock the secrets to knowledge and its practical application to life. Scientology considers itself to be a religious philosophy of life.

Despite its seemingly sincere intentions, *Reader's Digest* recently called Scientology a "dangerous cult" and a "thriving scam." Author Richard Behar said,

> The Church of Scientology, started by science-fiction writer L. Ron Hubbard to "clear" people of unhappiness, portrays itself as a religion. In reality the church is a hugely profitable global racket that survives by intimidating members and critics in a mafia-like manner.[3]

Reader's Digest notes that no mind-control cult in America prompts more calls for help than does Scientology. Cynthia Kisser, executive director of the Cult Awareness Network, says, "Scientology is quite likely the most ruthless, the most terroristic and the most lucrative cult the country has ever seen." Former Scientology leader Vicki Aznarah said, "This is a criminal organization day in and day out."[4]

In his earlier writings, Hubbard referred to Scientology as a science. But in 1955 he incorporated it as a religion. Hubbard served as head of the church and its only prophet until his death in 1986. In order to conform to the national tax regulations in regard to churches, auditors and processors became "ministers" and classrooms became "churches." Reporters Carroll Stover and JoAnne Parke note, "Ministers of the Church of Scientology perform legal marriages and baptisms which mention neither eternal salvation nor God."[5]

Theologian Horton Davies recognized that theology, in its traditional usage, is nonexistent in Scientology. He observes,

"Despite its quasi-religious vocabulary [Scientology] has no theology worthy of the name, and its use of such terms as 'spiritual' and 'infinity' as equal to 'God' and 'the Church' without reference to Jesus, the founder of the church, seems to be a verbal camouflage to escape taxation."[6]

A former World War II veteran and successful science-fiction writer, Hubbard developed Dianetics as a do-it-yourself approach to psychoanalysis. The publication of *Dianetics: The Modern Science of Mental Health* in 1948 initially sold over 100,000 copies (eventually revisions of it sold over 14 million copies). But Hubbard was severely censured by various states for operating an unlicensed medical school and giving out bogus degrees. An official report from Australia called it "the world's largest organization of unqualified persons engaged in the practice of dangerous techniques, which masquerades as mental therapy."[7]

Hubbard quickly switched Scientology to the status of a religion to avoid further legal problems. William Peterson called Scientology "a curious amalgamation of crude psycho-analysis, positive thinking, sensitivity training and indoctrination."[8]

Basic Theology

Hubbard's basic theory is that people are mentally "blocked" from realizing their full potential because of *engrams*, which are prenatal impressions received by the embryo in the womb. Robertson observes, "Scientology purposes to uncover and eradicate prenatal problems, compulsions, and inhibitions that have accumulated in the soul during [one's] past lives."[9]

The individual seeking help is called the "seeker" and the Scientologist is called an "auditor." He or she directs the seeker to find a personal route to relive the emotions that were filed in his prenatal memory bank. In addition to engrams, Hubbard also added *Thetans* (immortal spirits) during the sixties. These spirits were supposedly banished to earth 75 million years ago by a cruel galactic ruler named Xenu.

Scientology includes the terminology and practice of these elements:

> *Reactive mind:* The storehouse of unconscious memories where engrams are stored
>
> *Engrams:* Mental blocks from previous incarnations and prenatal experiences
>
> *Pre-clear:* The beginning scientologist or seeker
>
> *Auditor:* Scientology-trained private counselor
>
> *Dianetics:* The method of removing engrams from the reactive mind
>
> *Clear:* One who is mentally clear of all engram blockage. One who can think, evaluate, decide, and choose his own destiny
>
> *Analytical mind:* The conscious, active mind that perceives and reasons
>
> *E-meter:* An electropsychometer (two empty tin cans connected to a galvanometer) that acts like a lie detector to get the pre-clear to tell the truth

According to Robertson, the E-meter is used to reveal the engrams that must be identified, confessed, erased, and then detached from the Thetan. This process generally follows eight steps or "dynamics" of existence:

1. Self
2. Sexual
3. Group
4. Mankind
5. Animal
6. Universe
7. Spiritual
8. Infinity

The pre-clear can choose how far he or she will progress in these eight steps. No particular religious belief is required.

"Counseling" sessions may eventually cost $5,000 to $120,000 to "clear" all eight stages.

Much of Scientology's efforts are harmless pop psychology, but the organization has attracted intense criticism for claiming to be scientific and religious. Like a repackaged version of Christian Science, it is neither. Its harassment of members, ex-members, lawyers, and critics have won Scientology numerous enemies and critics who claim that its members are being held by intimidation, threats, and fear. The current leader, David Miscavige, intends to change that image through health care and drug treatment programs. But the basic elements of Scientology remain the same: shake off your engrams, create your own path to success, and if anybody gets in your way, stomp on them!

Divine Light Mission

Maharaj Ji

This cult represents a variation of the teaching of *siddha yoga*, in which the guru is worshiped as God. Divine Light Mission (DLM) was actually founded by Shri Hans Ji Maharaj, a wealthy and respected guru, known as the "Perfect Master." When he died in 1966, his eight-year-old son Maharaj Ji proclaimed that he was the reincarnation of his father. At his father's funeral, the boy announced, "Why are you weeping? The Perfect Master never dies. I am here among you. Maharaj Ji is here now. Recognize him, obey him and worship him."[1]

Suddenly the entire family, led by the boy's mother, and all the DLM followers fell down prostrate before the young incarnate deity. The cult instantly had something different and unusual—a boy guru. His disciples, called "premies," spread his message worldwide and called upon him to come to the United States. In July 1971, he left Delhi for Los Angeles aboard a TWA flight. His American devotees blasphemously announced, "He is coming in the clouds in power and great glory!"

Jack Sparks observes, "The boy guru was an instant success. His first Guru Puja ("worship") festival in Colorado in the summer of 1972 brought an estimated 2,000 converts. The bandwagon was moving. For two years he became the hottest thing on the guru circuit."[2]

Troubles began, however, in May 1974, when Maharaj Ji married his older secretary, Marolyn Lois Johnson, and renamed her Durja Ji. His mother denounced him and his excessive lifestyle, which now included nightclubs, dancing, drinking, and meat-eating! But the "Lord of the Universe" prevailed and retained control of the Divine Light Mission.

DLM's unique appeal was its adaptation of Christian terminology to sell Hindu concepts. This was done mostly by American converts who were familiar with such ideas, and Maharaj Ji accepted them. God was called "He" and spoken of in the terminology of personal relationship. Hitchhiking their doctrine off Jesus' teachings, DLM leaders used His statement, "The kingdom of God is within you" (Luke 17:21) to say that He taught that every person in the world has God inside him. Jesus is viewed as the best living Master of His time. He tried to help people get in touch with the divinity within themselves.

Like all Hindu-based cults, DLM teaches that salvation is unity with the divine god within ourselves. "Realize the god within" is the appeal of DLM. "Unite with god and all humanity through Guru Maharaj Ji" is its further appeal. "Rid yourself of the illusion that you are separate from god and immerse yourself in the creator."

The evangelistic arm of DLM is aggressive. The organization puts out a *Propagation Handbook*, a newspaper called *Divine Times*, numerous books, including *Meditation: The Missing Peace*, and a series of movies and videos. Most ex-cult members claim they were invited to friendly gatherings to hear *satsang* ("teachings"), only to be subjected later to indoctrination that lasted 10 to 12 hours a day for weeks at a time. Charges of brainwashing and hypnotism have been brought forward by several former cult members. "Give me your mind," the guru says. "I am ready to receive it." And many do just that. Meditating constantly on the guru, they lose all sense of themselves—and everything else.

The People's Temple

Jim Jones

November 18, 1978, is one of those dates that will live in infamy. It was on that day that the mass suicide of over 900 members of the People's Temple cult occurred in Guyana, South America. It had come after nearly a decade of political and social confrontation between the cult members and public officials.

The attempted investigation of the cult by California congressman Leo Ryan had ended in disaster. When the final tally was taken, over 900 people lay dead on the ground at Jonestown, five others at the Port Kaituma airstrip, and four more in the People's Temple at Georgetown.

A note written by one of the followers was found on the body of Jim Jones:

> Dad: I see no way out—I agree with your decision—I fear only that without you the world may not make it to communism—
>
> For my part—I am more than tired of this wretched, merciless planet and the hell it holds for so many masses of beautiful people—thank you for the only life I've known.[1]

There can be little doubt that the infamous suicide pact had been agreed on long before by members of the People's Temple. It was something they had rehearsed on numerous occasions, and when "Dad" gave the orders, nearly everyone complied. Jones himself had been shot in the head. So had Maria Katsaris, his mistress. Jones's wife, Marceline, was found poisoned, lying near the cult leader. But most will remember the 900 bodies of Jones's followers lying strewn across the grounds of the Guyana compound. Lying lifeless in the sun were whole families, parents and children, who had chosen to die together. It was an incredible and frightening sight.

Jim Jones was born in 1931, the only child of a poor family in the small farming community of Lynn, Indiana. The elder Jones was a member of the Ku Klux Klan, which had a large following in the rural community. There were six churches in the small town, and Jim loved to play church when he was a child. A neighbor recalled he would have about ten youngsters in the yard and would "preach" to them, line them up and make them march, and then hit them with a stick if they didn't comply. The neighbor remarked to his wife that Jim was either going to grow up to do a lot of good, or end up like Hitler!

Jim's early religious training came from Mrs. Orville Kennedy, who lived down the street from him and introduced him to the Nazarene faith. Thirty years later, in June 1976, Jones stopped in Lynn to visit Mrs. Kennedy, along with 600 of his followers, while on a bus tour across the Midwest.

Despite his religious interests, Jim Jones was a loner and known for having a bad temper. He attended Indiana University, where his roommate described him as being maladjusted. Jones dropped out of college after a while. In 1949, at age 18, he married Marceline Baldwin, four years his senior. By 1950, he had become pastor of a small church in Indianapolis. It was there he began to reject his racist background and proclaim what he called a biracial gospel. He eventually graduated from Butler University in Indianapolis and was ordained by the Christian Church (Disciples of Christ) in 1964.

Cultic Beginnings

As early as 1956, Jones had founded his own church, the People's Temple, in a racially changing neighborhood of Indianapolis. In addition to rearing his own children, Jones adopted seven children of various racial backgrounds during this period of time. His style of ministry appealed to both black and white families who were living in the transitional neighborhood.

Jones later made a trip to Philadelphia to visit Father Divine, a black preacher who claimed to be God and had total control over his adoring followers. About this same time, Jones began to claim to have divine premonitions and supernatural gifts of healing, which were taking up more time in the services than did the sermon. After a while, his ministry in Indianapolis grew to attract several hundred followers. They began to call him "Father" and "Prophet of God."

Jones was eventually appointed director of Indianapolis's Human Rights Commission by Mayor Charles Boswell because of his ability to work with interracial groups of people. But a series of financial setbacks, an IRS investigation of his personal finances, and his claim to have a vision of a coming nuclear holocaust soon led Jones to believe God was telling him to move the entire congregation to Redwood Valley, California. In June 1965, a hundred or more people followed Jones on his first trek to a new utopia.

During the time they were in Redwood Valley, Jones became an expert at dealing with local politicians. Instead of taking the confrontational approach he had used in Indianapolis, he began to court the favor of politicians and use it to his own advantage. It wasn't long, though, before Jones became restless in the rural setting of Redwood Valley. He began to load up buses with church members and take them to San Francisco's Fillmore District, where they distributed leaflets promoting his healing services.

Bold flyers read, "Incredible! Miraculous! Amazing! The most unique prophetic healing service you've ever witnessed! Christ is made real through the most precise revelations and miraculous healings in this ministry of His servant, Jim Jones!"[2] Services had now been expanded to include bands, gospel singing, dancing, and long impassioned appeals by Jones, who wore sunglasses and a satin-trimmed robe. Healings of elderly black women who had been seriously injured by such things as "malicious white drivers" were a common part of the services. The healings would be spectacular, bewildering, and even mystifying. Soon Jones was establishing People's Temples in San Francisco and Los Angeles, as well as the mother church in Redwood Valley.

As early as 1972, *San Francisco Examiner* religion writer Lester Kinsolving began criticizing Jones's ostentatious style and his claim to have raised more than 40 people from the dead. Kinsolving also became disturbed by the number of armed guards who constantly hovered about Jones and were always present in the services. Soured by the scoffing tone of the sensational *Examiner* series, Jones became hostile toward the media.

Playing Politcs

In September 1972, Jones bought an empty auditorium on Geary Boulevard for $122,000 and established what would become the infamous People's Temple of San Francisco. Upon arriving in town, Jones immediately befriended Reverend George Bedford of the Macedonia Missionary Baptist Church, one of the most respected black clergymen in the city. In a drastic reversal, he began a policy of total flattery toward the press, even bestowing $4,400 in grants to various newspapers for what he considered to be professional journalism. He also bought a 30-minute radio broadcast on KFAX, a religious station in the city.

During this time, Jones often sent his followers on political errands to win acceptance from the community. A positive editorial about him appeared in the *Washington Post*, which he used to his advantage. He soon began claiming a membership of over 7,000 and began publishing a small newspaper called *The People's Forum* with a circulation he declared to be in excess of 300,000. During the close race for mayor in 1975, hundreds of People's Temple members worked to get out the vote on behalf of George Moscone, who credited Jones with helping him win the election. And on October 18, 1976, Jones was nominated to a seat on the city's Housing Authority Commission. He also began supporting nearly every liberal politician in California, including Tom Hayden, formerly married to Jane Fonda. Jones himself favored a Communist form of government.

The real problems with the People's Temple were among the membership itself. Former cult members began to tell of arranged marriages, forced divorces, and promiscuous sexual practices among Jones' followers. His lengthy sermons often dealt extensively with sex, and at times he proclaimed himself the only person permitted to have sex. At least three pregnancies were attributed to Jones's involvement with female members. Homosexual relationships between Jones and male members of the cult were also widely reported.[3]

Kilduff and Javers observe, "Jones found sex a useful tool for controlling his Temple parishioners. Couples who thought of themselves as good Christians found, after engaging in adulterous and homosexual conduct, that they were liable to blackmail and subject to intense guilt."[4] He even established a marriage bureau, which in reality was a kind of ecclesiastical spy group that regulated every area of people's personal lives. In the meantime, Marceline Jones, Jim's wife, though deeply upset by her husband's philandering, was willing to overlook her husband's misconduct as she was showered with clothes, gifts, public attention, and special privileges.

The use of drugs by various followers, many of whom were supposed to be converted drug addicts, was also widely reported by ex-cult members. Guns and other concealed weapons had become part of the security force at the temple in The Redwood Valley, and they were more prolific than ever at the San Francisco headquarters. By 1973, all the trappings were in place that would lead to the disaster five years later in South America.

Move to Guyana

The Republic of Guyana (formerly British Guiana) had become independent in 1966 and was under a socialist government. As paranoia built within Jim Jones over his immoral conduct and illegal involvements, the desire to move to Guyana became intensified. Jones had visited the country in the late sixties on a "missions" trip. He immediately fell in love with the Victorian houses and Guyanese people. Their language was English, they were receptive to his brand of spiritual healing, and they had a socialist government. It was a perfect mix. By this time Jones had turned completely against American politics and was preaching a gospel of worldwide Communist takeover. Guyana seemed the ideal place for him to build his ultimate empire based on the vision of interracial communism.

In December 1973, four emissaries from the People's Temple visited Guyana in search of a site to build what would become Jonestown. Jones offered the government officials a large sum of money for an isolated location six miles from Port

Kaituma on which to build his "promised land." By 1975, 15 temple members were at Jonestown, clearing the land and building the complex that would soon gain international attention.

In the meantime, Jones was being bombarded by increasingly negative press and threats of investigations of the People's Temple in San Francisco. By the end of 1977, he and most of the congregation left San Francisco for Guyana, leaving behind only 100 people to send supplies. Those who made the trip signed away their cars, homes, and possessions to the People's Temple. Discipline at the campsite was strict and the early enthusiasm quickly gave way to an intense spirit of armed control. Many family members became concerned that their friends and relatives would not be allowed to leave, even if they chose to do so. Although Jones himself continued to say, "I reject corporal and physical punishment," later stories by former cult members indicated that that was not the case.

Threatened by lawsuits at home, Jones refused to leave Guyana. Over a period of time it became evident that his powerful control over the 900 members was such that he would not allow them to do anything that he did not choose to do himself.

Concerned that many of these people were being held against their will, California congressman Leo Ryan took a group of reporters to Guyana to investigate the complaints firsthand. His "invasion" of the compound exposed Jones and forced his hand.

Jim Jones preached a gospel of social welfare, spiritual healing, and self-indulgence. Like many other extremist cult leaders, he had stepped over the boundaries of human civility and knew it. His sexual indulgence caused him such great guilt and paranoia that he began to proclaim the self-fulfilling prophecy of coming destruction. "They will never destroy what we have, because we made the determination long ago that if they came after one of us, they would have to take us all on," one cult member wrote. "Martin Luther King perhaps

said it best," he continued, " 'A man who hasn't found something to die for isn't fit to live.' Well, we've found something to
die for and it's called social justice!"[5]

Jim Jones had attracted people to the People's Temple with
promises of food, clothing, shelter, and physical healing. He
used benevolence as a gimmick and also as an excuse for his
extravagant, immoral lifestyle. In the end, he chose to die
rather than to repent of his sin. Tragically, he influenced over
900 other people to line up and drink the cyanide-laced Kool-
Aid that had been prepared for the mass suicide at Jonestown.
The followers were so used to taking Jim's orders and letting
him have his own way that they obeyed without hesitation.
Believing him to be God's prophet, the cult members accepted
the mandate to kill themselves as though it had come from
heaven itself.

Today, the "new paradise" which Jones hoped to establish
is overgrown by the advancing jungle. The utopia he had
promised lies in a shambles, and the hopes and dreams of
nearly 1,000 of his followers have been obliterated forever.

The Branch Davidians

David Koresh

"There's a mad man living in Waco. Please, please, please won't you listen? It's not what it appears to be. We didn't want to hurt anybody. Just set our people free." These were the lyrics to the song "Mad Man from Waco," written by David Koresh about his encounter with the former Branch Davidian cult leader George Roden.

Unfortunately, David is the one who will go down in history as the madman of Waco, Texas. Believing himself to be King David incarnate and Jesus Christ Himself, David Koresh

193

died with 86 of his followers in the burning inferno that he had nicknamed "Ranch Apocalypse."

With a Bible in one hand and a gun in the other, Koresh, a 33-year-old, long-haired, high-school dropout used a mixture of biblical prophecy, fear, and personal persuasion to hold control over his followers. His blend of religion, sex, and violence led to their incredible act of self-destruction on April 19, 1993.

Koresh was born Vernon Howell in Houston, Texas, in 1959. After a failed career as a rock musician, Howell became involved with the Branch Davidians at age 18. The sect was a heretical branch of the Seventh-day Adventist Church in which Howell was reared. The Davidian Seventh-day Adventists were founded in the thirties by Victor Houteff, a prominent Los Angeles-area Adventist. He believed the return of Christ was imminent, but that it could not occur until there was a pure church that could receive Christ.

Houteff was banned by the Seventh-day Adventists and moved to a communal farm in Waco, Texas. He died there in 1955 and his widow, Florence, took over the leadership of the group. In 1959 she predicted the kingdom of God would arrive on Easter day. Hundreds of followers across the nation quit their jobs, sold their possessions, and made the trip to Waco. After the "great disappointment," most of the Davidians scattered. However, a small group of fifty stayed in Waco. That group later split and the splinter group, known as the Branch Davidians, came under the control of Ben Roden. After his death in 1978 he was succeeded by his wife, Lois.

In the meantime, Howell, the illegitimate son of 15-year-old Bonnie Clark, had grown up in Dallas, where he was raised as an Adventist. He dropped out of school in the ninth grade, studied the Bible, and learned to play the guitar. Disillusioned with the Adventists, he eventually made his way to Waco to join the Branch Davidians. Former cult members claim that Howell, then 23, had a sexual affair with 67-year-old Lois Roden, prophetess of the group. Howell later had a serious confrontation with her son, George, over the leadership of the

Branch Davidians, who were already housed at the Mount Carmel complex. The bitter competition between George Roden and Vernon Howell was so intense that Roden began wearing a gun around the compound. This was the first introduction of weapons into the Branch Davidian cult.

A New Name

Eventually Howell tired of Lois Roden and married 14-year-old Rachel Jones, the daughter of a Branch Davidian family. Lois Roden died in 1986 and Howell, with his family and a few friends, left the compound for about a year.

Eventually Vernon Howell changed his name to David Koresh. He actually believed he was the biblical David as well as the biblical Cyrus (Hebrew, *Koresh*), a Persian king who decreed the return of the Jews to Jerusalem. It was this belief that would eventually drive David Koresh to his ultimate and fiery confrontation with fate. Accepting the cult's belief that the King David of Israel would one day return to earth in order to pave the way for the Messiah, Koresh claimed himself to be David and, later on, the Messiah as well.

In a bizarre turn of events, Koresh returned to Mount Carmel in 1987 and challenged Roden for the leadership of the Branch Davidians. Roden dug up a coffin containing the corpse of an 85-year-old woman and announced that whoever could resurrect her back to life was the true leader of the Branch. On Halloween night, Koresh tried to have Roden arrested for corpse abuse. A local prosecutor, Denise Wilkerson, told him that she could not file such charges without some evidence, such as a photograph, of the actual corpse.

A few days later, on November 3, Howell and seven heavily armed friends invaded the grounds of Mount Carmel to get a picture of the corpse. A 20-minute gunfight ensued, and Roden was wounded. Koresh and his friends were charged with attempted murder and released on bond. Later, Roden was jailed for contempt of court, and Koresh moved his followers into the Mount Carmel complex.

In 1988, Koresh's accomplices were acquitted and his trial ended in a hung jury. As everyone filed out of the courthouse, Koresh invited the crowd, including the jury, out to Mount Carmel for an ice cream social![1] Roden was later sent to a state mental hospital for killing another man. It was clear by now that a kind of "insanity" ruled the Branch Davidians. From that point on, there were always armed guards at the Mount Carmel compound. As time passed, David Koresh's paranoia grew deeper and he began preaching an apocalyptic confrontation with local authorities. He was convinced the last days had already begun and that Armageddon was just around the corner.

"If the Bible is true, then I'm Christ," Koresh said in a taped message. The further he progressed into immorality, the more bizarre became his theology. *People* magazine stated, "He insisted that cult members begin each day at 5:30 A.M. with boot camp style physical training and no water. . . . The rest of the day was spent rebuilding the run down compound. Koresh, meanwhile, stayed in bed, not getting up until around 2 P.M. Then he would begin Bible classes, sometimes preaching for fifteen hours straight, while his exhausted followers tried to stay awake."[2] He controlled the group through isolation, constant activity, and fear of reprisal.

The Lamb of God

David Koresh believed he was the Lamb of God and that he had absolute control over the lives of his followers. Koresh insisted that female members wear long skirts and not cut their hair. He put them on strange diets of fruit and popcorn to keep them thin, and he eventually "married" 19 of them and fathered at least ten of their children. He believed that he was building the "House of David," and that his children would rule in God's future kingdom. In August 1989, he announced that he was the only one allowed to have wives and to procreate children. Every other marriage was annulled. Some couples left the cult at that point, but most stayed.

There were also charges of child abuse by former cult members. Many claimed that he beat even the youngest children until they were bruised and bleeding. One of his "wives" was Kiri Jewell, who was only 12 years old. She lived on the compound with her divorced mother, Sherri, who was 43. Her father, David Jewell of Michigan, was able to win a custody case and have Kiri removed from the compound. Another "wife" was Rachel's 12-year-old sister Michelle Jones.

"He was fixated with sex, and with a taste for younger girls," says Marc Breault, who belonged to the group from 1988 until 1989. He began to teach that all the women in the world belonged to him because he was the Son of God. Another former cult member, Elizabeth Barabya, said that he believed it was necessary for him to become a "sinful Jesus" so that he could properly forgive sinners on judgment day.[3]

Like Jim Jones before him, David Koresh became obsessed with a messianic complex and sexual perversion. Attempting to reconcile the two, he began to read his sexual intentions into almost every passage of Scripture. Hitchhiking his theology off the Branch Davidian belief that King David would literally return to the earth one day, Vernon Howell, alias David Koresh, believed that he was David in the flesh. Just as the Old Testament king had multiple wives, so Koresh rationalized that he could do the same today. He also believed that his procreation of children was actually building the House of David and preparing for the coming of the kingdom of God.

From an early age, David Koresh also had an intense interest in Bible prophecy. As a construction worker, he was often reported to be discussing prophecy and charting eschatological events. His interest focused on the seven seals of the book of Revelation (chapters 6-11). In this biblical prophecy, Christ Himself is the only One who can open the seals and pronounce the final judgment on the world prior to His return as triumphant Lord and King. Believing himself to be Christ, David Koresh believed that he personally would open those seals and bring about the final apocalyptic judgments on the

198 Angels of Deceit

world. His followers were so committed to him that ex-cult members Lisa and Bruce Gent said, "They will kill for him!"[4]

The Bureau of Alcohol, Tobacco, and Firearms (ATF) began investigating the Branch Davidians for several months. Neighbors had complained of automatic gunfire, and undercover agents had spotted numerous caches of illegal weapons. Continued reports of possible child abuse finally provoked the ATF into an armed confrontation at the Mount Carmel compound on February 28, 1993. After a 45-minute gun battle with federal agents at the cult's fortified headquarters east of Waco, Texas, four agents lay dead and 16 wounded. At least six members of the cult were believed to have been killed in the initial fight and Koresh himself was wounded by the gunfire. The bizarre confrontation shocked the public and gained the attention of the media. Hundreds of reporters descended on Waco, Texas, and began to wait out the 51-day ordeal while the compound was under siege by federal agents.

The 51-Day Siege

What had begun as an attempt to serve arrest and search warrants had turned into a 45-minute gun battle. Next, it became a 51-day siege. Jeeps, tanks, trucks, helicopters, 500 federal agents, and endless numbers of reporters descended on the perimeter of the Mount Carmel complex to await the surrender of the Branch Davidians.

Field operations were centered 250 yards from the compound across the bullet-pocked no-man's-land that separated the agents from their adversaries.[5] For the 500 federal agents, the siege became an endless succession of 12-hour work shifts. Electrical power was cut to the complex. Bright lights and loud music blasted the compound every night. Federal agents prepared their strategy, polished their weapons, and bolstered the perimeter.

In the meanwhile, the news media turned the ordeal into an outdoor camping extravaganza. The country road in front of Mount Carmel soon became strewn with lawn chairs, beach umbrellas, and camper trailers. Direct satellite linkups from the broadcast remote trucks made live coverage of the daily activities a nightly reality on the evening news.

Public Reaction

Within hours, public opinion became divided over the ATF's handling of the Mount Carmel incident. Many applauded the agency's intervention into what had been a growing crisis between the cult and its nervous neighbors. Others questioned the unusual display of force used to simply serve warrants, wondering if such a display had not provoked the armed response. Former McLennan County district attorney Vic Feazell called it a "vulgar display of power."[6]

More than 80 agents had been involved in extensive training and practice at Fort Hood for more than a week prior to the raid. Their plan had been to breach the front door in seven seconds, deploy the 80 agents from the trailers within 13 seconds, mount ladders and breach the upper-story windows within 22 seconds, and reach the cult's armory on the second floor in less than 45 more seconds. The entire operation was supposed to have taken two-and-a-half minutes.

The Dallas Morning News reported that the raiding party had assembled at the Bellemead Civic Center, which served as a staging area early on Sunday morning.[7] There they were joined by state and local law-enforcement officials and emergency personnel, who were briefed on the nature of the raid.

By the time the raiding party arrived at Mount Carmel, however, seven reporters from the *Waco Tribune-Herald* and a crew from KWTX-TV were already on the site. In the meantime, apparently, someone tipped off the Branch Davidians, and they were waiting with what turned into a 45-minute armed response.

The Fatal Decision

Intelligence reports of the possibility of a mass suicide had prompted the raid. FBI agent Bob Ricks repeatedly insisted that surrounding the compound and calling for Koresh's surrender would never have worked. In the meantime, constant negotiations were conducted by telephone. Eventually, 35 people, mostly women and children, were allowed to leave the compound. Koresh's own children and most of the adults remained holed-up inside.

Koresh, claiming that the federal authorities started the gunfight, promised to surrender to them after presenting a 58-minute taped message that was aired on radio. "I, David Koresh, agree upon the broadcasting of this tape to come out peacefully with all the people immediately," he said.[8] Several radio stations broadcast his rambling "sermon" about the seven seals of the book of Revelation and the coming apocalyptic judgment on America.

But when Tuesday, March 2, passed, Koresh refused to surrender. Claiming God told him "to wait," Koresh remained barricaded in the compound with about 90 cult members. During the 51 days of the siege, there was no more exchange of gunfire. Reporters were allowed to visit the compound, and a well-known Houston lawyer, Dick DeGuerin, was called in to represent the Branch Davidians. After several days of deliberations, DeGuerin indicated Koresh would soon surrender to federal authorities.

But after both Passover and Easter passed, Koresh showed still further signs of delay, claiming he wanted to write a book on the seven seals. Then newly appointed attorney general Janet Reno informed President Clinton she was authorizing an assault on the cult's compound. Claiming she was concerned about the welfare of the children inside, Reno made the decision to force them out.

"I just wanted to save the children," Reno stated. "But we obviously made the wrong decision."[9] The attempt to inject tear gas into the compound throughout the morning hours of April 19, 1993, apparently resulted in the cult members deliberately setting fire to the complex. The buildings were engulfed in flames as live ammunition exploded within, and the entire complex burned to the ground. Within 30 minutes,

90 people, including several women and children, died in the conflagration. David Koresh's prediction of a coming apocalypse became a self-fulfilling prophecy. But instead of being spared in the hour of judgment, the Branch Davidians perished in the flames.

Unification Church

Sun Myung Moon

The self-proclaimed Korean messiah was born on January 6, 1920, in a small village in what is now North Korea. His parents originally named him Yong Myung Moon. When he was ten years old, they converted to Christianity and joined the Presbyterian Church. Moon himself later attended a Pentecostal church as a teenager. Then on Easter Sunday, 1936, the 16-year-old Moon claimed to have a vision of Jesus while praying on a mountainside in Korea.

In this vision, Moon claimed that Jesus called him to fulfill His mission of bringing salvation to the world. According to Moon, Jesus failed in His original mission and was now commissioning the young Korean to be the new messiah. He would later proclaim that all mankind will be saved, hell will be abolished, and all the religions of the world will unite under the banner of Christianity and the Lord of the Second Advent (Moon himself).[1]

During the Japanese occupation of World War II, Moon studied at a Japanese university. In 1944, he returned to Korea and was married. After the war, in 1946, he moved to South Korea and spent several months with Paik Moon Kim, a self-proclaimed Korean Savior whose ideas greatly influenced Moon. In 1948, Moon was excommunicated from the Presbyterian Church for his heretical beliefs. He was later imprisoned in North Korea, but escaped in 1950 during the Korean War.[2]

In 1954, the self-ordained Reverend Moon founded the Holy Spirit Association for the Unification of World Christianity. In Korea it is known as the Tong-il Church, and in America and Europe it is known as the Unification Church. Its members are known to the general public as Moonies.

Ironically, Moon's wife of ten years divorced him in 1954. A year later he was arrested on morals charges related to his female followers, but was never convicted. In 1960, Moon married Hak Ja Han, who was 18 years old at that time and has been his wife ever since.

In 1957, Moon published his *Divine Principle*, which he claims is inspired of God. In it he builds his case that the *first Adam* and Eve failed to bring about a perfect humanity because Eve was seduced by Satan, who fathered Cain (who later killed Adam's son Abel). The *second Adam* was Jesus, who failed to find the second Eve and begin the physical restoration of the human race. Instead of unifying all mankind, Jesus was crucified. Moon denies the virgin birth, the deity of Christ, and His bodily resurrection. When Jesus saw He was going to fail, Moon claims, He began to teach about His second advent. The *third Adam* and Eve must now bring about physical salvation.

The third Adam is Lord of the Second Advent, or the new messiah, who was born in Korea in 1920.

America's Destiny

Moon also believes Israel, Europe, and England have all failed to bring in the kingdom of God on earth. It is now up to America to fulfill the messianic hope by accepting the Third Adam/Lord of the Second Advent/Moon himself!

In 1972, Moon began a series of preaching missions to the United States. As his movement grew he bought 680 acres of land near San Francisco for his Eden Awareness Training Center. He purchased a former Catholic seminary in Barrytown, New York, to use as a training institute. In time, he also bought the *Washington Times* newspaper and the Hotel New Yorker, which he converted into his headquarters.

On June 1, 1976, Moon addressed a rally of nearly 30,000 followers in Yankee Stadium in New York City. "It is my firm belief," he said, "that the United States of America was indeed conceived by God. . . . All the different races and nationalities of the world harmonized upon this land to create God-centered families, churches and the nation of America. . . . I have been teaching American youth a new revelation from God. . . . I know God's will is to save the world, and to do this America must lead the way. . . . This time our task is to build 'One World Under God.' . . . This new ideology will also be capable of unifying all the existing religions and ideologies of the world. . . . The Unification Church movement has been created by God to fulfill that mission."[3]

Moon's vision for a unified world religion with him as the new messiah grew out of his earlier experiences in an extremist underground Pentecostal group in Pyong Yang, North Korea. Cult expert James Bjornstad notes, "This group was deeply entrenched in mystical revelations, awaiting the impending appearance of a new messiah. They believed that Korea was the New Jerusalem of the Bible and that the messiah would be born in Korea—all elements which are found in Reverend Moon's theology and in the *Divine Principle*."[4]

Moon later claimed to have a mystical vision in which he overcame the spirit world and was recognized as the "Lord of creation." The *Divine Principle* says, "He fought alone against myriads of satanic forces, both in the spirit world and the physical world, and finally triumphed over them all."[5] Later, in *Master Speaks*, Moon described this incident in more detail:

> At that moment, he became the absolute victor of heaven and earth. The whole spirit world bowed down to him on that day of victory. . . . The spirit world has already recognized him as the victor of the universe and the Lord of creation.[6]

After this experience of spiritual illumination, he changed his birth name to Sun Myung Moon, which means, "Shining Sun and Moon." In 1972, he claimed to have another vision in which God called him to come to America to prepare people there for the second advent of Christ. From America he launched a worldwide missionary effort in 1975, sending crusade teams into several foreign countries.

Moon's Theology

The theology of the Unification Church is a blend of Christianity and Eastern mysticism. Dr. Young Oon Kim, professor at the Unification Theological Seminary, explains their beliefs in her book *Unification Theology and Christian Thought:*[7]

1. *God is energy.* God is pictured as the invisible essence of perpetual, self-generating divine energy. God is the force behind all matter. He is manifested in dual polarities (male and female, positive and negative). Thus, creation is the emanation of God's essence.

2. *Adam and Jesus failed to become the True Parents of Mankind.* Moon believes Adam and Eve were created as expressions of God's male/female polarity. Their goal was ideal marriage and the procreation of children free from inherited sin. However, before they could attain perfection, Eve

committed fornication with Lucifer, causing the spiritual fall of man. Through sexual union with Satan, Eve received a sinful nature, and, in turn, Adam also received the sinful nature of Eve. Thus, Adam and Eve failed to achieve deity and form a trinity with God. Jesus also failed in this mission. Though He was sinless, He was crucified before He could marry and have a sinless family.

3. *Divine Principle is the only way to salvation.* In Moon's theology, the Divine Principle has three steps:

    a. Maturing to spiritual perfection

    b. Marrying the ideal partner

    c. Producing perfect children

Moonies believe that Adam and Eve failed because they sinned and produced sinful children. They also believe Jesus failed because He was crucified before He could marry and produce children. Thus, it is left to Moon and his wife, called "True Parents" by the Moonies, to produce the perfect family.

Believing Moon to be the new messiah, Lord of the Second Advent, Moonies view his marriage to Hak Ja Han in 1960 as the marriage of the Lamb which is prophesied in Revelation 19. As he establishes his perfect family, he will help others to establish perfect families as well, and together they will build a perfect society. This explains their insistence on three year's celibacy (to reach perfection) before marriage, which must be approved by Moon himself. These marriages are generally performed in mass ceremonies on January 1 ("God's Day").

Reverend Won Chei, a leading Korean Presbyterian minister who has known Moon for many years, believes that Moon's concept of perfect marriage and perfect family stem from his earlier beliefs of sexual cleansing. Since Moon believes Adam and Eve were infected with sin sexually, he also believes perfect husbands must sexually "cleanse" their wives in order to rid the world of sin. This would then reverse the sin process. A woman's sexual intercourse with a perfect man (perfected in the spirit world) would eradicate her sinful nature.

Moon believes that he met Jesus in the spirit world and overcame Him. "We are the only people who truly understand the heart of Jesus, and the hope of Jesus," he has said.[8] *Divine Principle* claims that Moon "came in contact with many saints in paradise, and with Jesus, and thus brought into light all the heavenly secrets through his communion with God."[9]

Moon rejects the deity of Christ and teaches that his perfect humanity of the future will be greater than Jesus Himself. He also believes Jesus' death on the cross was a victory for Satan. He clearly states, "The cross has been unable to establish the Kingdom of Heaven on earth by removing our original sin."[10]

In order to spread his teachings, Moon's followers have developed an aggressive program of recruitment, peer pressure, and indoctrination. New converts are isolated from family, friends, and the outside world in general. The other Moonies literally become their family. Material possessions are usually surrendered to the church. Rigid daily schedules keep new believers inundated with constant lectures, drilling, praying, singing, dancing, long hours of hard work, and limited amounts of sleep. They are often charged up into emotional frenzies and harangued with guilt over any display of nonconformity.

Ken Boa notes, "All physical needs—housing, food, and clothing—are provided for Moon's followers. They no longer need money, and they make no decisions. Many who have observed these techniques see in them a classic pattern of brainwashing. It is not surprising that there have been nervous breakdowns and some suicides among Moon's followers."[11]

Moon's rejection of Christian doctrine is as evident as his arrogance about himself. In an interview with the *New York Times*, he said, "I am the foremost one in the whole world. Out of all the saints sent by God I am the most successful. I have talked with many masters, including Jesus Christ, on the questions of life and the universe. They have subjected themselves to me in terms of wisdom. After my winning the victory, they surrendered."[12]

In 1984, the Lord of the Second Advent was convicted of tax evasion and sentenced to prison in his beloved America. Since then, Moonies have attempted to promote the positive aspects of their beliefs—while awaiting the new messiah's release and the coming of his kingdom.

Church Universal and Triumphant

Elizabeth Clare Prophet

      Elizabeth Clare Prophet was born in Jersey City, New Jersey, in 1940. Her family dabbled in Christian Science and Theosophy. As a child she claimed to have a revelation that she had lived on the Nile River in Egypt in another life. As a teenager, she began reading books published by Guy and Edna Balladses' I AM cult, experimented with the occult, and became a trance medium.

      Known to her followers as Guru Ma, Elizabeth Clare

Prophet heads one of the more popular New Age cults. Founded in 1958 by her husband, Mark Prophet, the Church Universal and Triumphant (CUT) owns property in 36 states and six foreign countries. Some also consider the cult to be armed and dangerous. *Newsweek* recently reported that 5,000 CUT members have amassed a huge arsenal of weapons in a remote part of Montana, where they are awaiting the Battle of Armageddon.[1]

Mark Prophet claims he was urged to found his new religion by El Morya Khan, a leader of the Ascended Masters (spirit beings) known as the "Great White Brotherhood." Many of Prophet's ideas seem to have been borrowed from Guy and Edna Ballard, who founded the Saint Germain Foundation (also known as the "Great I Am" movement) in the thirties. They were Theosophists who taught that God is impersonal and unapproachable except by deified, human intermediaries. They have passed through reincarnation and have merged their consciousness with God. They are, therefore, the messengers (or masters) whom God now uses to reveal His truth.

These heavenly beings (Ascended Masters) impart hidden (occult) knowledge to human recipients known as "Enlightened Ones." Streett and Larson both observe that the Ballardses' teaching is very similar to ancient gnosticism (secret "knowledge" communicated to those who are enlightened).[2] Mark Prophet modernized and popularized their ideas, claiming to be the human spokesperson for the Great White Brotherhood, which included Jesus, Mary, Buddha, Confucius, El Morya Kahn, Kuthumi, Godfrey, and Saint Germain (an eighteenth-century French occultist).

Mark Prophet claimed to be a medium (or channel) for El Morya Kahn and other Ascended Masters. In 1958, he founded the Summit Lighthouse in Washington, D.C., as his headquarters. While holding seances and seminars for various clients, he met Elizabeth Clare Wulf in 1961. She also claimed to have made contact with the Ascended Masters. She told Mark she had her first spiritistic encounter at age three when she was surrounded by "angelic hosts." Over the years a variety of spirit beings communicated with her, including Saint Germain. They immediately formed a spiritistic team. He was 43 and she was 21 when they married in 1963.

Their popularity exploded and soon drew them into nationwide recognition in occultic circles. They claimed to be the sole appointed messengers of the Great White Brotherhood. They eventually moved their headquarters to Colorado Springs, produced a correspondence course called *Keepers of the Flame*, and wrote a 500-page book titled *Climb the Highest Mountain*, which chronicled their occult journey and systematized their teachings. In 1969, they founded Summit University in Santa Barbara, California, offering courses in astrology, astral projection, channeling, and other psychic topics.

Ma Takes Over

At the height of their success, Mark Prophet died from a massive stroke in 1973 at age 54. Elizabeth Clare, then 33, took over as the leader of the 30,000-member cult. She immediately deemed Mark the newest Ascended Master, communicating with the spirit name "Lanello." During an invisible (spirit realm) inauguration service, Lanello and the other Ascended Masters ordained Clare (who claims to be the reincarnation of the biblical Martha) to be the "Vicar of Christ on earth." Today she is viewed by her followers as the sole channel through whom the Ascended Masters communicate.

Nine months after Mark's death in 1973, Elizabeth married Randall King, one of her faithful disciples, only to divorce him four years later. And in 1975, she changed the cult's name to the Church Universal and Triumphant and moved the headquarters to Malibu, California. Assets from books, tapes, lectures, correspondence courses, and the sales of gold, silver, gems, and survival kits (in case of a Communist takeover) caused the cult to grow into a multimillion-dollar enterprise.

Eventually, the Ascended Masters declared her "Mother of the Universe." Her followers were to call her "Guru Ma."

Streett notes that her self-appointed elevations were enthusiastically accepted by her followers.[3] As the Divine Mother she lavishes herself with diamonds, rubies, and emeralds which she claims are spiritually charged with cosmic powers. Her church headquarters are luxuriously decorated with expensive paintings, statues, and crystal chandeliers.

Elizabeth now believes the hour has come for her to usher in the dawning of the Aquarian Age. She proclaims spiritual purification of the Violet Consuming Flame, which enables one to attain Christ-consciousness by the spiritual merit of Saint Germain. Streett notes that at a typical CUT service, Guru Ma enters the stage to the sound track of the movie *Chariots of Fire*. Her *chelas* (disciples) cheer wildly as the prophetess walks out dressed in white and bedecked with jewels, charms, and occult amulets.[4]

Services usually include a "spirit dictation" from the Ascended Masters, a multimedia presentation, a light show, chanting, meditative visualization, and a healing ceremony, with Guru Ma laying hands on the *chela's* forehead, the location of the mythical "third eye." A favorite incantation is, "I am that I am," an affirmation of self-deity which enables one's spiritual ascension.

Claiming divine revelation from the Ascended Masters, Elizabeth claims to be a messenger for the "Spiritual Hierarchy" commissioned to "speak the unspeakable."[5] In a work claiming to be "written" by El Morya, CUT acknowledges dependence on the ideas of the Ballards, Mary Baker Eddy, Helena Blavatsky, and Nicholas Roerich, who originated the idea of the Violet Consuming Flame.[6] One of the Ballardses' disciples, Godfrey Ray King, wrote, "Grace means the bringing of all into Divine Order, through Divine Love, and this is done by the use of the Violet Consuming Flame—the ONLY WAY in heaven or earth."[7]

The basic theology of the Church Universal and Triumphant (CUT) is an insidious blend of Eastern mysticism, watered-down Christianity, and occult "revelations."

1. *God is the Father-Mother Principle.* God is viewed as an impersonal force whose presence endows the creation with immortality. God is both male and female. The Father is the wisdom that planned the creation. The Mother is the love that gives it birth. Christ is the light that is the epitome of both wisdom and love.

2. *Jesus is not the Christ.* Jesus was merely a human being who taught us to recognize the "Christ" within ourselves. It is the Universal Christ, not Jesus, who is worshipped by the New Age church. "The Master's greatest desire was that they should not mistake the Son of Man (Jesus) for the Son of God (the Christ). . . . Should this confusion arise . . . the Savior knew that generations to come would not worship the Christ, but the man Jesus."[8] In contrast, the Bible says, "Who is the liar? It is the man who denies that Jesus is the Christ. Such a man is the antichrist—he denies the Father and the Son" (1 John 2:22).

3. *Salvation is by the merits of Saint Germain's Violet Consuming Flame.* Walter Martin states, "Salvation in I AM Theology is not biblical salvation!"[9] The self-realization that "I am God" damns and does not save. It involves the condemnation of one's soul by the self-affirmation of one's deity. Salvation by the blood of Jesus Christ is rejected as "the erroneous doctrine concerning the blood sacrifice of Jesus."[10] Guru Ma insures her *chelas* that God did not require the sacrifice of Christ as "an atonement for the sins of the world." Rather, salvation comes by the beneficent legacy of Saint Germain bought with the price of his love in order to procure the sin-cleansing experience of the Violet Consuming Flame that burns away our sins.

Tantric Yoga

Bhagwan Shree Rajneesh

Born as Rajneesh Chandra Mohan in a remote village in the province of Madhya Pradesh, the Bhagwan Shree Rajneesh ("The Blessed One Who Is God") claims that he came to enlightenment while completing a fast he had begun 700 years earlier in another life. He was obsessed with death from an early age. "Death stared at me before the thrust of life began," he reflects. "Aloneness became my nature."

Rajneesh's Hindu astrologer told his parents that he would "die" every seven years until the age of 21. It was then that he finally experienced his explosion into enlightenment. At seven, his grandfather died, and at 14, he nearly drowned. Throughout his teenage years he claimed to learn the lesson of total abandonment. He would dive off high bridges into rushing rapids, be sucked into the downward spiral, and reemerge again. The key: don't resist—cooperate with the divine purpose in all things.

Later he experimented with occult magic, telekinesis, and yogic breath control. "I became a universe to myself,"[1] Rajneesh explained. After intense meditation, a kind of cosmic desperation or suicidal drive overtook him: Become god or die! In time, all questions melted away and a "great void" was created in his mind. He claims that on March 21, 1953, he fell into a selfless, bottomless abyss of nothingness.

"I was becoming a nonbeing," he confessed. "I felt a great presence around me in the room . . . a great vibration . . . a great storm of light . . . I was drowning in it. . . . That night another Reality opened its door . . . the really Real. . . . It was nameless . . . but it was there."[2]

Something totally alien had overtaken Rajneesh at that point. He describes it himself: "That night I died and was reborn. But the one that was reborn has nothing to do with the one who died. . . . The one who died, died totally; nothing of him has remained. . . . After the explosion there is only void. Whatever was before is not me or mine."[3] Even his family members admit that he was not the same person as before.

By 1969, Rajneesh began initiating his first disciples, giving them a new name and a locket with his picture in it. In 1974, he moved to the wealthy Indian city of Poona. By the mid-seventies he was attracting visiting dignitaries, movie stars like Diana Ross, and even Ruth Carter Stapleton, Jimmy Carter's sister. He was also driving a Rolls Royce and a Mercedes-Benz, and living in opulent wealth. Devotees (*sannyasins*) in red-flamed robes crowded the streets of Poona to the delight of local storekeepers. Soon a rapidly expanding commune of 7,000 followers emerged, with thousands of others visiting regularly.

219 Bhagwan Shree Rajneesh 219

Gospel of Self-Indulgence

Unlike other gurus who preach self-denial, Rajneesh has become known as India's sex guru, preaching complete abandonment of the self by total indulgence. He openly preaches premarital sex, "open" marriages, and the abolition of the family. "Repression should not be a word in the vocabulary of the *sannyasin* [seeker]," his ads announced in *Time* magazine. He encourages tantric (sex) yoga, ecstatic dancing, disrobing, and even drug use as means of meditation. Sterilization of females to keep them from getting pregnant has also been a common practice. "The path to desirelessness is through desire," he admonishes his followers.[4]

Meditation at Rajneesh's *ashram* (village commune) includes Sufi dancing, where participants wear blindfolds, disrobe, and work themselves into an ecstatic trance. Claims of sexual abuse and physical violence eventually brought government action, and Rajneesh has continually moved from place to place in recent years to avoid legal confrontations.

At the height of his popularity, Rajneesh would sit dressed in a long purple robe on a raised platform in the Rajneesh Mundir temple in the city of Rajneeshpuram, Oregon. Fifteen thousand worshippers bowed before the smiling deity, chanting, "I go to the feet of the awakened one." Armed guards, machine guns, and helicopters protected the divine one on his 120-square-mile playground while the faithful worked 14 hours a day building the millennial city in America. But by 1985, he was deported from the United States after pleading guilty to two counts of federal indictments.

Tal Brooke believes that Rajneesh was possessed of the devil. He had that quality of perfect possession, a kind of antichrist who is "truly wired to the other side of the universe."[5] Brooke tells the story of Echart Flother, one of Rajneesh's key disciples, who tells of encounter-group rapes, enforced switching of sexual partners, forced homosexuality, crude abortions, and countless deaths and suicides at the Poona commune. Favorite women, like Laxmi, Rajneesh's

220 Angels of Deceit

number-one witch, were discarded penniless on the streets of India. Others told stories of a satanic covenant, spiritual vampirizations, robbing the soul of the desire for life, and leaving countless victims of mindless suicides.

"She was mad about him, crazy with Rajneesh," the old nun explained of Isabella, a Spanish girl of noble birth. "But Rajneesh used her and tossed her out. . . . She was a fragile bird and he crushed her. . . . But she kept believing in Rajneesh, saying that this was all a test of loyalty. . . . She ended up in the Poona asylum . . . babbling nonsense. . . . God! I tell you, he is the devil."[6]

The accounts of the Rajneesh cult indeed sound like the kingdom of darkness. They are not unlike the accounts of the ancient Druid orgies in England, where the great horned god sat enthroned as the evil one overseeing the whole filthy affair. These men are like little antichrists who exalt themselves as God, whose coming is "in accordance with the work of Satan displayed in all kinds of counterfeit miracles, signs and wonders, and in every sort of evil that deceives" (2 Thessalonians 2:9,10).

Jehovah's Witnesses

Charles T. Russell

Predicting dates for the second coming of Christ was a common practice in the nineteenth century. One of the most spectacular predictions was that of Charles Taze Russell (1852-1916). He believed Christ would return to the earth and usher in His kingdom by 1914. When questioned about the possibility of revising his date, Russell said, "We see no reason for changing the figures—nor could we change them if we would. They are, we believe, God's dates, not ours. But bear in mind that the end of 1914 is not the date for the *beginning*, but for the *end* of the time of trouble."[1]

Russell originally predicted that the Battle of Armageddon would occur in October 1914 and that the governments of the world would collapse and be replaced by the millennial kingdom of Christ on earth. But instead of Armageddon, World War I began in 1914, and Christ still has yet to appear!

Like all "biblical numerologists," Russell arrived at his date by a series of calculations. Believing that God worked in history in 115-year cycles, Russell said, "The time of the end, a period of 115 years, from A.D. 1799 to 1914 is particularly marked out in the Scriptures."[2] Seventh-day Adventists had earlier predicted 1844 as the date of Christ's return. When they missed their guess, some began to argue that the Greek word *parousia* (for "coming") could also be translated "presence." Thus, one could argue that Christ's presence was manifest even though He did not literally return.[3] This argument would later be seized by the Russellites to defend his false prediction.

Charles Russell was so sure he was right about 1914 that he wrote,

> The Kingdom of God has already begun, that it is pointed out in prophecy as due to begin the exercise of power in A.D. 1878, and that the battle of the great day of God Almighty of Rev. 16:14 which will end in A.D. 1914 with the complete overthrow of earth's present rulership is already commenced.[4]

Charles Russell was born in Allegheny, Pennsylvania, in 1852. His parents were Scotch-Irish Presbyterians, and Charles was a member of the Congregational church. But by the time he was 17, he had rebelled against the doctrines of election and eternal punishment and became an avowed skeptic. In 1870, however, he came under the teaching of Jonas Wendell, an Adventist who specialized in Bible prophecy.

Russell's interest in future events and the coming of Christ drove him to organize a Bible-study class of six members who met in Pittsburgh from 1870-1875. He was affectionately called Pastor Russell by the class, though he was never officially ordained. In 1876, Russell joined forces with N.H. Barbour of Rochester, New York, a disaffected Adventist who believed Christ would return in 1914. In 1877, Barbour and Russell jointly published a book entitled *Three Worlds,* in which they set forth 1914 as the "end of the times of the Gentiles."[5]

Russell later split from Barbour and began publishing a new periodical, *Zion's Watchtower and Herald of Christ's Presence*, on July 1, 1879. At that point Russell still believed Christ had already returned secretly and that His presence would continue until 1914, when He would win the Battle of Armageddon. In 1939, well after Russell's death, the Jehovah's Witnesses changed the periodical's name to *The Watchtower Announcing Jehovah's Kingdom.*

Zion's Watchtower

In 1881, Russell organized Zion's Watchtower Tract Society, which would become the forerunner of the Jehovah's Witnesses. In 1886, Russell published *The Divine Plan of the Ages*, the first of a seven-volume series entitled *Millennial Dawn* (later retitled *Studies in the Scriptures*). Millions of copies were printed and circulated by door-to-door distribution. Then in 1908, the society moved its headquarters to Brooklyn, New York.

As the twentieth century dawned, interest in Russell's 1914 prediction heightened. Several newspapers began carrying his articles and columns about Bible prophecies. He was a man of enormous energy. He traveled extensively, wrote voluminously, and promoted himself constantly. He said of his own writings that if one "merely read the 'Scripture Studies' with their references and had not read a page of the Bible as such, he would be in the light at the end of two years, because he would have the light of the scriptures."[6]

Russell's later years, however, were marked by several controversies. He had married Maria F. Ackley in 1879. She was an active Watchtower worker for several years, but in 1897 she left her husband. In 1903 she sued for legal separation. Then in 1913, Maria sued for a divorce on the grounds of "his conceit, egotism, domination, and improper conduct in relation to other women."[7]

About that time, perhaps to pay off the 6,000-dollar alimony settlement, Russell began selling miracle-wheat seeds in his magazine, claiming they would grow five times more than any other wheat seeds. His claim was later discredited in a sensational trial in which he attempted to sue the *Brooklyn Daily Eagle* for libel and lost. During the trial, his miracle wheat was proven to be inferior, not superior!

In June 1912, Reverend J.J. Ross, pastor of the James Street Baptist Church in Hamilton, Ontario, Canada, published a pamphlet against Russell and his views. Russell sued Ross for libel the following year. During the trial, Ross's lawyer asked Russell if he could read the Greek alphabet. Russell lied and said he could. When the lawyer handed him a Greek New Testament, Russell was forced to admit publicly that he was completely unfamiliar with the Greek language.

Charles Russell died aboard a train near Waco, Texas, while returning from a speaking trip to California on October 31 (Halloween), 1916. Russell was eventually replaced by "Judge" Joseph Rutherford, who had served as the Watchtower's legal counselor. He drastically reorganized the society and eventually led it to officially adopt the name *Jehovah's Witnesses* in 1931. Today the Jehovah's Witnesses claim over two million followers, despite Russell's original prediction that only 144,000 true witnesses would survive Armageddon and enter into the millennial kingdom.

Witness Theology

Jehovah's Witness theology may be summarized as follows:

1. *Denial of the Trinity.* They believe Jehovah God is the one true God, Jesus is not divine, and the Holy Spirit is not a separate person of the Godhead. Witness literature claims "such a doctrine (trinity) is not of God. . . . Satan is the originator of the trinity doctrine."[8]

2. *Jesus was a created being.* Witnesses believe, as did Russell, that Jesus never was and is not now equal to Jehovah. Prior to His incarnation, He was known in heaven as Michael the archangel. He was "a god," but not God, based upon their translation of John 1:1. They accept the idea of His virgin birth and sinless nature, but deny that His birth was an incarnation of God in human flesh. Only after His baptism was Jesus made Jehovah's High Priest, Messiah, and King by spiritual birth. Russell also denied the physical resurrection of Christ's body, teaching that He arose a spirit only.

3. *Penalty for sin is physical death.* Russell denied the doctrine of eternal punishment in hell. He believed hell (Hebrew, *sheol*) was the common grave or resting place of all mankind awaiting the resurrection. In place of eternal torment, he taught physical annihilation as the last judgment of the unrighteous who reject Jehovah and His kingdom.

4. *Salvation is limited to 144,000.* Jehovah's Witnesses divide the saved into two groups: 1) the "anointed" class, or 144,000 true Witnesses who reign with Christ in heaven, and 2) the "other sheep." These are the "Jonadabs," or friends of the Witnesses. They believe in Christ but are not born again, regenerated, sanctified, or anointed to be kings and priests. In other words, they are second-class believers who will live eternally on the earth.

The Jehovah's Witness statement of this view is found in *Let God Be True* (1946, revised 1952):

> All who by reason of faith in Jehovah God and in Christ Jesus dedicate themselves to do God's will and then faithfully carry out their dedication will be rewarded with everlasting life (Romans 6:23). The Bible plainly shows that

some of these, that is, 144,000 will share in heavenly glory with Christ Jesus, while the others will enjoy the blessings of life down here on earth.[9]

Russell originally taught that the end-time harvest would close by 1918 because every one of the 144,000 places in the Bride of Christ would be filled by true believers. But the enormous growth of the Jehovah's Witnesses and the great amount of time that has since lapsed forced Rutherford to make room for the "other sheep."

5. *The second coming began in 1914.* Charles Russell originally taught that the second coming of Christ began in 1878 and would culminate in 1914. When it did not, he shifted his view, claiming the second coming began on October 1, 1914, with the invisible "return" of Christ to earth to begin a time of waiting to establish the kingdom of God visibly. In the meantime, Jehovah's Witnesses believe that the church age ended in 1914, thus they meet in Kingdom Halls. They also believe that Christ's presence eliminates the validity of human governments; therefore, they salute no flag, hold no public offices, recognize no political or national authority, and refuse to do military service. In the meantime, today's "Russellites" go door to door warning of the coming Battle of Armageddon.

False Prophecies

Over the years the false prophecies of Russell, Rutherford, and Watchtower publications have been many:[10]

1877: "The end of this world ... is nearer than most men suppose."

1889: "The battle of the great day of God Almighty which will end in 1914 ... is already commenced."

1894: "1914 is not the date for the *beginning,* but for the *end* of the time of trouble."

1904: "The great time of trouble will be on us soon, somewhere between 1910 and 1912—culminating...October 1914."

1914: "Armageddon may begin next spring."

1915: "The present great war in Europe is the beginning of the Armageddon of the Scriptures."

1917: "We anticipate that the 'earthquake' will occur early in 1918 and that the 'fire' will come in the fall of 1920."

1920: "Deliverance is at the door...the old world order is ending."

1931: "Armageddon is at hand."

1939: "Armageddon is just ahead."

1940: "The Witness work for the theocracy appears to be about done."

1941: "Armageddon is surely near...within a few years."

1946: "Armageddon should come sometime before 1972."

1955: "The war of Armageddon is nearing its breaking out point."

1966: "A climax of man's history is at the door."

1969: "There is only a short time left."

1975: "Armageddon could come quickly, within a short time the terminal day of the lunar year 1975."

1980: "Do we have any way of knowing the time of Armageddon? Yes, we do."

Russell and his deceived followers would do well to heed Jesus' warning: "No one knows about that day or hour...but only the Father" (Matthew 24:36). Jehovah's Witnesses, Adventists, and a host of others have discredited themselves as false prophets by their constant date-setting. Then, to make things worse, they have developed elaborate systems of false doctrine to explain away their false prophecies. Jesus warned that one day false prophets would arise, claiming that He had come again in secret (Matthew 24:26). "Do not believe it," He said.

Mormons:
The Latter-day Saints

Joseph Smith

Joseph Smith (1805-1844) made some of the most preposterous claims any religious leader could ever make. Today, five million Mormons believe he was telling the truth. He claimed 135 revelations from God; said that angels appeared to him; proclaimed that he found and translated a sacred text on golden plates; taught that lost tribes of Jews came to prehistoric America; denounced all other churches as wrong; and declared that he was God's only true prophet.

Smith was born in 1805 in Sharon, Vermont. His family later moved to Palmyra, New York, in 1817. Confused over which church taught the truth, Smith read James 1:5: "If any of you lacks wisdom, he should ask God." Accordingly, in 1820, when he was 14 years old, he went into the woods, knelt in prayer, and asked God which was the true church. Then, said Smith, two "Personages" appeared and told him "they were all wrong" and that he should join none of them. Instead, he was to listen to Christ alone.[1]

On September 21, 1823, Smith claimed to have a second vision in which the angel Moroni appeared to him, telling him of a set of golden plates that contained the account of former inhabitants of the American continent and containing the "fullness of the everlasting gospel." The next day, Smith claimed to find the golden plates in the hill Cumorah outside of town.[2] They were deposited in a stone box with the Urim and Thummim and the breastplate of the high priest. He claimed he was not permitted to remove them for four years.

In the meantime, he married Emma Hale of Harmony, Pennsylvania. They eloped when Emma's father refused to consent to the marriage because Joseph wasted his time digging for money with the help of a "peepstone." Smith claimed on September 22, 1827, he was finally given permission to remove the golden plates which he was to "translate" from "Reformed Egyptian" with the aid of the Urim and Thummim, which served as a pair of "spectacles."

The Book of Mormon

Martin Harris, a farmer, agreed to finance the publication of Smith's translation. In 1829, Oliver Cowdery, a former schoolteacher, began to transcribe Smith's "translation." In time, Smith and Cowdery claimed that John the Baptist appeared to them and conferred upon them the priesthood of Aaron. Later, they claimed Peter, James, and John appeared on the banks of the Susquehanna River and conferred the (higher) priesthood of Melchizedek upon them. They now considered themselves true "prophets" of God.

Later, Cowdery, Harris, and David Witmer testified that an angel appeared to them holding the golden plates. This "Testimony of the Three Witnesses" appears in every copy of *The Book of Mormon*. Smith later called upon eight more men to testify of the validity of the golden plates (three of which later left the Mormon Church). When the "translation" was finished, Moroni took the plates back and they were never seen again—if indeed they had ever really been seen at all! In reality, no one but Smith ever "saw" the golden plates. A curtain separated him from Cowdery while he dictated the translation.

On March 26, 1830, *The Book of Mormon* was released for public sale in Palmyra, New York. On April 6, 1830, the Church of Jesus Christ of Latter-day Saints was officially organized at Fayette, New York, with six members. Smith and Cowdery ordained each other as elders and within a month they had 40 members, including Orson Pratt and Sidney Rigdon. In the meantime, Joseph Smith claimed to receive a revelation requiring a great move westward.

Westward Migration

Rigdon was instrumental in starting a church at Kirtland, Ohio. Soon 150 converts organized the United Order of Enoch as a spiritual commune. In January 1831, Joseph and Emma Smith traveled to Kirtland, and work on the first Mormon Temple was begun in 1833. However, financial problems soon plagued the work and Smith received a new revelation to move on to Missouri to build the temple. He purchased 63 acres at Independence for the sacred site to which he believed Christ would return to set up His kingdom.

Smith's bizarre doctrinal views and reports of polygamy at his communes soon brought mob violence against the Mormons. They were ordered out of Missouri in 1833. In February 1834, Smith had a revelation that "Zion" (Independence, Missouri) could be redeemed by force and gathered a 200-man militia called "Zion's Camp" and threatened to take back his property by force. This only increased the local hostility against the Mormons and set the stage for Smith's tragic assassination.

In the meantime, the church at Kirtland grew to over 1,600 members. Several "prophets" claimed divine revelations and Smith had to turn his attention to keeping order within his own ranks. In addition to *The Book of Mormon*, Smith claimed to receive other revelations of God: the *Doctrine and Covenants* and the *Book of Abraham*. Smith actually purchased four ancient mummies and some old papyri from a traveling lecturer, only to "discover" that two of the papyri were handwritten histories of Abraham and Joseph. Smith's "translation" of these documents revealed many "lost" truths, including the precedent for denying Negroes the Mormon priesthood—a position the Mormon Church only recently reversed.

In 1838, Smith and 600 followers returned to Missouri and laid out the town of Far West in Davies County. While he was there, Smith "identified" Adam-Ondi-Ahman, where Adam and his family supposedly lived after leaving the Garden of Eden! Soon Governor Boggs ordered the Mormons driven out of Missouri by force and they fled across the Mississippi River into Illinois.

In 1839, Smith established Nauvoo, Illinois ("beautiful plantation"), which prospered. Hundreds of converts were brought in to help build the city, a temple, a proposed university, and plans were even made for a 4,000-man militia to defend the "saints." It was in Nauvoo that Smith began to dream of a federal territory, a Mormon nation, separate from the legal intrusions of the United States government.

In 1843, Smith received his infamous "revelation" allowing for polygamy, based on the multiple wives of Old Testament kings, and threatened excommunication to all who would not adhere to it.[3] Many believe this "revelation" was intended to condone a practice that had already become widespread among the Mormons since female converts far outnumbered the males.

In 1844, Smith actually ran for president of the United States. His platform included freeing the slaves, annexing Texas, and replacing the two-party political system with a "theodemocracy." But later that year, Joseph Smith and his brother, Hyrum, were arrested for destroying the *Nauvoo Expositor,* an "apostate" (non-Mormon) paper that criticized the Mormons. Vowing to lose his life if necessary, the embattled prophet faced charges of insurrection against the state. Held in the city jail at Carthage, Illinois, Joseph and Hyrum were brutally murdered by an angry mob who broke into their cells and shot them.

In the confusion that followed, Smith's son, Joseph III, claimed rightful leadership of the Church—a fact which was historically confirmed by the recent discovery of a handwritten document dated January 17, 1844. In it, Joseph Smith said of his son, "He shall be my successor to the presidency of the high priesthood, a seer and revelator, and a prophet unto the church."[4] Eventually Joseph Smith III, his mother, and other members of Smith's family split from the main body of Mormons, who were now led by Brigham Young, president of the "Twelve Apostles." The Smith faction, emphasizing the lineal heritage of the prophet, formed the Reorganized Church of Jesus Christ of Latter-day Saints at Independence, Missouri, where they still hold title to the sacred temple site.

Brigham Young had first joined Smith in Ohio. He was now 43 years old and provided the mature leadership the Mormons needed. They were ordered out of Illinois, and began their famous trek west in February 1846, arriving in the Salt Lake Valley in Utah on July 24, 1847. There, isolated from the rest of America, the Mormon Church prospered for 30 years under Brigham Young's leadership. Between 1856 and 1860, some 3,000 converts pushed handcarts from Iowa City (then the end of the railroad line) a distance of 1,300 miles to Salt Lake City. When Young died in 1877, there were 140,000 Mormons. Members today include Senator Orrin Hatch, hotel magnate Willard Marriott, entertainers Donny and Marie Osmond, and the late Walt Disney.[5]

Prehistoric America

The theology of the Mormons is based upon their acceptance of Smith's *Book of Mormon* as a true revelation of God
and as an accurate history of prehistoric America. *The Book of
Mormon* makes fantastic claims about two ancient civilizations: 1) About 2250 B.C. a group of people (Jaredites) left the
Tower of Babel, crossed the Atlantic Ocean, and settled in
Central America; and 2) another group of righteous Jews (Nephites) left Jerusalem about 600 B.C. (before the Babylonian
captivity), crossed the Pacific Ocean, and settled in South
America. Some of the Nephites eventually migrated to North
America.

The Jaredites were totally destroyed because of spiritual
apostasy and internal strife. The Nephites met a similar fate
when they divided into two warring factions: Nephites and
Lamanites. The latter group wiped out the Nephites, but were
cursed by God with dark skin and became the American
Indians. Before the Nephites were destroyed in a great battle
near the hill Cumorah (Palmyra, New York) in A.D. 428, Christ
visited them on the North American continent, preached the
true gospel to them, and instituted baptism, communion, and
the prophetic priesthood. The abridgment of older Jaredite
records and the history of the Nephites was recorded by
Moroni, son of Mormon. They were buried in the hill
Cumorah for 1,400 years until the angelic Moroni revealed
them to Joseph Smith.

Mormon Theology

Mormons believe that the Bible is God's revelation to the
Jews and the East, while *The Book of Mormon* is His revelation
to the Americans and the West. Unfortunately, there is no
scientific, historical, or archaeological evidence to support the
claims of *The Book of Mormon.* Over 25,000 words and phrases
from the King James Bible appear verbatim in scattered sec-
tions of *The Book of Mormon,* including several from the New
Testament! References to advanced civilizations, two million

Jaredites, steel implements, and a compass all represent gross historical blunders made by the naive Smith as he "dictated" the book to Cowdery.[6]

Smith did predict that "at the rebellion of South Carolina . . . the Southern states would call on other nations, even the nation of Great Britain . . . and then war shall be poured out on all nations."[7] While there was indeed a Civil War some years later, Great Britain did not get involved, and "all nations" were not drawn into this conflict. Smith also prophesied that he would possess the house he built in Nauvoo "forever and ever" and that his seed would live there after him "from generation to generation."[8] But the house was destroyed after his death and his descendants moved to Independence, Missouri.

The "theology" taught in Smith's books and "revelations" include the following concepts:

1. *Plurality of gods.* Smith said, "The doctrine of the plurality of gods is as prominent in the Bible as any other doctrine. It is all over the face of the Bible."[9] Brigham Young remarked, "How many Gods there are I do not know. But there never was a time when there were not Gods and worlds."[10]

Mormons basically believe that God the Father had a father, and so on. They also believe that the gods were once men. In Smith's famous sermon at the funeral of Elder King Follett in1844, he said, "God himself was once as we are now, and is an exalted man, and sits enthroned in yonder heavens!"[11] Lorenzo Snow, fifth president of the Mormon Church, put it this way: "As man is, God once was; as God is, man may become."[12]

2. *Humanity of God.* Smith taught that God has a "body of flesh and bones" as tangible as a man's body. He also believed humans could become male and female gods. "Here, then, is eternal life," he said, "to know the only wise and true God; and you have got to learn how to be gods yourselves . . . from exaltation to exaltation, until you attain the resurrection of the dead . . . and sit in glory."[13] Brigham Young went so far as to

suggest that Adam was God. He said, "When our father Adam came into the garden of Eden, he came into it with a celestial body, and brought Eve, one of his wives, with him. . . . He is Michael the Archangel, the Ancient of Days. . . . He is our father and our God, and the only God with whom we have to do."[14]

3. *Sexuality of God.* Mormons identify Christ with *Jehovah,* the first born of *Elohim's* (God's) children. Thus, they distinguish two separate persons from the names of God. Jesus Christ, they believe, was the product of the physical union of God (*Elohim*) and the Virgin Mary. In turn, they believe Jesus was polygamously married to Mary, Martha, and the other Mary at the wedding at Cana! Since Mormons teach that only those whose marriages are sealed for eternity can ever become gods, it was virtually "necessary" for them to believe Jesus was married. Unmarried people can only hope to become angels.

4. *Salvation by works.* Mormons reject the doctrine of justification by faith. James Talmage, a leading Mormon theologian, calls it a "pernicious doctrine" which has exercised a great "influence for evil."[15] Mormons clearly teach that four elements are necessary for one's salvation: 1) faith, 2) repentance, 3) baptism, and 4) laying on of hands. Mormons believe that one must be baptized by immersion by the Mormon Church in order to be saved. All others will be lost.

5. *Celestial marriage.* Full exaltation (the highest degree of salvation) requires that a married couple be sealed to each other for both time and eternity in a temple ceremony. Those who have been so sealed will live together forever with their children and will continue to have sex and procreate more children for all eternity. In their original teachings, Mormons also believed men could be married to several wives for all eternity. Unfortunately, Jesus Himself said, "You are in error because you do not know the Scriptures or the power of God. At the resurrection people will neither marry nor be given in marriage; they will be like the angels in heaven" (Matthew 22:29,30).

6. *Exclusivity of salvation.* Joseph Smith believed that the "everlasting gospel" had been revealed to him alone in *The Book of Mormon.* He was convinced all who did not receive his message would be damned forever. Brigham Young said, "Every spirit that does not confess that God has sent Joseph Smith, and revealed the everlasting gospel to and through him, is of Antichrist."[16] Orson Pratt said of non-Mormon churches, "They have nothing to do with Christ, neither has Christ anything to do with them"[17]

7. *Return of Christ to America.* Mormons believe they are the tribe of Ephraim and are presently being gathered in the American West. They will eventually be taken to Zion (Independence, Missouri) by Christ at His return. The ten lost tribes of Nephites are hidden in the "land of the North" and they too will be brought to Zion when Christ returns. After a thousand-year millennium, everyone will go into eternity into one of three kingdoms:

  a. *Celestial*—Believing Mormons and their spouses, sealed for all eternity
  b. *Terrestrial*—Lukewarm Mormons and honorable people who repent of their rejection of the everlasting gospel
  c. *Telestial*—Unrepentant sinners who continue to refuse the everlasting gospel, but may yet repent and progress from one kingdom to another

Joseph Smith envisioned a very "earthly" kind of heaven: his God had a human body and several wives; Jesus was polygamously married to three women; believers could be married to several women; and everyone could keep having sex and producing more children for all eternity. The apostle Paul said of such false teachers that they were "lovers of pleasure rather than lovers of god" (2 Timothy 3:4). He added, "They are the kind who . . . gain control over weak-willed women, who are loaded down with sins and are swayed by all kinds of evil desires" (verse 6).

Transcendental Meditation

Maharishi Mahesh Yogi

Founded by Maharishi Mahesh Yogi, Transcendental Meditation (TM) is expressed as a nonreligious "path to God." A disciple of Guru Dev ("Divine Teacher"), Maharishi founded the Spiritual Regeneration Movement in 1968 in India and in 1959 in America. Targeting intellectuals, businessmen, and college students, TM promoters use Westernized terms, such as "Science of Creative Intelligence" to promote Hinduistic meditation. Today, TM is taught in over 100 countries, with 400 teaching centers in the United States alone. It has made incredible inroads into private schools, prisons, and businesses. Fortunately, a 1977 New Jersey Federal Court ruled that Transcendental Meditation is indeed a religion and cannot be taught in public schools.

Maharishi Mahesh Yogi was born Mahesh Brasad Warma in 1911 in Jabalpur, India. He graduated from Allahabad University with a degree in physics. Eventually he became a disciple of Guru Dev, who claimed to be a living avatar. It was Guru Dev who revived a technique of meditation which originated with the philosopher Shankara in the ninth century A.D. Maharishi ("Great Sage") spread this technique after his mentor's death in 1953. In 1967, he met George Harrison of the Beatles rock group in London. Harrison in turn persuaded the others, John Lennon, Paul McCartney, and Ringo Starr, as well as Mia Farrow, to join him on a pilgrimage to India to sit at Maharishi's feet. Soon the Rolling Stones and the Beach Boys became followers as well, and Transcendental Meditation became the fuel for the hippie movement. Maharishi, flowers in hand, appeared on magazine covers, did the talk show circuit, and went on a lecture tour funded by his newfound friends.

Promising peace and serenity, Maharishi made fantastic claims for the power of TM. But in time, the Beatles became disillusioned with what John Lennon called the "lecherous womanizer." His popularity faded and he retreated to Italy to repackage TM in nonreligious terms. Bob Larson observes, "Religious terminology was dropped in favor of psychological and scientific language. The Spiritual Regeneration movement became the Science of Creative Intelligence, and the Maharishi presented an image of a friendly psychotherapist rather than a Hindu monk."[1]

The new approach worked like a charm. Millions of Americans bought into the concepts of TM to reduce stress, expand their creativity, and open their minds. Maharishi's income jumped to $20 million a year. Introductory courses were offered to students for $85 and adults for $165. Inner peace and strength was guaranteed to everyone. Armed with a gospel of self-exploration, Maharishi appealed to the new generation of Americans. There was no message of repentance of sin or renunciation of life's pleasures. All one had to do to find salvation was meditate twenty minutes every morning and evening while repeating his own personally chosen *mantra.* During the TM initiation a devotional hymn, *puja* ("worship"), is sung by the instructor in Sanskrit before a flower-laden altar, which includes a picture of Guru Dev. Larson notes that among the lines recited are, "To lotus-born Brahma the Creator, to Shakti . . . I bow down . . . Vishnu . . . great Lord Shiva . . . I bow down . . . to Shri Guru Dev, I bow down."[2] After the prayer, the instructor whispers the secret Sanskrit word that is to become the devotee's personal *mantra.* This word may never be divulged—even to one's spouse—or it will lose its magical powers.

In 1975, Maharishi announced the dawn of the Age of Enlightenment and promised a new era of peace and prosperity as TM spread into wider usage. Later he launched the *Sidhi* program, where one could obtain supernatural powers for $3,000 to $5,000. Advanced meditators claim to have mastered dematerialization and the ability to fly—though none have ever been seen to do so by outsiders or on video. In the meantime, the Maharishi continues to travel in a Rolls Royce and a private helicopter from his international headquarters in Seelisberg, Switzerland.

26

A Light in the Darkness

*Helping Family, Friends,
and Kids Escape*

"Satan just walked through the front door!"
The words greeted Elder Terry and me as we entered a small Baptist church. I thought it was a strong indictment to lay on two clean-cut boys. Before we could recover and escape, the pastor had condemned us to hell in front of the entire congregation.[1]

Charles Rushing says that his first encounter with the gospel in no way endeared him to the Christian church. "In fact, it hardened my mind and heart against organized Christianity for many years," he explains.

Rushing was a Mormon missionary who was attempting to fulfill his obligation to serve the Church of Jesus Christ of Latter-day Saints when he first encountered born-again Christians. But their abusive treatment of him was so severe that nearly ten years went by before he was willing to listen to their message.

Bob and Gretchen Passantino have spent the past 20 years witnessing to cultists. They share the following advice: "At the core of successful witnessing to cult members is a commitment

243

to God's pattern of evangelism: 'The Lord's servant must not quarrel; instead, he must be kind to everyone, able to teach, not resentful. Those who oppose him he must gently instruct, in the hope that God will grant them repentance leading them to a knowledge of the truth, and that they will come to their senses and escape from the trap of the devil, who has taken them captive to do his will' (2 Timothy 2:24-26)."[2]

Bob and Gretchen explain that many cultists are sincere people who believe that they are worshiping and serving God. In most cases they are convinced that they have discovered truths about God which others desperately need to know. Bob and Gretchen observe that unless we can have empathy and identify with them, we will not reach them for Christ.

"If I've been deceived for 30 years," a Jehovah's Witness told them tearfully, "how can I know for sure that this is right? What if this is wrong and Jehovah rejects me for all eternity?"[3]

All of us who want to help those caught in a cult should have a desire to shine the light of the truth into the darkness of the spiritual deception into which the cultist has fallen. But shining the light down into the tunnel of spiritual darkness merely exposes the error into which the individual has fallen. We must also be prepared to lower the rope of hope in order to pull them out of the dilemma in which they find themselves so hopelessly caught.

Witnessing to the Cults

The Passantinos recommend using the golden rule of apologetics: Treat the cultist as you would want to be treated yourself. They go on to explain that even when we don't have all the answers, our compassion and sincere interest to search for the truth will encourage the cultist to take us seriously. But in order to be effective, we must learn to separate the deception of the cult from the sincerity of the cultist. Very few people ever get caught up in a cult because they want to be deceived. It is their search for the truth and for personal acceptance that often leads them into the cultic trap.

Balancing information with compassion is essential if we are going to be effective in helping family and friends to see the light of the truth. Some Christians have memorized lots of facts to quote to the cultist, but they end up sounding like a verbal machine gun in their attempt to obliterate the lies of the cult. In the process they often offend the individual to the point that he or she retreats even further into the cult for safety and security. On the other hand, there are Christians who have loads of compassion but very little information to help the cultist. They are genuinely concerned about the cultist's plight, but are not equipped to answer his or her questions.

If you and I are going to be truly effective in helping cult members face the truth about themselves and their leaders, we must be prepared to follow these basic steps:

1. *Know what you believe.* In order to present the gospel message in a plain but powerful manner, we must know the biblical basis for our own beliefs. There is no substitute for the truth. The best way to recognize the counterfeit is to become familiar with the genuine article. Just as bank tellers are taught to recognize counterfeit money by concentrating on the qualities and characteristics of the real thing, so you and I must know what we believe and why we believe it.

If you find yourself getting in over your head, admit it. Don't try to fake your way through the maze of Bible doctrine. If you don't know what you're talking about, the cultist will pick up on that immediately. Remember, honesty is the best policy! No one ever got deceived into believing the truth. You don't fight deception with deception. Jesus said, "Then you will know the truth, and the truth will set you free" (John 8:32).

2. *Expect your witness to make a difference.* Whenever you and I witness to a cultist or any other unbeliever, we are sharing the truth of God in the power of the Holy Spirit. The gospel that we present is the only true and living gospel. The doctrines of the cults are dry bones compared with the glorious gospel of Jesus Christ.

Because of this, we need to have the confidence that our witness can make a difference in the life of the cultist. It is not our ability to outthink, scheme, or maneuver the cultist that will bring him to genuine faith in Christ. Only the Holy Spirit has the power to do that. Only He can convict the mind and heart of the cultist to believe the truth of God's Word in a way that produces genuine, saving faith. Again, it is not our skill or ability to witness that wins the individual to faith in Christ. It is the power of the witness of the Holy Spirit who convinces men of their sin and their need of a Savior that draws them to a personal faith in Jesus Christ, the Son of God.

We have the same Great Commission that was given to the original disciples, to whom Jesus said, "All authority in heaven and on earth has been given to me. Therefore go and make disciples of all nations, baptizing them in the name of the Father and of the Son and of the Holy Spirit, and teaching them to obey everything I have commanded you. And surely I am with you always, to the very end of the age" (Matthew 28:18-20).

Think of the obstacles faced by the early disciples as they carried out those instructions. Judaism had lapsed into legalism, and the Roman Empire was overrun with paganism. Our Lord was asking these 11 men to take on the spiritual deception of the entire world! What is more, He gave them the assurance that they could succeed!

You and I cannot expect to win every cultist to Christ. But that doesn't mean we shouldn't try, for if we don't, then we will not win any of them. Our Lord's assurance is that if we share His truth with others, they will come to know the truth and trust the Savior.

3. *Ask the Holy Spirit to convict them.* You and I cannot win anyone to Christ by ourselves. Our reasoning will fall on deaf ears unless the Holy Spirit uses the Word of God to open the hearts and minds of those to whom we witness. Jesus promised that He would send the Holy Spirit upon the church after His ascension into heaven. "When he comes," Jesus said, "he will

convict the world of guilt in regard to sin and righteousness and judgment" (John 16:8).

Our Lord pictures the Holy Spirit as the One who will guide us into all truth. It is the ministry of the Spirit to point men toward the Savior by convincing them of their sin and their need of salvation. Our witness is like a finger pointing men to God. And the work of the Holy Spirit is an irresistible force, drawing them to Himself. Therefore, our witness must be coupled with the fervent prayer that the Holy Spirit touch the heart of the unbeliever with the conviction of his sin, the love and compassion of the Savior, and the reality of personal salvation.

4. *Understand what the cult believes and teaches.* The more one knows about the beliefs and practices of the cult whose member he is trying to win to Christ, the more effective his witness is likely to be. You don't have to become an expert in the theology of a particular cult in order to reach someone caught up in that group. But if you don't understand what the cult believes, it may be difficult for you to present an effective witness.

Each cult has its own particular belief system and vocabulary. For example, Mormons make a distinction between the Holy Spirit and the Holy Ghost. They believe that anyone who professes Christ could possess the Holy Spirit, but only highly committed Mormons can receive the Holy Ghost. Jehovah's Witnesses believe that Jesus is *a* Son of God, but not *the* Son of God. Adventists believe that Jesus will still return to the earth in the future, but they believe He already began that process in 1844.

Be prepared for the cultist to argue his strongest points with you. Most Adventists, for example, want to talk about Sabbath worship, not the prophetic date 1844. Mormons will try to emphasize the legitimacy of Joseph Smith's angelic revelation. They will not want to defend the actions of early Mormons and their polygamist pronouncements or conflicts with the law.

Remember that cultists are not that much different from evangelical Christians. Many of them do not even know the history of their particular movement. Badgering a Jehovah's Witness about Charles Russell's divorce or a Christian Scientist about Mary Baker Eddy's husbands will be no more effective than the cult member reminding you of the spiritual failures of professing believers within your denomination.

Cult experts consistently emphasize that it is more important to present the truth of the gospel of salvation by grace than to point out the personal failures of the cult's leaders.

5. *Know the facts and stick to them.* Don't allow yourself to be sidetracked from the facts. Always include a clear presentation of the gospel. It is the message of the death, burial, and resurrection of Christ on our behalf that is the power of God unto salvation (1 Corinthians 15:1-4). The early Christians in the book of Acts spent more time presenting the truth than they did attacking error. Their witness was centered on the truth that they believed and the experience they had had with the risen Christ. While they addressed the concerns and questions of a pagan society, their tactic was essentially to show a better way.

Most cults emphasize the distinctions of their belief system. As a result, their followers are usually well versed in a limited area of teaching. Adventists will quote dozens of verses about the Sabbath. Jehovah's Witnesses will focus on the coming of Armegeddon and how to avoid it. Mormons will talk about the importance of the family and the eternality of marriage. Scientologists will emphasize the importance of finding better ways to deal with your personal problems.

Remember, cultists are not mindless idiots. In most cases, they are convinced there is a rationale for their beliefs. In fact, they are often so convinced they are right that it is almost impossible for them to break out of their cultic mind-set to even begin to consider other viewpoints about their teaching. That is why it is important to concentrate on the core biblical doctrines concerning the person and nature of God the Father, Jesus Christ the Son, the nature of man's sinfulness, and the plan of salvation. Peripheral issues such as the nature of the priesthood, the mode of church government, or the timing of the second coming are not crucial to the issue of one's personal salvation. Stick to the major truths of biblical doctrine. Don't allow yourself to be pulled off the track into the quagmire of secondary side issues.

6. *Don't assume you know what the cultist believes.* Show your personal interest by asking him or her to tell you what they believe about various issues. This is important for at least two reasons. First, unless you are an expert or an ex-cult member, it is highly unlikely that you fully understand the entire belief system of a particular cult. Second, many cult members do not believe everything their religious group teaches. Many cult members, like many church members, are not well versed in what they believe. Others may know what they believe personally, but their personal beliefs may not be consistent with what the cult officially teaches. For example, not all Mormons reject other Christian believers as heretical. While this is the official position of the Mormon Church, it is not necessarily the personal position of every individual Mormon.

Arrogance and ignorance about the cult's beliefs will automatically turn off the cultist to whom you are trying to witness. It may be necessary to say something like, "I had always thought that your group believed thus and so. Could you explain to me your beliefs in light of the group's teaching on this matter?" This will give the cultist an opportunity to explain his or her own position. It will also enable you to evaluate whether his or her personal position is consistent with the group's public belief system.

7. *Guard your motivation for witnessing.* Watch your attitude. Don't get involved in a lengthy, heated argument with the cultist. Present the truth in such a way that it becomes evident that your witness is coming from the sincerity of your heart. Be sure to guard against a self-righteous I'll-show-them attitude. That will only turn people off to the truth you are attempting to show them.

When the heat of your argument becomes greater than the light of the gospel, you will lose the convert! Ex-cult members who become born-again converts almost universally testify that it was the spirit of love and kindness that eventually attracted them to the truth. Sincerity will go a lot further than hostility when it comes to shining the light into the darkness. The sincerity of your motives is just as important as the clarity of your message. Combining content with compassion is a vital ingredient to winning converts from the cults.

8. *Share your personal testimony.* Cultists can argue doctrine all day long. But they can't deny the reality of your personal testimony. The apostle Paul faced constant rejection from his fellow Jewish countrymen. But they could not deny the dramatic nature of his personal conversion. He had gone from being a Christ-hater to a Christian leader who spread the gospel everywhere he went. In sharing his testimony with King Agrippa, who was a Gentile, Paul explained that his conversion had opened his eyes to the truth of Jesus Christ. When Agrippa questioned whether Paul was attempting to persuade him to become a Christian, the apostle answered that he wished all who were listening to him would come to experience what he had.

While each believer's personal conversion is unique to himself, it is difficult to refute. Even the most staunch cultist cannot help but be impressed by the reality of one's personal testimony. It is not easy for the cultist to dismiss such a testimony as being irrelevant. Whether he or she responds visibly at that moment may not be clear, but the seed of truth has been sown in his or her heart. In many cases this is the beginning of the cultist's willingness to listen to the genuine gospel message.

9. *Be patient in your witnessing.* Remember that cult members are at various stages of belief within their own system. Some are new converts themselves. They may not be all that sure what they believe or how to articulate it. This is why the Mormons and Jehovah's Witnesses usually send people out in pairs. One is usually a trainer and the other a trainee. The

trainee is more likely to become confused when asked to defend his or her position. The trainer is more likely to become argumentative in the same situation. You and I must bear in mind that every cult member is at a different stage of deception in regard to his or her beliefs.

Newer cult members can be reached by being challenged to defend the cult's beliefs. Try to get them away from their literature and focus their attention on the Bible itself. "Can you show me that in the Bible?" is a question they need to be asked again and again. Most advanced cult members may need to be challenged to defend the more heretical elements of their doctrine. Ask them, "How could you possibly believe that in light of these passages of Scripture?"

It is also possible you may find yourself witnessing to someone who has already become disillusioned with what the cult teaches and believes. In such a situation, it is important to be fair and avoid cynicism. Once a person begins to admit to himself that he may have been deceived into believing error, it is natural for him to question the sincerity of other religious beliefs. The cult member may begin to wonder if maybe what you believe is not just another cult as well!

We need to be patient, therefore, with every cult member. You and I may not readily discern where that person is in his own pilgrimage of spiritual deception. Hostility, criticism, and sarcasm will only drive him further into confusion and distrust. No one wants to believe he has been foolish enough to be deceived. Such admissions usually come only after deep and serious soul-searching. It takes a great deal of sincerity to admit you have been deceived. At first, some may express anger and resentment for this deception. Others may appear confused and spiritually numb. Still others will want to go back and evangelize to the entire cult, only to have the door slammed in his or her face. We must be patient in dealing with each person in light of his or her own needs, struggles, and potential.

10. *Leave something for the cultist to read.* Many of the cults have succeeded because of their printed materials. Even if they

face initial rejection, they will leave literature at your door which can be read later. We need to do the same thing! The power of the printed word is unsurpassed. Spoken words can be forgotten, but printed material can be read over and over again. If possible, leave some literature that will help a person further understand your witness to him. This can include gospel tracts, booklets, and books that clearly explain the plan of salvation. You may want to include literature that will help someone to better evaluate the cult in which he is a member. Information on the various cults are available at your local Christian bookstore. You can also consult organizations that specialize in reaching and ministering to those who are caught in a particular cult. The list at the end of this chapter will help you to become familiar with those resources.

You don't have to have been in a cult to win a cult member. But you will need to understand some of their beliefs in order to present the gospel in a manner that effectively counters those beliefs. A Jehovah's Witness will insist that he believes in Jesus, but he believes in the Jesus of the Watchtower, who is less than a divine Savior. He does not believe in the Jesus of the New Testament.

Mormons claim to believe in God, but they actually believe in many gods. In fact, they believe that men themselves can become gods. New Agers talk about Jesus, but they are referring to the cosmic Christ, not Jesus of Nazareth, the Savior who shed His blood for our sins. Christian Scientists talk about salvation from our sins, but they do not mean the reality of sin—rather, they are talking about the illusion of sin. To them, salvation takes place in the mind when one refuses to believe that sin, sickness, and death exist. Dismissing the painful realities of life is viewed as finding salvation. It has nothing to do with the blood of Christ that was shed on the cross as an atonement for our sins.

Making the Break

Remember, cult members are not the devil. They are simply deceived. In *Moody Monthly* magazine, Jim Morud tells the story of Ashley and her break from Mormonism. She said, "I had been a Mormon for 21 years, and I knew *The Book of Mormon* backward and forward, but I knew little about the Bible. I was shocked to see there was such a difference between the Mormon concept of God, and that of the Bible."[4]

Faced with the deception in which she had been trapped for so long, Ashley eventually prayed to receive Christ as her personal Savior. Even then, she struggled at times with her newfound faith, feeling that she had disappointed her family and betrayed her heritage. Her relationship with her mother was particularly strained. In time she realized she was going through a normal grieving process. Eventually she went to her mother and reached out to her to express God's unconditional love. Even though her mother did not respond at first, Ashley continued to show loving acceptance until her mother finally acknowledged she had been wrong in the way she reacted to her. In time, Ashley was able to share her beliefs about her faith in Christ with her mother. She was also able to point out some of the flaws in Mormon theology.

Interestingly, Ashley's mother sees the flaws in her belief, but they don't seem to bother her. She is still emotionally bound to the church and cannot let go of the concept of temple marriage: being married for all time and eternity, and having her children sealed to her forever. It is this concept, more than Mormon theology itself, that holds Ashley's mother to the cult.

Each one of us wants to be used of God to help our family and friends see the truth. But we must realize that each cult member is hooked by a different lure.

Some are attracted to a cult intellectually. They have become convinced that what the cult believes is actually true. This is often the case with the followers of Herbert and Garner Ted Armstrong. They are convinced that evangelical Christians are deceived about some of the things they believe (such as the date of Christmas or Easter), and that they have discovered the real truth of the Bible. Intellectual converts can only be reached by intellectual arguments that force them to reevaluate their own beliefs.

Some cult members are emotional converts. They become hooked on the cult because it appeals to their emotional needs for security, love, and acceptance. Ex-moonies emphasize that it was the warmth and love of the group that attracted them to the cult. The Unification Church does not generally sponsor public intellectual debate on its beliefs. Rather, it has used the approach of appealing to lonely and idealistic students who are looking for acceptance and ideal causes rather than specific truths. The Children of God cult has taken this concept to the extreme of "flirty fishing," which uses the opposite sex to attract converts. In order to win back emotional converts, we must show them the genuine love of Christ and the acceptance of a group of supportive Christians who will minister to them.

The third category is *brainwashed converts.* These are tragic individuals who have become so totally brainwashed by the constant indoctrination, rigid routines, and constant activities of the cult that they do not have time to consider what it is they actually believe. Intellectual arguments and emotional acceptance will be of no avail. Unfortunately, these kinds of converts must often be deprogrammed in order to bring them to a point where they can honestly sit back and evaluate the cult for what it really is.

Hank Hanegraaff concludes his powerful book *Christianity in Crisis*[5] with the observation that the real tragedy of spiritual deception is not that it always leads to destruction. Certainly our hearts go out to cult members like those of the People's Temple, or the Branch Davidians, who gave their lives for a lie. But the real tragedy, Hanegraaff notes, is to live a long and prosperous life "without ever using it to serve the Master." While a few lives are lost in extremist cults, there are many millions of lives being lost for eternity in the dozens of cults that have gained popular acceptance with their messages of spiritual deception.

Notes

Chapter 1—Falling into the Darkness

1. A.T. Pierson, *The Bible and Spiritual Life* (Fincastle, VA: Scripture Truth, n.d., reprint of 1887 Exeter Hall Lectures), p. 169 emphasis added.
2. C.S. Lewis, *Mere Christianity* (New York: Macmillan, 1960), pp. 53-54.
3. Mary Baker Eddy, *Science and Health with Key to the Scriptures* (Boston: Trustees, 1925), p. 150.
4. Ibid., pp. vii-viii.
5. Hank Hanegraaff, *Christianity in Crisis* (Eugene, OR: Harvest House, 1993).
6. "Children of the Apocalypse," *Newsweek* (May 3, 1993), p. 30.
7. "Sect Leader Charismatic, Dangerous," *USA Today* (March 2, 1993), A1.
8. "Zealot of God," *People* (March 15, 1993), p. 43.
9. *Atlanta Journal* (March 1, 1993), A6.
10. **"Cult of Death,"** *Time* (March 15, 1993), p. 38.
11. "Thy Kingdom Come," *Newsweek* (March 15, 1993), p. 54.
12. Ibid., p. 55.
13. 2 "Mass Suicide Ends Waco Standoff," *USA Today* (April 20, 1993), p. A1.

Chapter 2—The Cultic Mentality

1. Paul Martin, *Cult-Proofing Your Kids* (Grand Rapids, MI: Zondervan, 1993); excerpts in *Christian Counseling Today* (January 1993), pp. 40-41.
2. Described in detail by Carroll Stoner and JoAnne Parke, *All God's Children* (Radnor, PA: Chilton Books, 1977), p. 233.
3. Dave Breese, *Know the Marks of the Cults* (Wheaton, IL: Victor Books, 1984), p. 42.
4. Christopher Edwards, *Crazy for God* (Englewood Cliffs, NY: Prentice-Hall, 1979), pp. 160-176.
5. Martin, *Cult-Proofing Your Kids.*
6. Ibid.
7. Alan Bloom, *The Closing of the American Mind* (New York: Simon & Schuster, 1986), pp. 25-85.
8. Ibid., p. 34.
9. Ibid., p. pp. 82-85.
10. Harold Bussell, *Unholy Devotion: Why Cults Lure Christians* (Grand Rapids, MI: Zondervan, 1983), pp. 61-72.
11. Breese, *Know the Marks of the Cults.*
12. Ibid., p. 42.
13. Jim Morud, "Making the Break," *Moody Monthly* (November 1992), p. 19.
14. Anthony Hoekema, *The Four Major Cults* (Grand Rapids, MI: Eerdmans, 1984), pp. 127-128.
15. Latayne C. Scott, *The Mormon Mirage* (Grand Rapids, MI: Zondervan, 1979), pp. 233-237.
16. Hoekema, pp. 196-200.
17. Ibid., pp. 297-312.
18. Irvine Robertson, *What the Cults Believe* (Chicago: Moody Press, 1983), pp. 74-86. Cf. also Moon, *Divine Principle* (Washington, D.C.: Holy Spirit Association for Unification of World Christianity, 1973), p. 511ff.
19. Quoted by Ronald Enroth, *A Guide to Cults & New Religions* (Downers Grove, IL: InterVarsity Press, 1983) p. 19.
20. Quoted by Jim Morud, "Making the Break," p. 18.
21. See Edwards, *Crazy for God,* p. 200.
22. See Elliot Miller, *A Crash Course on the New Age Movement* (Grand Rapids, MI: Baker Book House, 1989), pp. 17-18.

Chapter 3—A Crash Course in Spiritual Deception

1. Christopher Edwards, *Crazy for God* (Englewood Cliffs, NY: Prentice Hall, 1979), pp. 171-173.
2. Irving Hexham and Karla Poewe, *Understanding Cults and New Religions* (Grand Rapids, MI: Eerdmans, 1986), pp. 106-109.
3. Walter R. Martin, *The Kingdom of the Cults* (Minneapolis: Bethany Fellowship, 1968), pp. 63-65; 113-115; 156-175; 223-224.
4. Elena S. Whiteside, *The Way: Living in Love* (New Knoxville, OH: American Christian Press, 1972), p. 178.
5. *The Way* (September-October 1974), p. 7.
6. Josh McDowell and Don Stewart, *Understanding the Cults* (San Bernardino, CA: Here's Life Publishers, 1986), p. 142.
7. Moses David, *Reorganization, Nationalization, Revolution!* (Rome: Children of God, 1978), DO# 650.
8. Cf. Carroll Stoner and JoAnne Parke, *All God's Children* (Radnor, PA: Chilton Book Co., 1977), p. 65ff. and the compelling inside story by Berg's daughter, Deborah Davis (Linda Berg), *The Children of God* (Grand Rapids, MI: Zondervan, 1984).

9. Una McManus and John Cooper, *Dealing with Destructive Cults* (Grand Rapids, MI: Zondervan, 1984), pp. 119-120.
10. Ibid., p. 118.
11. See examples cited by John Ankerberg and John Weldon, *Cult Watch* (Eugene, OR: Harvest House, 1991), pp. 297-329.
12. Adapted from the eyewitness account by *San Francisco Chronicle* staff correspondents in *The Suicide Cult* (New York: Bantam Books, 1978), pp. 168-170.
13. Ibid., see also Phil Kerns, *People's Temple—People's Tomb* (Plainfield, NJ: Logos International, 1979).
14. Ibid., p. 178.
15. Quoted in *Larson's Book of Cults* (Wheaton, IL: Tyndale House, 1984), p. 367.
16. *You May Survive Armageddon into God's New World* (Brooklyn, NY: Watchtower Bible and Tract Society, 1955), p. 342. Cf. Anthony Hockema, *The Four Major Cults* (Grand Rapids, MI: Eerdmans, 1984), pp. 307-312.
17. *Discourses of Brigham Young* (Salt Lake City: Deseret Book Co., 1954), p. 435.
18. Series of Pamphlets, No. III., p. 8. Quoted by Hoekema, *The Four Major Cults* (Grand Rapids, MI: Eerdmans, 1984), p. 63.
19. Hoekema, pp. 139-140.
20. Mary Baker Eddy, *Science and Health with Key to the Scriptures* (Boston: Trustees, 1934, first published 1875), pp. 456-457.
21. Ibid, p. 583.
22. *What Is Spiritualism?* Spiritualist Manual Revision of 1940. Quoted by Walter R. Martin, *Kingdom of the Cults* (Minneapolis: Bethany Fellowship, 1965), p. 209.
23. Ibid, p. 210.
24. *Many Mansions*, p. 107. Quoted by Martin, *The Kingdom of the Cults*, p. 210.
25. Ibid., p. 250.
26. Ibid., p. 246.
27. Ibid., p. 312.
28. Sun Myung Moon, "Our Shame," *Master Speaks* (March 11, 1973), p. 3.
29. Moon, *The Way of the World*, p. 20. Quoted by Josh McDowell and Don Stewart, *Understanding the Cults* (San Bernardino, CA: Here's Life Publishers, 1982), p. 134.
30. L.E. Froom, *The Prophetic Faith of our Fathers* (Washington, D.C.: Review & Herald, 1954), IV, p. 463.
31. Quoted by Adventist author F.D. Nicholl, *The Midnight Cry* (Washington, D.C.: Review & Herald, 1945), p. 458.
32. Hoekema, *The Four Major Cults*, p. 94.
33. Ibid., pp. 137-143.
34. Cf. Ronald Enroth, et. al., *A Guide to Cults & New Religions* (Downers Grove, IL: InterVarsity Press, 1983), pp. 104-105; Walter Martin, *Kingdom of the Cults*, pp. 87-101.
35. See Jehovah's Witness publications *Qualified to Be Ministers*, pp. 283-297 and *You May Survive Armageddon*, p. 252ff. See also Hoekema, *The Four Major Cults*, pp. 287-297.
36. Jack Sparks, *The Mind Benders* (Nashville, TN: Thomas Nelson, 1977), p. 135.
37. "Zealot of God," *People* (March 15, 1993), pp. 38-43.
38. "Radical Sheik,"*Newsweek* (March 15, 1993), p. 32.
39. Una McManus and John Cooper, *Dealing with Destructive Cults* (Grand Rapids, MI: Zondervan, 1984), p. 117.
40. Christopher Edwards, *Crazy for God*, p. 145.

Chapter 4—Apostles of Error

1. Allan Streett, *The Cult Invasion* (Dallas: Lighthouse Books, 1980).
2. "The Messiah of Waco," *Newsweek* (March 15, 1993), pp. 56-58.
3. Quoted by Jim Morud, "Making the Break," *Moody Monthly* (November 1992), pp. 18-20.
4. Herbert W. Armstrong, *Autobiography* (Pasadena: Ambassador College Press, 1967), pp. 294-298.
5. R.B. Thieme, *Living Grace* (Houston: Berachah Church, 1968) pp. 10-11. See also *The Blood of Christ* (1972) and *Super Grace Life* (1973).
6. R.B. Thieme, *Super Grace Life*, p. 45.
7. See Stewart Custer, *What's Wrong with the Teaching of R.B. Thieme, Jr.?* (Greenville, SC: Bob Jones University Press, 1972).
8. Ronald Enroth, et. al. *A Guide to Cults & New Religions* (Downers Grove, IL: InterVarsity Press, 1983), pp. 17-19.
9. Ibid. pp. 19-21.
10. R.B. Thieme, *The Blood of Christ* (Houston: Berachah Church, 1973), p. 1.
11. *The Watchtower* (September 1, 1979), p. 8; J.F. Rutherford, *Religion* (Brooklyn: Watchtower Bible and Tract Society, 1940), p. 104. Cited by John Ankerberg and John Weldon, *Cult Watch* (Eugene, OR: Harvest House, 1991), pp. 63-64.
12. *Doctrine and Covenants* (Salt Lake City: Church of Jesus Christ of Latter-day Saints, 1968 edition), 1:30.
13. Orson Pratt, *The Seer* (April 1854), p. 255.
14. Bruce McConkie, *Mormon Doctrine*, 2d edition (Salt Lake City: Bookcraft, 1977), p. 626; and *Doctrinal New Testament Commentary* (Salt Lake City: Bookcraft, 1976), Vol. 2, pp. 113, 366, 458-459, 506-507.
15. Quoted by W.J. Peterson, *Those Curious New Cults* (New Canaan, CT: Keats Publishers, 1973), p. 95.
16. Sun Myung Moon, "Holy Wine Ceremony," *The Blessing Quarterly* (Spring 1977), p. 5.
17. Brooks Alexander, "The Rise of Cosmic Humanism," *SCP Journal* (Winter 1981-82), pp. 3-4.

18. Ronald Enroth, *Youth Brainwashing and the Extremist Cults* (Grand Rapids, MI: Zondervan, 1977), pp. 133-146.
19. *Let God Be True* (Brooklyn, NY: Watchtower Bible and Tract Society, 1952), pp. 100-102.
20. *Times and Seasons* (August 1, 1844). Quoted by Walter R. Martin, *The Kingdom of the Cults* (Minneapolis: Bethany Fellowship, 1968), p. 179.
21. Brigham Young, *Journal of Discourses*, Vol. I, p. 50. Cf. Martin, p. 178.
22. Lorenzo Snow, *Millennial Star*, Vol. 54. Cf. Martin, p. 178.
23. Mary Baker Eddy, *Science and Health with Key to the Scriptures* (Boston: Trustees, 1934), pp. 152, 302, 517.
24. Ibid.
25. *The Plain Truth* (November 1963), pp. 11-12.
26. *Why Were You Born?*, pp. 21-22. Quoted by Martin, p. 307.
27. H.P. Blavatsky, *Key to Theosophy* (Point Loma, CA: Aryan Theosophical Press, 1913); *Studies in Occultism* (Point Loma, CA: Theosophical University Press, n.d.), p. 134.
28. Martin, pp. 246-247.
29. Garner Ted Armstrong, *The Real Jesus* (New York: Avon Books, 1977), p. 2.
30. Eddy, p. 330.
31. *The Truth Shall Make You Free*, pp. 47-49. Quoted by Martin, *The Kingdom of the Cults*, p. 51.
32. Brigham Young, *Journal of Discourses*, pp. 50-51.
33. J. Fielding Smith, ed., *Teachings of the Prophet Joseph Smith* (Salt Lake City: Deseret Press, 1958), pp. 370-372.
34. *New York Times Magazine* (May 30, 1976), p. 19.
35. Eddy, p. 327, emphasis added.
36. James Talmage, *Articles of Faith* (Salt Lake City: Church of Jesus Christ of Latter-day Saints, 1957), p. 479.
37. Anthony Hoekema, *The Four Major Cults* (Grand Rapids, MI: Eerdmans, 1963), p. 126.
38. Paul V. Wierwille, *Receiving the Holy Spirit Today* (New Knoxville, OH: The Way International, 1972), p. 148, emphasis added.
39. Martin, *The New Cults*, pp. 290-292.
40. Enroth, *A Guide to Cults & New Religions*, p. 21.
41. Harold Bussell, *Unholy Devotion: Why Cults Lure Christians* (Grand Rapids, MI: Zondervan, 1983), p. 77, emphasis in original.

Chapter 5—Riders of the Cosmic Cicuit
1. Tal Brooke, *Riders of the Cosmic Circuit* (London: Lion Publishing, 1986), p. 11.
2. Ibid., pp. 12-14.
3. Ibid., p. 37.
4. Ibid., p. 28.
5. Bob Larson, *Larson's Book of Cults* (Wheaton, IL: Tyndale House, 1982), p. 71.
6. Douglas Groothuis, *Unmasking the New Age* (Downers Grove, IL: InterVarsity Press, 1986), p. 140.
7. Bhagwan Shree Rajneesh, *I Am the Gate* (New York: Harper & Row, 1977), p. 17 emphasis in original.
8. Ibid., p. 15.
9. Swami Prabhavananda, *The Upanishads: Breath of the Eternal* (New York: Mentor, 1957), p. 70.
10. Ibid., p. 73.
11. Groothuis, *Unmasking*, p. 110.
12. Swami Prabhavananda, *The Song of God: Bhagavad Gita* (New York: Mentor, 1951), p. 36.
13. Irvine Robertson, *What the Cults Believe* (Chicago: Moody Press, 1983), p. 109.
14. Ibid., p. 109.
15. Ibid.
16. Larson, *Book of Cults*, p. 72.
17. *Back to Godhead* (No. 36, p. 2).
18. Ibid.
19. *Back to Godhead* (No. 47, p. 1).
20. Kenneth Boa, *Cults, World Religions and You* (Wheaton, IL: Victor Books, 1979), p. 185.

Chapter 6—The New Age Rage
1. Sanaya Roman and Duane Packer, *Opening to Channel: How to Connect with Your Guide* (Tiburon, CA: H.J. Kramer, 1987), p. 127.
2. C.S. Lewis, *The Screwtape Letters* (London: Collins, 1964), p. 25.
3. Shakti Gawain, *Creative Visualization* (San Rafael, CA: New World Library, 1978), p. 15.
4. Ibid., p. 18.
5. Ibid., pp. 36-40.
6. Ibid.
7. Elliot Miller, *A Crash Course on the New Age Movement* (Grand Rapids, MI: Baker Book House, 1989), p. 15.
8. Ibid., p. 16.
9. For a general survey of New Age ideas, see the "Spiritual Counterfeits Project" study by Karen Hoyt, *The New Age Rage* (Old Tappan, NJ: Revell, 1987), pp. 21-32.
10. See the insightful study of transpersonal psychology by William Kilpatrick, *The Emperor's New Clothes: The Naked Truth About the New Psychology* (Westchester, IL: Crossway Books, 1985). See also Garth Wood, *The Myth of Neurosis* (New York: Harper & Row, 1986); and Jay Adams, *The Biblical View of Self-Esteem, Self-Love, and Self-Image* (Eugene, OR: Harvest House, 1986).

258 Notes

11. Dave Hunt and T.A. McMahon, *The Seduction of Christianity* (Eugene, OR: Harvest House, 1985), pp. 77-84.
12. See Teilhard de Chardin, *The Future of Man* (New York: Harper & Row, 1964); *Man's Place in Nature* (London: Collins, 1966); *The Vision of the Past* (New York: Harper & Row, 1966). For an analysis of his teaching, see N.M. Wildiers, *An Introduction to Teilhard de Chardin* (New York: Harper & Row, 1968); and G.D. Jones, *Teilhard de Chardin: An Analysis and Assessment* (Grand Rapids: Eerdmans, 1969).
13. Teilhard de Chardin, *Hymn of the Universe* (New York: Harper & Row, 1961). He argued that the convergence of all material and psychic forces will eventually combine in an *implosion* of energy forces.
14. Fritjof Capra, *The Turning Point* (Toronto: Bantam Books, 1982), p. 22.
15. Ibid., p. 302.
16. Miller, p. 65.
17. Donald Keys, *Earth at Omega: Passage to Planetization* (Boston: Branden Press, 1982), p. iv.
18. John White, "Channeling: A Short History of a Long Tradition," *Holistic Life* (Summer 1985), p. 20.
19. Margot Adler, *Drawing Down the Moon* (Boston: Beacon Press, 1979), p. v.
20. Hunt and McMahon, *Seduction of Christianity*, pp. 120-136.
21. Morton Kelsey, *The Christian and the Supernatural* (Minneapolis: Augsburg, 1976), pp. 113-123.
22. Douglas Groothuis, *Unmasking the New Age* (Downers Grove, IL: InterVarsity Press, 1986), p. 144.
23. Shirley MacLaine, *Out on a Limb* (New York: Bantam Books, 1984) p. 236.
24. Ron Rhodes, *The Counterfeit Christ of the New Age Movement* (Grand Rapids, MI: Baker Book House, 1990), pp. 15-18.
25. Ibid., p. 19.

Chapter 7—Voices from the Dark Side
1. Elliot Miller, *A Crash Course on the New Age Movement* (Grand Rapids, MI: Baker Book House, 1989), p. 24.
2. Ibid., pp. 21-22.
3. Marilyn Ferguson, *The Aquarian Conspiracy* (Los Angeles: J.P. Tarcher, 1980). Her claim that there are "legions of conspirators" at every level of government, society, and education is certainly overstated, but accurately reflects the hopes and dreams of New Age "evangelists."
4. Reproduced and quoted by Constance Cumbey, *The Hidden Dangers of the Rainbow* (Shreveport, LA: Huntington House, 1983), pp. 13-15.
5. Ibid.
6. Miller, p. 197.
7. Ibid., p. 107.
8. Ibid., p. 122.
9. Jon Klimo, *Channeling* (Los Angeles: J.P. Tarcher, 1987), p. 185.
10. *Seattle Times* (July 28, 1986), Section B. "Jonah" claimed Jesus did not die on the cross but had an out-of-body experience, married a druid princess, and had children.
11. R.J. Burrows, "The Coming of the New Age," in *The New Age Rage*, Karen Hoyt, ed. (Old Tappan, NJ: Revell, 1987), p. 21.
12. Terry Cole-Whittaker, *How to Have More in a Have-Not World* (New York: Fawcett Crest, 1983), p. 3.
13. Jane Roberts, *Seth Speaks* (Englewood Cliffs, NJ: Prentice Hall, 1972), pp. ix-x.
14. "Ramtha—An Exclusive Interview with His Channel J.Z. Knight," *Holistic Life* (Summer 1985), p. 30.
15. "Lazaris, Awakening the Love" (videotape) and "Lazaris, the Consummate Friend" (publicity flyer). Quoted by Miller, p. 237.
16. Miller, p. 177.
17. Cumbey, p. 7.

Chapter 8—Satan and His Angels
1. Benjamin Camfield, *A Theological Discourse of Angels and Their Ministries* (London: St. Paul's Churchyard, 1678), p. A3.
2. C.S. Lewis, *The Screwtape Letters* (New York: Macmillan, 1961), p. 3.
3. Jerry Johnston, *The Edge of Evil* (Dallas: Word, 1989), pp. 17-19.
4. Maury Terry, *The Ultimate Evil* (Garden City, NY: Doubleday, 1987), p. 511.
5. Arthur Lyons, *The Second Coming: Satanism in America* (New York: Dodd Mead, 1980), p. 5.
6. Merrill Unger, *Demons in the World Today* (Wheaton, IL: Tyndale House, 1972), p. 18.
7. John Ankerberg and John Weldon, *Cult Watch* (Eugene, OR: Harvest House, 1991), p. 248.
8. Elliot Miller, *A Crash Course on the New Age Movement* (Grand Rapids, MI: Baker Book House, 1989), p. 177.
9. Bob Larson, *Straight Answers on the New Age* (Nashville, TN: Thomas Nelson, 1989), p. 133.
10. Ronald Enroth, "Occult," in *Evangelical Dictionary of Theology*, Walter Elwell, ed. (Grand Rapids, MI: Baker Book House, 1984), p. 787.
11. Ezekiel 28:12-17.
12. Ankerberg and Weldon, pp. 262-263.
13. S.M. Warren, *A Compendium of the Theological Writings of Emmanuel Swedenborg* (New York: Swedenborg Foundation, 1977), p. 618.

Chapter 9—Playing with Fire
1. Jerry Johnston, *The Edge of Evil* (Dallas: Word, 1989), pp. 3-4.
2. John Ankerberg and John Weldon, *Cult Watch* (Eugene, OR: Harvest House, 1991), p. 253.
3. Michael Harner, *The Way of the Shaman* (New York: Bantam Books, 1986), p. 54.

4. See the excellent survey by Bob Larson, *Straight Answers on the New Age* (Nashville, TN: Thomas Nelson, 1989), pp. 306-311.
5. Ibid., p. 309.
6. See J.K. Van Baalen, *The Chaos of the Cults* (Grand Rapids, MI: Eerdmans, 1960), pp. 62-84.
7. K. Boa, *Cults, World Religions and You* (Wheaton, IL: Victor Books, 1979), pp. 130-135.
8. Larson, pp. 249-253.
9. Geoffrey Dean, "Does Astrology Need to Be True?" *The Skeptical Inquirer*, Vol. II, No. 2, p. 167.
10. Sybil Leek, *My Life in Astrology* (Englewood Cliffs, NJ: Prentice-Hall, 1972), p. 11.
11. Boa, p. 110. See also John W. Montgomery, *Principalities and Powers* (Minneapolis: Dimension Books, 1975).

Chapter 11—Herbert W. Armstrong
1. Herbert W. Armstrong, *The Autobiography of Herbert W. Armstrong* (Pasadena, CA: Ambassador College Press, 1967), pp. 298.
2. Personal letter to Robert Sumner, editor of the *Biblical Evangelist* (Nov. 27, 1958). Cited by Josh McDowell and Don Stewart, *Understanding the Cults* (San Bernardino, CA: Here's Life Publishers, 1982), p. 155.
3. Roderick Meredity, "The True Church—Where Is It?" *The Plain Church* (March 1963), p. 44.
4. *The Inside Story of the World Tomorrow Broadcast*, pp. 7-11. Cited by Walter Martin, *The Kingdom of the Cults* (Minneapolis: Bethany Fellowship, 1970), p. 306. Cf. H.W. Armstrong, *The United States and the British Commonwealth in Prophecy*, p. 184.
5. *Tomorrow's World* (May-June 1970), p. 18. Cited at length by Salem Kirban, *Armstrong's Church of God* (Chicago: Moody Press, 1973), pp. 22-23.
6. See photo reproduction of this article in Kirban, *Armstrong's Church of God*, centerfold insert.
7. H.W. Armstrong, *Why Were You Born?*, pp. 21-22. Cited by Martin, p. 307, emphasis in original.
8. *The Plain Truth* (November 1962), pp. 11-12.
9. H.W. Armstrong, "What is the True Gospel?" *Tomorrow's World* (January 1970), p. 7, emphasis in original.
10. D.J. Hill, "Why Is God the Father Called a Father?" *Tomorrow's World* (September 1970), p. 28.
11. Ibid.
12. H.W. Armstrong, *All About Water Baptism* (Pasadena, CA: n.d.), p. 1.
13. H.W. Armstrong, *The Mark of the Beast* (Pasadena, CA: Ambassador College Press, 1957), p. 10.
14. A. Roberts and J. Donaldson, *The Ante-Nicene Fathers*, Vol. I (Grand Rapids, MI: Eerdmans, 1950), pp. 62-63, 199-207.
15. *The Plain Truth* (June 1953) and *Tomorrow's World* (May-June 1970), p. 21, emphasis in original.

Chapter 12—David Berg
1. Bob Larson, *Larson's Book of Cults* (Wheaten, IL: Tyndale House, 1984), p. 124.
2. Quoted by Alan Streett, *The Cult Invasion* (Dallas: Lighthouse Books, n.d.), article on "Children of God."
3. Deborah (Linda Berg) Davis, *The Children of God: The Inside Story* (Grand Rapids, MI: Zondervan, 1984).
4. Ibid., p. 3.
5. Ibid., p. 11.
6. Ibid., p. 29.
7. Ibid., p. 190.
8. "Dad's Little Diamonds," *Mo Letter*, no. 994, par. 47.

Chapter 13—Edgar Cayce
1. Bob Larson, *Larson's Book of Cults* (Wheaton, IL: Tyndale House, 1984), p. 243.
2. Ibid., pp. 242-248.
3. Ibid., p. 246.
4. Ibid., p. 247.

Chapter 14—Jeane Dixon
1. Streett, *The Cult Invasion*, (Dallas, Lighthouse Books, n.d.), article on "Jeane Dixon."
2. Ibid.

Chapter 15—Mary Baker Eddey
1. Anthony Hoekema, *The Four Major Cults* (Grand Rapids, MI: Eerdmans, 1984), p. 172.
2. Hoekema, p. 173. See also Walter Martin and Norman Klann, *The Christian Science Myth* (Grand Rapids, MI: Zondervan, 1955), p. 14. They quote from page 388 of the *Quimby Manuscripts*.
3. Mary Baker Eddy, *Science and Health with Key to the Scriptures* (Boston: Trustees, 1934), p. 107.
4. Ibid., pp. 456-457.
5. Mary Baker Eddy, *Miscellaneous Writings* (Boston: Trustees, 1924), p. 21.
6. Eddy, *Science and Health*, p. 472.
7. Ibid., p. 584.
8. Ibid., p. 331.
9. Mary Baker Eddy, *The First Church of Christ, Scientist, and Miscellany* (Boston: Trustees, 1941), p. 181.

Chapter 16—L. Ron Hubbard
1. *L. Ron Hubbard: The Man and His Works* (nationally distributed magazine published by the Church of Scientology), pp. 3-9.

2. *Scientology: Results and Successes* (published by the Church of Scientology), p. 44.
3. Richard Behar, "Scientology: A Dangerous Cult Goes Mainstream," *Reader's Digest* (October 1991), pp. 87-92. Condensed from *Time* (May 6, 1991).
4. Ibid., p. 88.
5. Carroll Stoner and JoAnne Park, *All God's Children: The Cult Experience* (Radnor, PA: Chilton, 1977), p. 48.
6. Horton Davies, *Christian Deviations* (Philadelphia: Westminster Press, 1972), p. 109.
7. William Peterson, *Those Curious New Cults* (New Canaan, CT: Keats Publishing, 1973), p. 90.
8. Ibid.
9. Irvine Robertson, *What the Cults Believe* (Chicago: Moody Press, 1983), pp. 124-125.

Chapter 17—Maharaj Ji
1. Quoted by Kenneth Boa, *Cults, World Religions, and You* (Wheaton, IL: Victor Books, 1979, p. 188.
2. Jack Sparks, *The Mind Benders* (Nashville: Thomas Nelson, 1977), p. 66.

Chapter 18—Jim Jones
1. Quoted by Marshall Kilduff and Ron Javers, *The Suicide Cult* (New York: Bantam Books, 1978), p. xiv.
2. Ibid., p. 33.
3. Ibid., pp. 53-55.
4. Ibid., p. 55.
5. Ibid., pp. 199-200. For an inside account by a former cult member, see Phil Kearus, *People's Temple/People's Tomb* (Plainfield, NY: Logos International, 1979).

Chapter 19—David Koresh
1. See the excellent article by Barbara Kantrowitz, et. al., "The Messiah of Waco," *Newsweek* (March 15, 1993), pp. 56-58.
2. "Zealot of God," *People* (March 15, 1993), pp. 38-43.
3. "Cult of Death," *Time* (March 15, 1993), p. 38.
4. Ibid., p. 37.
5. "Cult Seige Driving Waco Wacky,"*USA Today* (March 22, 1993) pp. A1-2.
6. "Sect Dead May Total 10," *USA Today* (March 3, 1993), p. A26.
7. "ATF Official Backs Raid" *Dallas Morning News* (March 27, 1993), p. A26.
8. "Cult Death Toll May Rise," *Atlanta Constitution* (March 3, 1993), p. A1.
9. "Texas Cult's Fiery, Tragic End," quoted in *Atlanta Journal* (April 20, 1993), p. 1.

Chapter 20—Sun Myung Moon
1. Sun Myung Moon, *Divine Principle* (Washington, D.C.: Holy Spirit Association, 1973), pp. 189-191.
2. See the excellent history of Sun Myung Moon in Ken Boa, *Cults, World Religions and You* (Wheaton, IL: Victor Books, 1979), pp. 167-177.
3. Sun Myung Moon, *God's Hope for America* (New York: Bicentennial God Bless America Committee, 1976), pages are unnumbered.
4. James Bjornstad, *The Moon Is Not the Son* (Minneapolis: Bethany Fellowship, 1976), p. 31.
5. Moon, *Divine Principle*, p. vii.
6. Sun Myung Moon, *Master Speaks* (March-April 1976), MS-3, pp. 4ff.
7. Y.O. Kim, *Unification Theology & Christian Thought* (New York: Golden Gate Publishing Co., 1975).
8. Sun Myung Moon, *The Way of the World*, p. 20.
9. Moon, *Divine Principle*, p. 16.
10. Ibid., p. 178.
11. Boa, p. 174.
12. *New York Times Magazine* (May 30, 1976), p. 19.

Chapter 21—Elizabeth Clare Prophet
1. "Cultic America: A Tower of Babel," *Newsweek* (March 15, 1993), pp. 60-61.
2. Bob Larson, *Larson's Book of Cults* (Wheaton, IL: Tyndale House, 1984), pp. 265-269; Streett, "CUT/Gura Ma" article.
3. Streett, ibid.
4. Ibid.
5. Mark and Elizabeth Prophet, *Climb the Highest Mountain* (Los Angeles: Summit Lighthouse, 1975), pp. xxii-xxvi.
6. El Morya, *The Chela and the Path* (Colorado Springs: Summit Lighthouse, 1975), pp. 121-122.
7. Godfrey Ray King, *Unveiled Mysteries* (Chicago: Saint Germain Press, 1939), p. 7.
8. *Climb the Highest Mountain*, pp. 301-302.
9. Walter Martin, *The New Cults* (Ventura, CA: Regal Books, 1985), p. 231.
10. Prophet, pp. 279-280.

Chapter 22—Bhagwan Shree Rajneesh
1. Vasant Joshi, *The Awakened One: The Life and Work of Bhagwan Shree Rajneesh* (San Francisco: Harper & Row, 1982), p. 23.
2. Rajneesh, *The Discipline of Transcendence* (Poona, India: Rajneesh Foundation, 1978), Vol. 2, pp. 313-314.

3. Ibid.
4. Quoted by Larson, *Larson's Book of Cults* (Wheaton, IL: Tyndale House, 1984), p. 191.
5. Tal Brooke, *Riders of the Cosmic Circuit* (London: Lion Publishing, 1986), p. 85.
6. Ibid., pp. 141-142.

Chapter 23—Charles T. Russell
1. *Watchtower* (July 15, 1894). Quoted by Gordon Duggar, *Jehovah's Witnesses: Not Just Another Denomination* (Smithtown, NY: Exposition Press, 1982), p. 38, emphasis in original.
2. C.T. Russell, *Thy Kingdom Come*, p. 23. In *Studies in the Scriptures* (Brooklyn, NY: Watchtower Bible and Tract Society, 1917). Quoted by Duggar, p. 37.
3. For a survey of Adventist beliefs, see Anthony Hoekema, *The Four Major Cults* (Grand Rapids, MI: Eerdmans, 1984), pp. 89-169. On Russell's Adventist roots, see John Gerstner, *The Theology of the Major Sects* (Grand Rapids, MI: Baker Book House, 1960), pp. 19-40.
4. C.T. Russell, *The Time Is at Hand* (Brooklyn, NY: Zion's Watchtower, n.d.) p. 101.
5. Cf. details in Hoekema, p. 225.
6. *Watchtower* (Sept. 15, 1910), p. 298.
7. Cf. details in H.H. Stroup, *The Jehovah's Witnesses* (New York: Columbia University Press, 1945), pp. 9-11.
8. *Let God Be True* (Brooklyn, NY: Watchtower Bible & Tract Society, 1952), p. 100.
9. Ibid., p. 298. Quoted by Hoekema, p. 279.
10. Duggar, pp. 103-106.

Chapter 24—Joseph Smith
1. Joseph Smith, *The Pearl of Great Price* (Salt Lake City: Church of Jesus Christ of Latter-day Saints, 1952), p. 4.
2. Ibid., pp. 48-51.
3. See the detailed history in Hoekema, *The Four Major Cults* (Grand Rapids, MI: Eerdmans, 1984), pp. 9-29, and L.C. Scott, *The Mormon Mirage* (Grand Rapids, MI: Zondervan, 1979), pp. 1-55.
4. "Founder Settles 137-Year-Old Dispute," cf. *Christianity Today* (April 24, 1981), p. 42.
5. Allan Streett, *The Cult Invasion* (Dallas: Lighthouse Books, n.d.), article on "Church of Jesus Christ of Latter-day Saints."
6. See detailed study in Walter Martin, *The Kingdom of the Cults*, pp. 165-175.
7. Smith, *Doctrine and Covenants* (Salt Lake City: Church of Jesus Christ of Latter-day Saints, 1968 edition), Sect. 87.
8. Smith, *Doctrine and Covenants*, Sect. 124.
9. J.F. Smith, ed., *Teachings of the Prophet Joseph Smith* (Salt Lake City: Deseret Press, 1958), pp. 370-372.
10. J.A. Widstoe, ed. *Discourses of Brigham Young* (Salt Lake City: Deseret Press, 1954), pp. 22-23.
11. Smith, ed., *Teachings of the Prophet Joseph Smith*, pp. 345-346.
12. *Millennial Star*, p. 54. Quoted by Hoekema, p. 39.
13. Smith, ed., pp. 346-347.
14. Quoted by Hoekema, p. 40.
15. James Talmage, *A Study of the Articles of Faith* (Salt Lake City: Church of Jesus Christ of Latter-day Saints, 1957, first published 1899), p. 479.
16. *Discourses of Brigham Young*, p. 435.
17. Series of Pamphlets, No. III, p. 8. Quoted by Hoekema, p. 63.

Chapter 25—Maharishi Mahesh Yogi
1. Bob Larson, *Larson's Book of Cults* (Wheaton, IL: Tyndale House, 1984), p. 336.
2. Ibid., p. 338.

Chapters 26—A Light in the Darkness
1. Charles Rushing, "Who's That Knocking at Your Door?" *Moody Monthly* (October 1985), pp. 96-97.
2. Bob and Gretchen Passantino, "Next Time They Knock," *Moody Monthly* (November 1992), pp. 23-25.
3. Ibid., p. 24.
4. Jim Morud, "Making the Break," *Moody Monthly* (November 1992), p. 19.
5. Hank Hanegraaff, *Christianity in Crisis* (Eugene, OR: Harvest House, 1993), p. 323.

Basic Bibliography
on the Cults

Ankerberg, John and John Weldon. *Cult Watch*. Eugene, OR: Harvest House, 1992.

Breese, Dave. *Know the Marks of the Cults*. Wheaton, IL: Victor Books, 1984.

Brooke, Tal. *Riders of the Cosmic Circuit*. Herts, England: Lion Publishing, 1986.

Bussell, Harold. *Unholy Devotion: Why Cults Lure Christians*. Grand Rapids, MI: Zondervan, 1983.

Dobson, Ed and Ed Hindson. *The Seduction of Power*. Old Tappan, NJ: Revell, 1988.

Edward, Christopher. *Crazy for God*. Englewood Cliffs, NJ: Prentice-Hall, 1979.

Enroth, Ronald. *Youth, Brainwashing the Extremist Cults*. Grand Rapids, MI: Zondervan, 1977.

_____. *A Guide to Cults & New Religions*. Downers Grove, IL: InterVarsity Press, 1983.

Groothuis, Douglas. *Unmasking the New Age*. Downers Grove, IL: InterVarsity Press, 1986.

Hanegraaff, Hank. *Christianity in Crisis*. Eugene, OR: Harvest House, 1993.

Hexham, Irving and Karla Poewe, *Understanding Cults and New Religions*. Grand Rapids, MI: Eerdmans, 1986.

Hoekema, Anthony. *The Four Major Cults*. Grand Rapids, MI: Eerdmans, 1984.

Horton, Michael, ed. *The Agony of Deceit*. Chicago, IL: Moody Press, 1990.

Hoyt, Karen. *The New Age Rage*. Old Tappan, NJ: Revell, 1987.

Hunt, Dave and T.A. McMahon. *The Seduction of Christianity*. Eugene, OR: Harvest House, 1985.

Larson, Bob. *Larson's Book of Cults*. Wheaton, IL: Tyndale House, 1984.

Martin, Walter. *The Kingdom of the Cults*. Minneapolis: Bethany Fellowship, 1985.

Mather, G.A. and L.A. Nichols, *Dictionary of Cults, Sects, Religions and the Occult*, Grand Rapids, MI: Zondervan, 1992).

McDowell, Josh and Don Stewart. *Understanding the Cults*. San Bernardino, CA: Here's Life Publishers, 1982.

McManus, Una and John Cooper. *Dealing with Destructive Cults*. Grand Rapids, MI: Zondervan, 1984.

Miller, Elliot. *A Crash Course on the New Age Movement*. Grand Rapids, MI: Baker, 1989.

Passantino, Robert and Gretchen. *Answers to the Cultist at Your Door*. Eugene, OR: Harvest House, 1981.

Peterson, William. *Those Curious New Cults*. New Canaan, CT: Keats Publishing, 1973.

Stoner, Carroll and JoAnne Parke. *All God's Children*. Radnor, PA: Chilton, 1977.

Sparks, Jack. *The Mind Benders*. Nashville: Thomas Nelson, 1977.

Cult Resource Centers

There are nearly 700 organizations that specialize in cult research and evangelism. Each group has specialized areas of interest and concentration. The following information will help you know where and how to get started.

The *Directory of Cult Research Organizations* lists 652 of these agencies. An invaluable resource for pastors, church leaders, teachers, and Christians concerned with evangelizing cultists, it is available for $6 (plus $2 shipping) from Cornerstone, 920 W. Wilson, Chicago, IL 60640. Or, you can call (312) 989-2080.

Additional information is available from the cult research organization coalition, Evangelical Ministries to New Religions (EMNR). You may contact EMNR by writing Bob Passantino, Executive Director, P.O. Box 2067, Costa Mesa, CA 92628.

When you contact an agency, be sure to include a stamped, self-addressed, business-size envelope. Remember to pay for materials and consider making a donation. Nonprofit organizations often have very limited budgets.

Answers in Action
P.O. Box 2067, Costa Mesa, CA 92628   (714) 646-9042

Christian Apologetics Project
P.O. Box 105, Absecon, NJ 08201

Christian Research Institute
P.O. Box 500, San Juan Capistrano, CA 92693   (714) 855-9926

Cornerstone Apologetics Research Team
920 W. Wilson Ave., Chicago, IL 60640   (312) 989-2080

Home Mission Board Southern Baptist Convention
1350 Spring Street NW, Atlanta, GA 30367

Personal Freedom Outreach
P.O. Box 26062, St. Louis, MO 63136   (314) 388-2648

Spiritual Counterfeits Project
P.O. Box 4308, Berkeley, CA 94704   (415) 540-5767

Watchman Fellowship
P.O. Box 7681, Columbus, GA 31908   (404) 576-4321

Witness, Inc.
P.O. Box 597, Clayton, CA 94517   (415) 672-5979